Model Minority Masochism

Model Minority Masochism

Performing the Cultural Politics of Asian American Masculinity

Takeo Rivera

OXFORD
UNIVERSITY PRESS

Oxford University Press is a department of the University of Oxford. It furthers
the University's objective of excellence in research, scholarship, and education
by publishing worldwide. Oxford is a registered trade mark of Oxford University
Press in the UK and certain other countries.

Published in the United States of America by Oxford University Press
198 Madison Avenue, New York, NY 10016, United States of America.

© Oxford University Press 2022

All rights reserved. No part of this publication may be reproduced, stored in
a retrieval system, or transmitted, in any form or by any means, without the
prior permission in writing of Oxford University Press, or as expressly permitted
by law, by license, or under terms agreed with the appropriate reproduction
rights organization. Inquiries concerning reproduction outside the scope of the
above should be sent to the Rights Department, Oxford University Press, at the
address above.

You must not circulate this work in any other form
and you must impose this same condition on any acquirer.

CIP data is on file at the Library of Congress

ISBN 978–0–19–755749–5 (pbk.)
ISBN 978–0–19–755748–8 (hbk.)

DOI: 10.1093/oso/9780197557488.001.0001

1 3 5 7 9 8 6 4 2

Paperback printed by Marquis, Canada
Hardback printed by Bridgeport National Bindery, Inc., United States of America

For Rafaela, Edward, Miyuki, Raymond, and Emiliano

Contents

Acknowledgments ix
Introduction xiii

1. Vincent Chin's Wedding: Techno-Orientalist Becoming and Asian American Liberalism   1

2. Bludgeons and Becomings: Vincent Chin, Suspenseful Reveal, and the Limits of the Legal   30

3. An Asian Is Being Whipped: The Afro-Asian Superego in the Theater of Philip Kan Gotanda   42

4. Never Stop Making Them Pay: Greg Pak's *Hulk*, Moral Masochism, and Asian American Ressentiment   68

5. Asians Never Stare into Your Eyes: Affective Flatness and the Techno-Orientalization of the Self in Tao Lin's *Taipei* and Tan Lin's *Insomnia and the Aunt*   92

6. White Skin, Yellow Flesh: Transhumanist Erotohistoriography in *Deus Ex: Human Revolution*   120

Coda: Sankyoufocoming   140

Notes 149
Bibliography 167
Index 179

Acknowledgments

I can scarcely believe how fortunate I am to have the community of support, mentorship, and affirmation that has been with me since the earliest days of this book's journey. This book, like every book, is as much the product of treasured relationships as it is of its author. First, I would like to thank Norman Hirschy at Oxford University Press for believing in and supporting this project—I am indebted to his immense generosity and patience. Thanks to everyone at all levels at OUP who has helped bring this book to fruition—editing, logistical coordination, promotion, and design—such as Lauralee Yeary and Preetham Raj. Thank you also to the two anonymous reviewers who provided stellar suggestions for editing the manuscript—such feedback allowed me to deepen my understanding of my own work. Thanks also to the Boston University Center for the Humanities for its generous financial assistance in the publication of this book.

This project owes its early genesis to the intellectual community at the University of California, Berkeley, where I underwent graduate training. My dissertation cochairs, Colleen Lye and Shannon Steen, were magnificent in their rigor and training, and I cannot thank them enough for everything they have done for me, both as a scholar and as a human being. The same goes to the rest of my dissertation committee: Juana María Rodríguez, Abigail DeKosnik, and Mel Y. Chen, all of whom were vital to the development of ideas written here and have provided support both intellectual and personal on levels I'll never be able to fully repay. The list of both mentors and staff from my UC Berkeley years, all of whom contributed either directly to mentoring this work or helped produce an environment that made writing this possible, is quite long. But to make an attempt, immense thanks to Philip Kan Gotanda, SanSan Kwan, Shannon Jackson, Brandi Wilkins Catanese, Robin Davidson, Michael Mansfield, Peter Glazer, Michael Omi, Lok Siu, Catherine Cole, Angelia Marino, Julia Fawcett, Joe Goode, Maura Tang, Lisa Wymore, Paola Bacchetta, Zeus Leonardo, David Kim, Wil Leggett, Marni Davis, Grace Leach, Megan Lowe, and Josh Hesslein. Thanks to treasured friends who helped me get through grad school and often offered vital interlocution in this project's early stages: Jerry Zee, Joshua Williams, Christopher Fan, Margaret Rhee, Kim Tran, Trent Walker, Chenxing Han, Paige Johnson, Seán McKeithan, Thea Gold, Miyoko Conley, Martha Herrera-Lasso, Caitlin Marshall, Natalia Duong, Omar Ricks, Hentyle Yapp, Iván Ramos, Juan Manuel Aldape Muñoz, Jeff Yamashita, Daniel Valella, Natalee Kehaulani, Giancarlo Salinas, Karin Shankar, Megan Hoetger, Michelle Potts, Adam Hutz, Ianna Hawkins Owen, Toshi Pau, Caleb Luna, Amanda Su, Aparna Christian Schoff-Nagler, Marc Boucai, Gowri

Vijayakumar, Anna Torres, Aparna Nambiar, Lashon Daley, Miyuki Baker, Bélgica del Río, and Jess Dorrance, among many others.

This book matured and deepened immeasurably since I joined the faculty at Boston University, and I cannot thank my colleagues enough for providing such a supportive intellectual home. The publication of this book simply would not have been possible without the generous support of Susan Mizruchi and Robert Chodat, spectacular mentors and friends. Several senior faculty at BU have taken a particularly active role in helping me adjust to my role as faculty and actively providing feedback on my work, most notably Carrie Preston, Louis Chude-Sokei, Maurice Lee, and Cati Connell, for whom my gratitude knows no bounds. I am grateful for the many friends and interlocutors I have had at BU; to name a non-exhaustive list of those who have been vital in helping develop this project and my work at BU more generally, they are: Anne Austin, Sean Desilets, Marie McDonough, Jennie Row, Joseph Rezek, Erin Murphy, Amy Appleford, Anna Henchman, Larry Breiner, Sanjay Krishnan, Anthony Petro, Jack Matthews, Petrus Liu, Karen Warkentin, J. Keith Vincent, Anita Patterson, John Paul Riquelme, Tamzen Flanders, Hunt Howell, Saida Grundy, Crystal Williams, and Hyo Kyung Woo. A very special thank you to Jena DiMaggio for her vital work in the final formatting of this manuscript, and to Karl Kirchwey for sponsoring these efforts and supporting this project in a myriad of other ways. Special thanks also to Korine Powers, Kristin Lacey, Ken Alba, and Nicole Rizzo for cat-sitting and camaraderie. Thanks again also to the Boston University Center for the Humanities for financial and institutional support for the production of this book.

This work has also been supported by a remarkable faculty fellowship at the Charles Warren Center at Harvard University. Thanks to Ju Yon Kim and Lorgia García-Peña for organizing and leading a truly spectacular cohort—I should note here that Harvard University's tenure denial of García-Peña, one of the foremost scholars in her field, was a profound travesty. Gratitude to the entirety of my cohort for providing a truly utopian ethnic studies academic community: Denise Khor, Marisol LeBron, Robert Diaz, Jason Ferreira, Anjali Nath, Allen Isaac, Nicole Guidotti-Hernandez, Umayyah Cable, Courtney Sato, Hannah Waits, Tina Shull, and Christina Davidson. Thanks to Arthur Patton-Hock, Monnikue McCall, and Syed Zaman for all of their coordination to make the fellowship possible.

There are so many other outstanding scholars I have not yet mentioned but have nevertheless had a considerable impact in the development of this project. Yoon Sun Lee, Rebecca Schneider, and Leticia Alvarado lent their considerable talents to a full-day manuscript workshop at Boston University, and their rigorous feedback was vital for the final stages of revisions. Special thanks to many other academic friends and colleagues I have not mentioned already, many of whom have provided many forms of help in the development of this project over the years: Douglas Ishii, Timothy Yu, Loan Dao, Vivian Huang, Theo Davis, Elizabeth Freeman, Terry Park, Christopher B. Patterson, erin Khuê Ninh, Mimi Thi Nguyen, Caroline Hong, Mai-Linh Hong, Long Le-Khac, Renee Hudson, Vivian Shaw, Evyn Lê Espiritu Gandhi, Victor Bascara, Lisa Nakamura, Vincent Pham, Lori Kido Lopez, Amanda Phillips,

Tara Fickle, Kimberly McKee, Jennifer Ho, and many others. Also, enormous thanks to the staffs of both the University of Michigan Bentley Historical Library and the UC Berkeley Ethnic Studies Library for their assistance in archival research.

Furthermore, I would not have gone to this PhD program if not for the academic, artistic, and political grounding I had in my undergraduate and master's years at Stanford University. I remain deeply indebted to Harry J. Elam, Scott Herndon, Andrea Lunsford, Cherríe Moraga, and David Palumbo-Liu, vital mentors who formed the foundations of my early intellectual development. Deep thanks also to Cindy Ng, Shelley Tadaki, Anne Takemoto, Wendy Goldberg, Astrid Fellner, Korina Jocson, Gordon Chang, Saikat Majumdar, Stephen Hong Sohn, and the late Sekou Sundiata, all of whom played enormous roles in my development as an Asian Americanist scholar and activist alike. Enormous special thanks to two old friends in particular, who provided enormous help not only in personal encouragement, but also expertise: Kunyu Ching, who provided invaluable guidance in my publishing considerations, and William Lowell Von Hoene, who developed vital concept art for the book cover. Thanks to my many other friends from that period who have continued to be a guiding light to this day: David Lai, Tammie Nguyen, Charlie Wang, Bryan Cauley, Yang Lor, Timmy Lu, Linda Lee, Mark Liu, Hai Binh Nguyen, Lan Le, Theresa Zhen, Pahua Cha, Lilian Thaoxaochay, Rich Liu, Rachel Yong, Henry Tsai, Luke Taylor, Spencer Chu, Mark Otuteye, Famia Nkansa, Jessica Jones Lewis, Chelsea Steiner, Sophie Hwang, Chika Okafor, Jason Sierra, Dylan Keil, Dawn Maxey, M. Scott Frank, Philana Omorotionmwan, Liane Al-Ghusain, and Alex Mallory. Furthermore, thanks to Gloria Brown, Robert Walker, and Teresa Willis at the Buck Foundation for their enormous financial support of my entire academic career.

Thanks also to Bryan Thao Worra and Eric Tran for generously allowing me to reproduce their gorgeous work in these pages, and to Arnold Pan at *Amerasia Journal* for allowing reproduction of my previously published work. And a second thanks to Bryan Thao Worra and the LaoMagination collective for what is, in the time of this writing, a truly humbling collaboration in developing visual art inspired by the content of this book. A shorter version of Chapter 6 was published in *Amerasia* as "Do Asians Dream of Electric Shrieks?: Techno-Orientalism and Erotohistoriographic Masochism in Eidos Montreal's *Deus Ex: Human Revolution*."

Thanks also to the thousands of service workers at BU, Harvard, Berkeley, and Stanford—janitors, food servers, and the countless others who form the oft-unacknowledged backbone of university life. Institutions owe you the very best.

I also must acknowledge the many instructors and mentors I had from my K–12 years without whose early guidance this book would never come to be: Leslie Moitoza, Ray Cobane, Terrence Elliott, Fritz Pointer, Michael Schwartz, Adolph Bertero, Richard Holmquist, Gary Carlone, Emilie Wilson, the late Patricia Horrigan, Cheryl Woolery, Gabby Bay, Bonnee Christian, and Carol Butcher.

I can never sufficiently express my love and gratitude for my parents Julia Otake Rivera and Charles Rivera, once members of the Asian American Movement themselves, who raised me with a passion for social justice and antiracism. I hope this work embodies what they always had me aspire toward. Much love also to my brother, Sien Rivera.

Finally, the deepest gratitude possible to my wife, Diana Austria Rivera, who has borne witness to the entirety of this process, has consoled me innumerable times when my resolve wavered, and has been my most brilliant and important interlocutor. This book would be nothing without her, and neither would I. And as I write this, my child Hikaru is experiencing his first days in this world—I hope that one day, these words written by his father can help him better understand himself one day, one way or another.

Introduction

> *What then may I do*
> *but cleave to what cleaves me.*
> *I kiss the blade and eat my meat*
> *I thank the wielder and receive,*
> *while terror spirits*
> *my change, sorrow also.*
> —Li-Young Lee, "The Cleaving" (excerpt)

Chun Hsien Michael Deng was not killed for being Asian American; rather, he became Asian American through being killed. In 2013, 18-year-old Deng, a college freshman at Baruch College, attended a hazing ritual in the Poconos as a pledge to Pi Delta Psi, an Asian American fraternity. Deng sought out a community of young Asian American men whose identity hinged upon an understanding of Asian American masculinity tied to "knowing one's history"—founded in a fledgling period of post–Vincent Chin Asian American consciousness in the 1980s, Pi Delta Psi was a fraternity that took Asian American history seriously, utilizing the entire history of Asian exclusion in the United States as the source of its community and solidarity. Recounting the 1982 murder of Vincent Chin, the destruction of Korean American groceries during the 1992 Los Angeles riots, and other incidents of anti-Asian violence, Pi Delta Psi drew upon Asian American studies as its libidinal wellspring, ensuring its members were aware of the suffering of fellow Asians, even if the members themselves had not been subjected to such violence themselves before.

It was with this ethos that Pi Delta Psi structured its hazing rituals—its senior members inflicted racial suffering onto the pledges that would mirror these historical injustices. After a weekend of education and reflection on the plight of Asians in America, Deng was subjected to "the Glass Ceiling," a hallowed test for the survival of Asian American manhood, named after the liberal metaphor for the limits to Asian upward mobility in organizational management. As Jay Caspian Kang describes in lurid detail,

> First, a pledge is blindfolded and separated from his assigned "Big," an older fraternity brother, by a line of brothers whose arms are linked together. For the most part, this line signifies the barrier between glumly accepting America's vision of emasculated, toadying Asian men and the great promise of success and masculine fulfillment. As his Big calls out his name, a pledge, or "Little," crosses his arms across his chest and walks toward his Big's voice. He soon runs into the

line of brothers, who call him "chink," "gook" and whatever other racial slurs they can muster. The verbal abuse lasts for 10 minutes or more. In the second stage, the pledge is instructed to push through the wall of brothers, who in turn shove him back toward his starting spot. The third stage isn't much different from the second: The pledge is still wandering blindfolded toward his Big's calls, but instead of being pushed, he is knocked to the ground or, in some chapters, even tackled.

[...]

While all this is happening, the pledge is supposed to be thinking about his parents and the sacrifices they made as immigrants, the humiliations they faced and the oppressive invisibility of Asian lives in America. The pushing, the tackling and the racial abuse are meant to be the physical expression of their struggle. That final walk, in which the pledge is shepherded to his Big by all of the fraternity's members, is intended to teach him that solidarity with his fellow Asians is his only hope of making it in a white world. (2017, 10–11)

It is a scene of torture that imagines a telos of transcendence, dressed in a tragicomically absurd re-enactment of racial injury. The pledges, who themselves are presumed to not yet have achieved a prior state of Asian American politicization, are subjected to the vicarious, modeled abuse of white racism in order to emerge as new Asian men, and in grotesque irony, it is their elder guides who perform the role of white supremacist tormentor. However, for Michael Deng, there would be no transcendence. When it was his turn at the Glass Ceiling, Deng was slammed into the ground from a fraternity brother running at full speed, from which he did not get up. The fraternity brothers eventually brought Deng inside, deliberated for hours before finally deciding to drive him to Geisinger Wyoming Valley hospital. After slipping into a coma, Deng died from head injuries that, if treated hours earlier, may have been recoverable.

This transpired thirty-one years after Vincent Chin succumbed from head injuries beside his mother in June 1982, incurred from resentful white autoworkers, an event that was considered foundational for the Asian American narrative of Pi Delta Psi, and in turn, this book. Chin's death was significant because he was Chinese American but taken for Japanese in a period of profound Japanophobia; his death consolidated signification of a panethnic, politicized sense of what it meant to be Asian American. I will detail the Vincent Chin case at much greater length in the first chapter, but suffice it to say that Chin's death inadvertently helped define contemporary Asian American identity—he became Asian American through death. But in a sense, so did Deng, except his Asian American Bildungsroman was delivered by Asian hands rather than white ones. Meanwhile, the fraternity brothers who inflicted the violence themselves modeled white racist violence in order to establish the performatic scenario to make the pedagogical point viable; they became white precisely to disabuse their pledges of the naiveté of model minority innocence. Under the schema of Pi Delta Psi, the entrance fee to Asian American masculinity is subjection, a bludgeoning as a claim to authenticity, to be undone and even destroyed by a history that becomes, coercively, one's own. Put simply, for some, to become an Asian American man is through the theater of sadomasochism, sometimes with catastrophic results.

I am not suggesting that the case of Deng is somehow paradigmatic or representative of all Asian American subject formation. Nor do I suggest, as Jay Caspian Kang does in a rather ahistorical flourish, that the incident demonstrates that Asian America is "mostly meaningless." In fact, Kang's widely circulated essay on the topic ultimately points to the futility of the Asian American formulation in general, which is in direct opposition to my position here. Rather, the incident demonstrates quite the opposite: that it metonymically demonstrates the paradoxical, contradictory affective investments cathected onto Asian America, that Asian Americanness simultaneously contains an excess of meaning and a lack of clarity. It is tempting to declare, as Kandice Chuh does, that Asian America's excess of itself demands a critical turn toward subjectlessness, since as she rightly points out, there exist "constraints on the liberatory potential of the achievement of subjectivity, […] that a 'subject' only becomes recognizable and can act as such by conforming to certain regulatory matrices" (2003, 9). It is ironically because of my full agreement with Chuh's assessment of the essentialist subject that I find its interrogation to be imperative; such a violent enactment of racialized Asian American masculinity in the Deng case demonstrates a yearning for *subjective* narrative, of a racial rather than a specifically ethnic marker, inaugurated by a decimation of self and other—or self-as-other—and made intelligible by panethnicity. Indeed, the liberatory potential of "the" "Asian American subject" is circumscribed by its very definition—and yet it possesses a fascinating, masochistic allure. That allure is at the crux of this project.

This incident, and this writing, occur at a crossroads for Asian American cultural politics, decades removed from the rise of radical Asian American panethnicity, in a period in which Asian Americanness is increasingly instrumentalized to consolidate racial neoliberal hegemony. As Wen Liu observes, "The shifting paradigm of race from violent exclusion to compartmentalized inclusion places Asian Americanness at a historical juncture—to either move forward toward postracial neoliberalism and turn into a profitable cultural commodity or recuperate the nostalgic formation of Asian American nationalism and profess allegiance to U.S. racial liberalism" (2018, 422). This division that Liu describes[1]—postracial neoliberalism and nostalgic racial liberalism—adroitly captures the current angst of contemporary Asian American cultural politics more broadly. Yet, even as Asian America has transitioned away from "violent exclusion," I would contend that both of these strands are nevertheless tethered to and draw meaning from the kinesthetics of self-violence we see in the Deng case, a form of race making through masochism.

This book, *Model Minority Masochism: Performing the Cultural Politics of Asian American Masculinity*, asks what it means for Asian Americanness to discover itself in the process of its own destruction. It explores where we affectively locate the presence of panethnic, racialized, gendered Asian America, through regimes of self-stereotype, self-punishment, and other modalities of subjectivation that, in a different age, the cudgel of normativity would label as "perverse." We find it in Asian American performance, literature, theater, and video games. The killing/becoming of Michael Deng is an extreme but poignant example of an Asian Americanness premised precisely through the performance of unraveling.

The Model Minority and Theories of Asian American Subjectivity

First and foremost, model minority masochism is a theory of Asian American subject formation that centers the psychic and affective effects of the model minority "myth," based on the material positionality of Asian Americans of the past half-century. This theory presents a critique of model minority ideology itself but also serves as an analytic of its adherents and detractors alike. Whether as an antiblack "racial wedge" or as ideological fodder for the denial of Asian American racial suffering, the model minority has been a stubborn phantasm impeding the project of Asian American radical politics and has thus been the persistent specter of Asian Americanist critique. Indeed, the racialization of Asian Americans in the United States cannot be separated from model minority ideology (which I will henceforth abbreviate to "model minoritarianism"), which is in turn intertwined with the economic and affective dimensions of modernity. In Colleen Lye's words, the Oriental in America demonstrates "a putatively unusual capacity for economic modernity, extend[ing] to moments when the affect of the racial discourse has been hostile ('yellow peril') as well as admiring ('model minority')" (2005, 3). The model minority is oft mentioned but rarely firmly defined; loosely, the model minority is the minoritized subject who, despite their ostensible marginalization, is able to prosper and successfully assimilate into the dominant society. Although not limited to Asian Americans (the label has, at times, been applied to upper-middle-class gay communities and African immigrants, for example), the model minority has been most persistently wedded to Asian Americans, and there are few racial demographics in North America for which the model minority is more constitutive. For the purposes of my argument here, the model minority is only secondarily "cultural," although culturally essentialist underpinnings of the model minority run the gamut from assimilationist to orientalist, from a purported propensity for adaptation and assimilation to a maintenance of "Confucian values" that emphasize hard work and education.[2] This aspect of model minoritarianism is more obviously "myth," and I will not belabor a refutation here. Rather, I emphasize primary focus on the political-ideological function of the model minority in the maintenance of U.S. racial formation. In the United States, the model minority has principally served two ideological purposes within racial discourse: first, to provide evidence for the prominence of meritocracy over the structural barriers faced by nonwhite peoples, and second, to implicitly blame less "successful" minoritized populations for their own subjugation (most notably, but not exclusively, those racialized as Black). Moreover, as Tara Fickle has recently and incisively observed, the model minority coagulated in the 1960s around Japanese

Americans not only as exceptional minorities, but as exceptional Americans in *general*, perceived as obedient capitalist subjects relative even to whites, prompting white Americans to catch up (2019, 90).

For much of its life as a field, Asian American studies has tended to actively disprove or discredit the model minority as a myth, either insisting that (1) Asian Americans have been and continue to be subject to considerable racism and structural barriers, and (2) the model minority does not adequately reflect the socioeconomic diversity of Asian Americans, which can correlate loosely according to disaggregated identity. Thus, anti–model minority critique locates the model minority as a harmful stereotype produced by a white racial order, one that can cause harm to both Asian Americans (such as the increased pressure to "succeed," via stereotype threat) and to non-Asian people of color. Consequently, since its radical beginnings with the Third World Liberation Front strikes at San Francisco State and UC Berkeley in 1968, and continuing through a wide range of demographic and ideological shifts, Asian American studies has often sought to idealize what Christopher Lee has termed "the ideal critical subject,"[3] that is to say, an Asian American subject position that has achieved a kind of Lukácsian racial "consciousness" against white racism. Asian American cultural critique has often accordingly read Asian American literature and theater in terms of its "resistant" potential, seeking out characters and thematics that adequately demonstrate a rejection of whiteness and an assertion of Asian American identity, whether in the vein of so-called "cultural nationalism" of Frank Chin, of feminist empowerment in Maxine Hong Kingston, or of a resistance against logocentric intelligibility in Theresa Hak Kyung Cha. Tellingly, the first major scholarly study of Asian American literature, Elaine Kim's *Asian American Literature: An Introduction to the Writings and Their Social Context* (1982), values Asian American works primarily by their resistant potential rather than their aesthetic attributes, a tendency that persists in the field to varying degrees to this day. This premise possesses a range of problematics, most notably that "Asian America" is itself what Susan Koshy provocatively called "a fiction," an imagined community insofar as it is overwhelmingly diverse in terms of its diasporic cultural origins, but also in imagining its politically "resistant" position against white racism when, as David Palumbo-Liu has written, the position of Asian America has certainly structurally fluctuated between "of color" and honorary whiteness. Moreover, a persistent problem is that judgment of the resistant potential of anti–model minority Asian American literature is not persistent in what precisely it is resisting, whether that be "assimilation" (understood variably as cultural, such as through ethnic marking, or political, understood as allegiance to racially reactionary political positions), racist policy, or economic adherence to (racial) capitalism. To take the internment of Japanese Americans as an example, those Issei (immigrants) who chose to accept incarceration (with the saying "shigata ga nai," or, "it can't be helped") but who remained anti-assimilationist with regard to their cultural practices, exercised a different form of resistance than Nisei "No No Boys," who primarily spoke English and willingly adopted mainstream "American" cultural mores but refused to serve in the U.S. armed forces. Who is more of a "model minority" in this contrast depends entirely upon the lens through which we judge complicity—cultural, sociopolitical, economic, et cetera.

One component of this problematic is that we principally take the "model" of "model minority" in its adjectival, rather than in its verb, or even noun, form. *What, precisely, does the model minority model?* And then, conversely, what model of minority does the model minority produce? I suggest conceptualizing the model minority (or perhaps, minority *modeling*) as a scenario, which is, according to Diana Taylor, "a meaning-making paradigm that structure[s] social environments, behaviors, and potential outcomes" (2013, 28). The scenario includes narrative "but also demands that we also pay attention to milieux and corporeal behaviors such as gestures, attitudes, and tones not reducible to language" (Taylor 2013, 28)—that is, the scenario is as constructed by affect and performance as it is by the familiar story it signifies. The model minority is phantasmal yet instantly recognizable because of its performatic, scenario quality; it can be simultaneously exemplar and sellout, but its modeling tends toward the gravitational pull of social domination along variable axes.

Yet, the modeling may also pull in its opposite direction, as well—there is also the *model anti-model minority*, the "ideal critical subject" of Asian American consciousness referenced earlier. To nod to Homi Bhabha, to "model" is almost, but not quite, to mimic. Bhabha's mimic is a postcolonial figure who positionally resembles the model minority, the assimilated, educated native who threatens the colonial-racial order with their uncanny resemblance. Not unlike the model minority and the perpetual foreigner, "The ambivalence of colonial authority repeatedly turns from *mimicry*—a difference that is almost nothing but not quite—to *menace*—a difference that is almost total but not quite" (Bhabha 1994, 131). However, unlike the mimic, the model minority is marked less by uncanny resemblance to whiteness than by an aspiration to white ideals; resistance to this accordingly supplants those ideals with other ones. Within cultural productions associated with Asian American panethnicity, and certainly within literary representation, "resistance" tends be legible more through affect than through actual political position, and it very frequently takes on masculine characteristics. Frank Chin's work is particularly emblematic of this trend, misogynistically configuring performative masculine "authenticity" as the route to *resisting* the pull of whiteness, the will to servility to white institutions, cultures, and bodies. In Chin's mode, it is an affective disposition to favor whiteness, more than any materialist imperative, that forms the meat of resistance. As Việt Thanh Nguyễn has noted, many artists and scholars who have committed to an Asian American politic would go so far as to limit Asian Americanness to those who perform the required "resistant" identity, dismissive of those Asian Americans who are satisfied with the status quo of capitalist white racism.[4] Frank Chin, after all, derided Asian Americans with model minority inclinations as "Uncle Tom minorities." Nguyễn writes, "critics tend to evaluate resistance as positive and accommodation as negative, without questioning the reductiveness of such evaluations" and suggests instead an Asian Americanist scholarship accounts for the flexible strategies of Asian Americans who "pick and choose their tactics of struggle, survival, and possible assimilation" (2002, 7).

Thus, with Foucauldian irony, the principal mode of resistance to the model minority reproduces its transitive structure, modeling what it means *to model*. Anti–model minority resistance becomes modeling by other means.

I assert that it necessarily follows that the signifier "Asian American," as problematic as it is, must also incorporate the politically less savory presence of those subjects who are an anathema to Asian American cultural resistance, that is, the dreaded "good subjects," model minorities, the "hard-working, successful" nonwhites discursively positioned in an antiblack racial paradigm to invalidate the structural oppression against other subjects of color. Queer of color critics may note that my configuration bears some similarity to José Esteban Muñoz's formulation of disidentification, that is,

> like a melancholic subject holding on to a lost object, a disidentifying subject works to hold on to this object and invest it with new life. [. . .] it is the reworking of those energies that do not elide the 'harmful' or contradictory components of any identity" (1999, 12)

There is certainly a disidentificatory element to this theoretical project, although I believe it would be accurate to say that my project here is more accurately an exposure and undoing of, and meditation on, prior disavowal. As historical monographs by Ellen D. Wu and Madeline Y. Hsu have detailed,[5] the production of the Asian American model minority throughout the twentieth century is not entirely the result of a white racial hegemony but is partly the result of the strategic racial positioning by Asian Americans themselves, especially by Chinese and Japanese Americans. Strategic self-stereotyping as ideal conformists to the U.S. social order, while simultaneously self-orientalizing to associate "Asian values" as congruent with both U.S. capitalist culture and heteronormative sexual and kinship relations, allowed Chinese and Japanese Americans to adapt to the changing political circumstances between the United States, Japan, and China, particularly in response to Japanese American internment and anticommunist anxiety toward China.

Thus, to put it obtusely, the "model minority" is not merely a "myth"; or, rather, it is not a historical untruth, socioeconomically speaking. Certainly, in addition to being a scenario, the model minority is a myth in the Barthesian sense, a semiological system of signification that "points out and ... notifies, it makes us understand something and it imposes on us" (Barthes 1972, 87). Yet, it is a scenario actively embraced by some, if not many, Asian American subjects. So when Frank Chin provocatively decries Asian Americans as "racial Uncle Toms," he refers to both the Asian American positionality of accommodation *and* the presence of Asian American actors who comply with and further such racial ideologies (although again, this production is more consistently affective than ideological). The masculinist "cultural nationalist" project of which Frank Chin is emblematic does not deny the presence of the model minority (which is often coded in femininized, homophobic language), but it abjects the model minority as "false" Asianness. And although generations of

Asian Americanist critique have long since consigned the casual misogyny of Chin's work to the dustbin of history, the specter of the accommodationist racial Uncle Tom remains, haunting the Asian Americanist project as a constitutive Other, a supposed falsehood that lures Asian Americans into white supremacist and/or bourgeois accommodation. My point here is that from the perspective of Asian American subject formation, we must take seriously the model minority not as an object of immediate disavowal to support the reigning primacy of exclusion as the ontological condition of Asian Americanness, but rather as a foundation for the psychic and affective condition of being racialized as Asian in the United States; that is, as a fabric inextricably woven into Asian American subjectivity itself.

Nevertheless, there remains a degree of peril in addressing the very notion of Asian American subjectivity, particularly when, as I have stated earlier, Asian America is itself a socially constructed political affinity rather than a clearly defined diasporic ethnic community. I would even argue that "Asian America" is no less "mythological" than the model minority itself (except that Asian America, of course, serves as the model minority's ideological camera obscura). Given the diversity of ethnicities, nationalities, genders, and sexualities within "Asian America," it becomes particularly difficult to produce generalized studies of Asian American subjectivity per se. Lisa Lowe's influential 1991 essay "Heterogeneity, Hybridity, Multiplicity: Asian American Differences" called for the broadening of Asian Americanist scholarship beyond "master narratives of generational conflict and filial relation" (1996, 63) as dominated within Chinese and Japanese American writings, and it also gestured toward a transnationalization of Asian American studies at large. In a similar vein, as mentioned earlier, Kandace Chuh's 2003 monograph *Imagine Otherwise*, following Derrida, calls for "subjectless discourse" within Asian Americanist thought. Such indispensable texts push Asian American studies against an all-encompassing essentialism, and the momentous effects these texts have had on the field are undeniably warranted. Yet, as invaluable as they are, I would argue that neither Lowe nor Chuh's project evades the Asian American subject altogether, but, rather, they diversify, deconstruct, and problematize who and what that subject is. And moreover, even as we recognize the impossibility of a singular Asian American subject, it is necessary to understand the attachments it engenders. Although I fully sympathize with the caution against "master narratives" within the study of Asian American subjectivity, such critiques can obfuscate the fact that Asian America is inescapably a kind of "master narrative" itself, constructed with both political and aesthetic intentionality, with and against the figure of the model minority.

This is not to say that there is an "essential" Asian America, or that it has any "inherent" attributes but, rather, that it is performative: it manifests itself through its own utterance. Insofar as model minoritarianism becomes problematically equated with Asian Americanness, "Asian American" becomes as much a structural position as a demographic category. Although I embrace the problematic Asian American subject as an analytic, I do so rejecting the liberal identitarianism that privileges individual identity as an a priori attribute of difference. After all, it is a Foucauldian truism that subject formation cannot be analyzed without an analytic of power and the gaze that consigns it. The word "subject" invokes both *subjectivity* and *subjection*; one can only become a *subject* by being *subjected*, whether through ideological interpellation or discursive subjectivation.[6] In the case of racialized subjects such as Asian Americans, subject formation and racialization bleed into one another even (or especially) in the formation of an identity politically oppositional to racialization.[7] Thus, although racialization does not necessarily mean destiny, it remains constitutive of racial subject formation; in other words, minoritized racial subject formation does not solely occur "against" or "in spite of" racialization but also *with* it. Concerning Asians in North America, racialization in its multiple and well-tread aspects—orientalism, yellow peril, model minoritarianism, and so on—has produced a range of psychic quandaries for those ensnared in its interpellating optic. In other words, theorization of "the" Asian American subject is, at best, a metonymic diagnosis of the historical, material, and ideological forces that carve the social position that produces the subject in the first place.

Consequently, in the early 2000s, paralleling a similar trajectory in queer and Black studies, there arose a psychoanalytic turn to analyze the interiority of Asian American subjectivity as a consequence of this relationship to racial power, inaugurated first by David Eng's 2001 *Racial Castration*, and followed by Anne Cheng's 2002 *The Melancholy of Race* and Karen Shimakawa's 2002 *National Abjection*. Across these psychoanalytic writings, Asian American subjectivity is modeled after various iterations of lack brought upon by racial injury, such as the absence of the (normative white) phallus in Eng's case. Cheng's *Melancholy of Race* is particularly paradigmatic in this sense. Interpreting Freud, Cheng explains how melancholia, contrasted with mourning, is a pathological state of being "psychically stuck" (2000, 8) on the lost object, and that, furthermore, "The melancholic eats the lost object—feeds on it, as it were" (2000, 8) so that "the melancholic subject fortifies him- or herself and grows rich from the empowerment" (2000, 8) even as the melancholic subject denies the persistence of the mourned object. The initial subject of Cheng's racial melancholia is the white subject, as she explains that "[d]ominant white identity in America operates melancholically—as an elaborate identificatory system based on psychical and social consumption-and-denial" (2000, 11). Then Cheng asks, "What is the subjectivity of the melancholic object? Is it also melancholic, and what will we uncover when we resuscitate it?" (2000, 14), suggesting then that the (racialized) object of melancholy becomes a melancholic subject herself. The racialized melancholic pathologically feeds upon the lack, requiring the absence of the object in order to stabilize meaning.[8]

As invaluable as these studies are, these texts do not centrally examine the role of the model minority itself in Asian American subjectification. Melancholic lack powerfully accounts for the psychic exclusion of Asian Americans from the broader U.S. body politic and sociality; exclusion is central to these analytics, sidestepping the history of Asian Americans' conditional *inclusion*. Although one can make the historical argument for an Asian American exceptionalism regarding exclusion (e.g., via the notion that the 1882 Chinese Restriction Act was the first race-based form of legislated immigration exclusion in the United States), even within these measures of exclusion, there was the production of an ideal assimilated Asian American subject. To reference Madeline Hsu again, the 1882 Restriction Act was as much a process of curation as it was one of xenophobic exclusion, establishing "*gateways* that permitted admission to peoples deemed assimilable but also strategic" (2015, 8), such as students and professionals. According to Ellen Wu, even the Japanese American internment camps contained key elements to coerce the cultural assimilation of incarcerated Nisei, such as the encouragement of baseball play and, of course, armed services enlistment into the 442nd Regiment and the 100th Infantry Battalion. As a consequence, model minoritarianism even haunts many of the paradigmatic events of Asian American exclusion upon which theories of exclusion-based Asian American subjectivity are based.[9]

To be clear, I am not arguing that model minoritarianism is necessarily an ontological component of Asian American subjecthood. Rather, I posit that the model minority has been underestimated as a historically constitutive (rather than merely antithetical) component, something that must be "overcome" or rejected rather than a despised ingredient of Asiatic racial form, and that it must be considered *alongside* the conditions of lack (i.e., melancholia, castration) or exclusion (abjection). Consequently, I belabor that the model minority is not only a racial position, but a class position. This is not solely because the model minority's "success" is measured in capitalist metrics, although this is certainly an essential component. Bearing in mind Cedric Robinson's forceful argument that early bourgeois capitalism drew its ideological formations from racism, that the laboring and ruling classes even within early modern Europe were understood to be separated by origin, bloodline, and later, culture, racial formation is a defining feature of capitalist modernity, and all capitalism is already racial capitalism. To say that the model minority is antiblack ideology is an understatement—the ideological ambition of the model minority is nothing short of the preservation and expansion of racial capitalism itself. Model minority masochism is the affective tissue that coheres this formation, but, as I will explain, it also paradoxically congeals around the Asian American efforts to oppose it.

Given the particular positioning of Asian Americans as model minorities, I posit that masochism provides a more comprehensive analytic for Asian American subjecthood. This masochism maps onto both the subject formation and the cultural politics of the conditionally accepted model minority.

Masochism Theory

By "model minority masochism," I mean an affective response to model minority racialization that blurs the boundaries between subjugation, pleasure, and moral authority. Model minority masochism is simultaneously an affective process and a cultural politics,[10] a model of subjectivity that often embraces rather than eschews its status of otherness and subordination.

It is first important to clarify: What is masochism? Like the model minority, masochism remains a moving signifier. Colloquially, masochism implies pleasure from pain, although it would be more accurate to say that masochism represents the surrendering of control to achieve sensation, to feel and become through unbecoming. Although much of contemporary literary analysis of masochism owes much of its foundation to the psychiatry of Richard von Krafft-Ebing, the psychoanalytic frameworks developed by Sigmund Freud and Jacques Lacan,[11] as well as relational psychoanalysts such as Melanie Klein,[12] I draw principally from the post-psychoanalytic theories articulated by Gilles Deleuze and Amber Jamilla Musser. Deleuze, in his influential *Coldness and Cruelty*, theorizes masochism from its literary origins, the writings of Leopold von Sacher-Masoch, from whom the word "masochism" is derived. Departing from Freud, Deleuze's post-psychoanalytic description of masochism locates it as a phenomenon that manifests primarily as aesthetic form. In contrasting sadism and masochism, Deleuze writes,

> We are no longer in the presence of a torturer seizing upon a victim and enjoying her all the more because she is unconsenting and unpersuaded. We are dealing instead with a victim in search of a torturer and who needs to educate, persuade, and conclude an alliance with the torturer in order to realize the strangest of schemes. This is why advertisements are part of the language of masochism while they have no place in true sadism, and why the masochist draws up contracts while the sadist abominates and destroys them. (1989, 20)

Key to Deleuze's notion of masochism is the pursuit of external torture, and the formation of an alliance with that torturer. But also within the masochistic paradigm exists a reliance on contracts and agreements, cathecting erotic energy onto the social contractarianism of liberal modernity.

Moreover, according to Deleuze, suspension and disavowal primarily drive the masochistic apparatus, which aims to replace the father's moral authority with that of the mother's. Consequently, although still male centric like Freud's and Lacan's models, Deleuze's masochism attempts to recuperate the feminine, although ultimately in the service of a male ego, attempting to birth "a new sexless man" who is no longer dependent on masculine control. Deleuze argues that this is achieved through masochistic coldness:

> The coldness of the masochistic ideal ... is not the negation of feeling but rather the disavowal of sensuality. It is as if sentimentality assumed in this instance the superior role of the impersonal element, while sensuality held us prisoner of the particularities and imperfections of secondary nature. The function of the masochistic ideal is to ensure the triumph of ice-cold sentimentality by dint of coldness; the coldness is used here, as it were, to suppress pagan sensuality and keep sadistic sensuality at bay. Sensuality is disavowed, and no longer exists in its own right; thus Masoch can announce the birth of the new man "devoid of sexual love." (1989, 52)

Thus, Deleuze's masochism possesses an affective and aesthetic character rather than just a psychic one, premised upon the disavowal of sensuality.[13]

While Deleuze enables the literary critique of masochism, contemporary queer theory has considered its utopian potentials, equally within the critical project of queer negativity (including Leo Bersani and Lee Edelman) as well as its often-opposed queer of color critique (e.g., Nguyen Tan Hoang, Darieck Scott, Juana María Rodríguez, Leticia Alvarado, Elizabeth Freeman, and Ariane Cruz). The former, owing largely to Michel Foucault's early theorizations of S/M,[14] is characterized by Kadji Amin as possessing a "liberationist negativity" (2017, 95), finding self-annihilation as a form of idealized liberatory practice.[15] The latter queer of color critics tend toward theorizing penetrability and bottoming (which are certainly not identical to masochism but offer a similar heuristic premise) as a form of reappropriation for the raced subject, allowing the trauma of history to reorganize and detach from prescribed affects of terror and instead resignify through the jouissance of sexual pleasure. Both species of optimistic valuations place hope in masochism's ability to reorganize social relations, and to point to the particularly disruptive possibilities of bottoming against a heteropatriarchial racist order.

A compelling example of optimistic masochism can be found in Nguyen Tan Hoang's *A View from the Bottom: Asian American Masculinity and Sexual Representation* (2014). Nguyen's project lays out a project of bottomhood "not as a fixed role, an identity, or a physical act, but as a position—sexual, social, affective, political, aesthetic—[that] facilitates a more expansive horizon for forging political alliances" (2014, 3). Nguyen's queer examination of Asian American masculinity configures bottomhood not as a position of immediate subordination, but one of sexual agency and power within Asian American cultural production. Asian American gay bottomhood, for Nguyen, becomes "a hermeneutic, a tactic of information ... a tactic of joy" (2104, 24) deployed by "subjects that do not seek to overcome injury but those that have learned to live with past and present damage, in particular, everyday injuries marked by gender, race, and sexuality, that cannot find relief or make amends through legitimate social or political means" (2014, 25). Nguyen's assessment of bottomhood is ultimately quite optimistic, reading bottomhood—roughly the "masochistic" position—as a recuperative strategy to reconfigure past trauma. However, although Nguyen's queering of the relationship between power and pleasure within the site of Asian American masochism remains essential to my own argument, Nguyen's theoretical optimism leads to a potential utopianism to bottoming that does not fully encompass the multiple trajectories of power relations enacted upon Asian American subjectivity. Its model of Asian American subjectivity also remains attached to the prior Asian Americanist premise of exclusion and lack, as opposed to incorporating the heterogeneous vectors of power associated with the model minority.

Ultimately, I remain skeptical of both pessimistic and optimistic readings of masochism; I mean to deploy masochism in its descriptive rather than prescriptive capacities. Accordingly, I draw from the work of Amber Jamilla Musser, who boasts neither an optimistic nor pessimistic reading of masochism; instead, Musser is most interested in how masochism offers a theory of the subject at large. In the opening of *Sensational Flesh: Race, Power, and Masochism*, Musser writes,

> Usually understood as the power to abdicate control in exchange for sensation—pleasure, pain, or a combination thereof—[masochism] is a site where bodies, power, and society come together in multiple ways.... As such, masochism allows us to probe different ways of experiencing power. (2014, 1)

Although Musser herself complicates this definition throughout her book, what is crucial in this working definition is the often-counterintuitive intersection of pleasure and power that transcends its origins. "What begins as a literarily influenced sexual practice," continues Musser, "morphs into a universal aspect of subjectivity, a way to describe a type of relationship between self and other, a subversive mode of desubjectification or resistance to dominant forms of power, and finally a privileged mode of personhood" (2014, 2). I follow Musser's conceptualization of masochism as not only a sex act, but also an analytic. And the stakes of this analytic rise dramatically when hailed into a minoritized, "oppressed" position that critically engages the paradox of what it means to take pleasure from one's own oppression, or at least, from some relationship to it. Importantly, Musser indicates that masochism is a mode of desubjectification, a form of actively undoing the subject. Yet, even as it desubjectivizes, it also simultaneously remains a "universal aspect of subjectivity," meaning that the undoing of the subject does not mean its dissolution. Masochism captures the subjectivity that coheres around self-inflicted incoherence, which is descriptive of the model minority that haunts Asian American panethnicity.[16]

To crystalize my previous points, and to gesture to my next ones, I posit here five theses of model minority masochism:

1. First, Asian Americans, insofar as Asian Americans have been historically constructed as a panethnic identity formation, have had a masochistic relationship to the model minority scenario.
2. Second, the model minority is constructed equally in economic terms as it is in racial ones. The metric upon which the minority is successfully "modeling" is according to bourgeois ideologies of attainment and uplift.
3. Third, the model minority is itself a masochistic social relation. Modeling, similar to mimicry, follows a perverse pattern, projecting an idealization to which the subject should submit.
4. Fourth, model minority masochism follows either a primary or secondary configuration. In the primary configuration, model minoritarianism is undifferentiated and direct, entailing submission and obedience to the economic-racial ideal—capitalist whiteness. In this configuration, model minoritarianism takes on techno-orientalist traits. In the secondary configuration, model minoritarianism operates as disavowal, resisting the temptation of capitalist whiteness to aspire to transcendence, which often takes the form of an idealized Blackness.

5. Fifth, model minority masochism is a gendered affect, often (but not necessarily) drawing upon phallocentric anxieties or pleasures of feminization to produce its heterogeneous masculinities.

My argument here is that Asian American subjectivity is best understood precisely through this desubjectification, and equally, self-objectification. Asian American subjectivity becomes itself through its own undoing. This is in part due to the impossibility of the singular Asian American subject—in other words, its very constructedness—but also the affective investments with and against model minoritarianism that produce the Asian American as a legible subject of power, existing liminally between strategic inclusion and radical otherness. Pulled doubly by the diametrically opposed moral authorities of assimilation and "good" subjecthood and the resistant anti–model minority imperative of "bad" subjecthood, masochism manifests in Asian American subjectivity in both directions: the pleasure of being stereotyped, or additionally, assimilated, as well as the pleasure of self-punishment from enjoying being stereotyped or assimilated.[17]

Model minority masochism must account not only for exclusion, but also inclusion, as flawed and contingent model minority inclusion may be. Masochism's function as *both* a technology of subjectification *and* a moral economy maps onto the model minority paradigm, since masochism possesses an internal logic of accommodation and subversion at once. I wish to consider how such formulations affect the affective fabric of Asian Americanness itself; thus, I consider model minority masochism to be, among other things, *a cultural politics*—or, perhaps, what Ariane Cruz has termed a "politics of perversion" (2016, 10)—one that shapes the Asian American self as much as it does the moral logic of a liminally interpellated panethnic community.

Masculinity, Techno-Orientalism, and the Machinations of Gender

Amber Jamila Musser, reading both Simone de Beauvoir's and Jean-Paul Sartre's unflattering descriptions of masochism, points to objecthood as central to masochism. "Masochism is an obsession with the state of being an object" (2014, 65), writes Musser, primarily referring to Beauvoir's argument that the female masochist is preoccupied with being the object of desire for the male. Continuing to a reading of Sartre, Musser adds that "[i]n masochism, the subject imagines him- or herself as relying entirely on the Other for existence, thereby attempting to more fully become an object for the other and to annihilate his or her own subjectivity and transcendence" (2014, 79). Read alongside Judith Butler's argument that the subject "is dependent on power for one's very formation" (1997, 9), masochism structurally thwarts itself; it is at once necessary for the minoritized subject for their own legibility and simultaneously signals a desire for annihilation of that very legibility.

Due to masochism's preoccupation with objecthood, the ostensible surrender of agentic subjectivity, I suggest that for Asian Americans, masochism often manifests in a peculiar form specific to the historical substance of Asiatic racial form. Since Colleen Lye suggests that "the Asiatic [is] a figure for the unrepresentable" (2005, 7), she asks, "how is the unrepresentable to be visualized? Does it have a human body? If not, what shape, as a whole or in part, does it take?" (2005, 7). Regarding the white U.S. literary consciousness, Lye suggests that we should not assume that Asiatic racial form has unmediated access to the human. But this ambivalence around Asiatic humanity does not only exist in the white American naturalist literature of Lye's study, but also within the double consciousness of Asian American cultural production itself; across multiple Asian American works, we see this instability of the human, a "thinglikeness" within Asianness. To invoke Mel Chen's groundbreaking theory of animacies, we could say that Asianness indexes an affective difference of animacy away from a "humanity" whose paragon is inescapably white, male, and normative.

Thus far, I have discussed masochism and the model minority in fairly ungendered terms. The discussion of objecthood so central to the study of masochism has a long history, particularly in the construction of ideal femininity, but has been most rigorously and recently theorized in Asian Americanist scholarship by Anne Anlin Cheng in *Ornamentalism* (2018). Cheng argues that the femininity of Asian women in the "West"—whom she provocatively labels "yellow women"—occupies a perihuman position between object/thing and person. She then deploys "ornamentalism" as a term, which "names the perihumanity of Asiatic femininity, a peculiar state of being produced out of the fusion between 'thingliness' and 'personness'" (2018, 18). Cheng powerfully argues that the discursive production of the "ornament" and the "orient" bear some mutually constitutive overlap, especially in terms of the yellow woman's synthetic qualities, and that "racial personhood can be assembled not through organic flesh but instead through synthetic inventions and designs, not through corporeal embodiment but rather through attachments that are metonymic and hence superficial, detachable, and migratory" (2018, 19).

In a sense, my elaboration of model minority masochism provides a complementary theorization. Cheng's description of the "ornamental" construction of Asiatic femininity encompasses more than "yellow women"—the ornamental, objectlike, feminized status of the Orient as something to be possessed and beheld is a key epistemological component of orientalism at large, regardless of the gender of those caught in the gaze. But where Cheng considers the perihuman femininity of Asian women from the 19th through 21st centuries, I focus principally on Asian American masculinity from the late 20th century to the contemporary moment. This masochistic Asian American masculinity is both reactive to and commingled with this Asiatic ornamental feminization, against which we can consider much of the Asian American Movement to be a reaction. Through masochism, contemporary Asian American masculinity is also caught within the ornamental thingliness that Cheng ascribes to Asiatic femininity, but it finds its relationship to the synthetic through other gendered means: the machinic and the digital.

I reference here a body of literature that concerns itself with the relationship of Asian racial form with technological production, an affinity that has been termed "techno-orientalism," which I would argue is also a key instantiation of model minority masochism. David Morley and Kevin Robins were the first to elucidate this new iteration of orientalism, describing how the Japanese have been variously configured in Western discourse as "little yellow men" or "ants" (1995, 147) who, through forms of mimesis, were attempting to "steal America's soul" (1995, 149–151). Morley and Robins configure Japan as being simultaneously a future and a past, a temporal dystopia where robots and samurai simultaneously represent the loss of selfhood and personhood so arduously won through the development of liberal modernity in white society. Techno-orientalist critique emphasizes how Asian subjects and Asian bodies take on traits of not only the synthetic, as in ornamentalism, but the machinic. Associations of Asians with the machinic are not exceptional in their racialization; as Louis Chude-Sokei has convincingly argued, Karel Čapek drew heavily upon the figure of the enslaved African as inspiration for the original robot. But the techno-oriental remix of this racial formation presents a curious cocktail when mixed with Yellow Perilist anxieties, which often map conveniently upon ones surrounding postmodernity. Indeed, as Sau-Ling Wong and Rachel C. Lee write, "Asians have been contradictorily imagined as, on the one hand, machine-like workers, accomplishing 'inhuman' feats of 'coolie' manual labor, and on the other, as brainiac competitors whose technological adeptness ranges from inventing gunpowder to being good with engineering and math" (2003, xiv). Wendy Chun writes that such orientalism "seeks to orient the reader to a technology-overloaded present/future ... through the premise of readable difference, and through a conflation of information networks with an exotic urban landscape" (2006, 177). Techno-orientalism also takes on aspects of mass reproducibility and an absence of originality,[18] a consequence of the machine-like incapacity to originate. Echoing Morley and Robins, Adrian Johns describes the binary of 1980's American Japanophobia: "Almost routinely, now, one side was identified as 'American' and 'creative,' the other as Japanese and, implicitly, imitative" (2010, 454). Indeed, Asian subjects and Asian bodies take on traits of the synthetic altogether; as Sianne Ngai elaborates, Asianness is racially coded as not only "silent, inexpressive, and ... emotionally inscrutable" (2005, 93), but consequently less "animate," on the spectrum "between the organic-vitalistic and the technological-mechanical, and between the technological-mechanical and the emotional" (2005, 95).

While critique of techno-orientalism has recently flourished within Asian American cultural studies—evidenced, for example, by Stephen Hong Sohn's "Alien/Asian" special issue in *MELUS* (2008) and the field-consolidating anthology *Techno-Orientalism: Imagining Asia in Speculative Fiction, History, and Media* co-edited by David Roh, Betsy Huang, and Greta Niu (2015)—much of the critique of techno-orientalism has largely focused on representation. Yet, the discussion of techno-orientalism can be expanded considerably further beyond stereotypical representation; techno-orientalism is itself a *technology* of subjectification, woven not only into the interpellating hail of white supremacist racial formation, but also within the optics of self-actualization among the racialized. Moreover, I suggest that undergirding Asian American techno-orientalism is model minority masochism, more specifically, that techno-orientalism as practiced by Asian Americans is one of the key instantiations of model minority masochism.

Already, it should be apparent that there are parallels between techno-orientalism and the model minority, both in terms of the attributes they index—relentlessly hard-working, eminently useful, enmeshed success in science and technology—and how they are similarly disavowed within Asian American cultural politics. I would go so far as to argue that the techno-oriental is the grotesque personification of the model minority itself, providing the figure with an optic vocabulary, replete with both the promises and perils of an increasingly technologized society. Insofar as Asianness becomes associated with a laboring body—once the coolie, now the Asian tech worker—Asiatic racial form shifts according to the status of material labor conditions. And as contemporary neoliberal society becomes increasingly enmeshed in high technology and new media, the boundary between human and machine in general grows increasingly blurry. Techno-orientalism, then, provides an essential imaginary and visual vocabulary for masochistic self-objectification. Concurring with Musser's assessment that "masochism is a mobile entity whose meanings shift depending on context" but nevertheless "hovers around ... discussions of pleasure and racialization" (2014, 167), I argue that masochism becomes a fruitful yet amorphous analytic for techno-orientalism and its discontents. My assertion, then, is that techno-orientalist racialization, as it pertains to masculine Asian American subjects, can best be analyzed through masochistic self-objectification.

Furthermore, techno-orientalism illuminates the means by which this Asian American model minority masochism is, in fact, gendered. As a tradition of feminist modernist scholarship has convincingly argued, the fear of becoming-machine has been associated with a terror of castration.[19] Mechanization becomes associated not only with the endlessly reproducible Taylorist embodiment within capitalist industrialism, but also with a panic of feminization, the removal of self-determinist agency at the core of modern Western masculinity. The female, then, is consigned to the machine position, instrumentalized like the femininized labor with which she is associated.[20] To become the machine, in other words, is to assume the position of the patriarchally consigned feminine, the *used* as opposed to the *user*.

Although the position of the female machine has been thoroughly reappropriated—most emblematically, of course, by Donna Haraway's iconic "A Manifesto for Cyborgs"—the becoming-machine becomes something of a threat, in particular, to hegemonic masculinity. The techno-orientalization of the Asian American *masculine* subject, then, engenders not only a masochistic relationship, but also a valence of feminization, of ornamentalism. Similarly, it is worth noting that the very dialectic between the "resistance" of the bad subject and the "accommodation" of the model minority good subject maps onto a problematic, heteronormatively masculine/feminine binary. Just as the anxiety over techno-orientalism is an often-misogynist anxiety over feminization, so might the anxiety over being or becoming a model minority.

We should pause to consider these implications in conversation with preexisting studies on Asian American masculinity. As David Eng, Celine Parreñas Shimizu, and Nguyen Tan Hoang have each already illuminated at length, Asian American masculinity finds itself variously "castrated" or "straitjacketed," cast in incomplete, feminized manhood relative to hegemonic white heteromasculinity. These prior studies of Asian American masculinity rightfully argue that this disruption of masculinity may possess a productive element, queering and potentially dismantling an allegiance to the patriarchal logic of white supremacy itself.

Moreover, this manuscript offers, in many respects, a critique of the most hegemonic dimensions of contemporary Asian American subjectivity, and these most hegemonic dimensions have tended toward the most privileged sectors of Asian American identity formation—the cis heteromasculine, the East Asian, and largely upper-middle class. Overwhelmingly, the cultural productions in this text largely (although not exclusively) fit this demographic profile, precisely because of their hegemonic status within Asian American subjectivity. The vital importance of scholars such as Lowe and Chuh is to imagine beyond this hegemonic construction, or beyond subjectivity altogether, since such subjectivity has been moored to these dominant figurations for so long—I share the same objective but through opposite means, turning *to* these masculine logics in order to understand and disassemble their operations. It is, I believe, an appropriately masochistic move.

Method, Theory, and the Suspenseful Reveal

It should be apparent from the preceding pages that the humanistic theoretical traditions I draw from are exceedingly diverse: psychoanalysis, queer Marxism, Foucauldian poststructuralism, technocultural theory, and phenomenology, among others. Ultimately, from a methodological standpoint, this book resides most definitively in performance studies and queer of color critique, fields whose methodological hybridity reflects my own refusal of theoretical "allegiance." Queer theory has, by and large, committed to an ethico-politics of disrupting normativity; Judith Butler, for example, has argued forcefully for the reconcilability between Althusserian/Foucauldian models of the subject and psychoanalytic ones in *The Psychic Life of Power*. Similarly, within performance studies, the intellectual threads vary vastly in order to account for the performance (or performing object), the audience, and the mise-en-scène that encompasses them.

Because of the scope of model minority masochism within Asian American masculinity, I have chosen an eclectic range of objects across multiple media, including more rarefied objects such as avant-garde theater and alternative literature, as well as new media objects from popular culture such as comic books and video games. Doing so allows me to center panethnic masculine Asian American subjectivity itself, rather than any particular literary or aesthetic form, as the primary object of study. Nevertheless, I treat each medium differently, relative to its particular relationship to content and form, and consider how each object in each medium builds upon that which precedes it. Moreover, the objects chosen are overwhelmingly male and East Asian American—as stated earlier, I make this choice intentionally, precisely because male East Asian Americans have historically had the easiest, least ambiguous claims to Asian American panethnicity more broadly, in both its model minority and resistant valences. I certainly risk reifying East Asian masculine hegemony by doing so, but model minority masochism is principally a critique of these most dominant, visible iterations of Asian American masculine subjectivity. It is my hope that, by both provincializing and interrogating this segment of relative privilege within Asian American panethnicity, I can contribute toward the dislodging of its hegemony, while at the same time illuminating the scope of its influence. I should also explicitly clarify that by no means is this book a critique of Asian American "emasculation"; not only is this topic already quite well trodden, but analytically, this text has no political investments in any "restoration" or "redemption" of masculinity, heteromasculinity especially (if anything, quite the opposite).

Moreover, this book is not a historical treatise. Nevertheless, I would like to offer a humble historiographic framing to explain why the focus of this text is from 1982 to the present. Loosely speaking, contemporary panethnic Asian American subject formation can be traced to three key periods. The early period, from 1968 to 1982, can best be described as a radical period—"Asian America" was in a nascent activist phase (particularly in California) alongside the Black Power and Chicano Movements that variously contended with diverse anti-imperialist, internationalist, and also cultural nationalist articulations, conceptualizing "Asian American" as principally a coalitional, resistant identity. In this period, dominated by Asian Americans who were descendants of pre-1965 immigration waves, the model minority was acknowledged as "real" but forcefully excluded from the Asian American political project. Then, from 1982 to 1992, is what I consider the liberal period; as the first chapter seeks to establish, the murder of Vincent Chin in Detroit in 1982 and the activist aftermath Americanized Asian American discourse, paradoxically attempting to dispel the model minority as "myth" while incorporating the model minority's aspirational logics. This period saw a vast expansion of "Asian American" identity as a mainstream panethnic identifier and successfully incorporated a broader, non-activist population into its fold. The current period, from 1992 to the present, is what I consider the period of Asian American neoliberalism, marked by the 1992 Los Angeles riots and the corresponding spectacle of "roof Koreans," characterized by explicit antiblackness, the erosion of Third World coalition, and an active, celebratory incorporation of Asian Americans into technocratic neoliberalism. This book covers subjects principally from the second and third periods—liberal and neoliberal formulations of Asian American subjectivity—but some texts yearn nostalgically for the first radical period, with many authors having emerged from that time themselves.

The first two chapters serve as a temporal/historical launching point for the narrative of the larger project, reading the event of Vincent Chin's murder as a crucial moment that binds together contemporary Asian American subjectification, techno-orientalism, and masochism. In Chapter 1, I read the racially motivated murder of Vincent Chin in 1982 not only as a profound event of domestic 1980s Japanophobia, but also as a pivotal social drama that enacted the techno-orientalist interpellation of today's contemporary Asian American subject. The landmark 1988 film *Who Killed Vincent Chin* presents a documented sequence of a large, carnivalesque gathering in which a crowd of predominantly white American adults bludgeon Japanese cars using sledgehammers with intense, vengeful abandon. While Frank Eaman, the defense attorney for Vincent Chin's murderer, claims that "it's a quantum leap … to say you're angry at, uh, Japanese imports and then hate Oriental people," the embodied public practice of violence produces a vital discursive, affective link between violence against a technological threat—the Japanese automobile—and the slaying of Vincent Chin at the hands of disgruntled white autoworkers Ronald Ebens and Michael Nitz. Using this scene as a foundation, I assert that through the Japanophobic 1980's white American imaginary, the Asian body became conflated with that of the automobile itself, and that conversely Vincent Chin underwent a Deleuzian "becoming-car," setting a precedent for the techno-orientalist subject position that Asian Americans continue to occupy in the North American logic of late capitalism. Examining the murder of Chin and its aftermath, I explore the death of Vincent Chin on two levels: (1) the murder by Ebens and Nitz as a performative choreography that transmuted Chin from human to machine, and (2) a gesture toward examining the discursive aftershocks of Chin by way of persisting techno-orientalism that informs contemporary Asian American subject formation and identity performance, particularly in the consolidation of Asian American liberalism. Furthermore, through archival research of the documents of the American Citizens for Justice (ACJ), the organization that mobilized the Asian American community to protest the light sentences given to Ebens and Nitz, I argue that the discourse surrounding the Asian American protest was configured primarily to counter techno-oriental racialization and the affective "coldness" associated with the orientalized, but countering this racialization also necessarily entailed a politics of respectability that performed Asian American assimilation into liberal democracy. Chin was, after all, slain after emerging from a strip club on the eve of his wedding, but only the wedding would be mentioned by ACJ publicity (with the strip club referred to generally as a "bar"). The sexual/masculine aspects of Chin's murder were understandably downplayed, but by casting Chin posthumously as both moral paragon and "normative" in his Americanness (in other words, model minority), the ACJ inadvertently reinforced the very logics of techno-orientalism that had impelled Chin's demise. Doing so furthermore established a masochistic relationship between the death/becoming-car of Chin and Asian American subject formation.

The second chapter is an immediate sequel to the first, examining two staged performances contending with the murder of Vincent Chin that transpired in the decades that followed his death: Ping Chong's 1995 play *Chinoiserie* and Philip Kan Gotanda and Frank Wu's trial re-enactment at UC Hastings in 2013. Each of these is considered a performance in the larger social drama of the Chin murder, each reconfiguring model minority masochism. I argue that *Chinoiserie* continues the liberal cultural politics laid by the ACJ while imbuing the Chin event with libidinal force through a masochistic aesthetic of suspenseful reveal. *Chinoiserie* teases the Chin murder throughout its narrative, offering it as a final climactic *jouissance* of a China/America dialectic, concluding a rhythm that lurches the audience ever closer to its end. In contrast, the UC Hastings re-enactment imagines masochism otherwise, subjecting the Chin narrative itself to masochistic scrutiny in order to reveal the systemic inadequacy of a liberal legal system to provide redress.

Chapter 3 then presents a psychoanalytic examination of "resistant" Asian American masochism premised upon the disavowal of the model minority through an idealization of Blackness. I frame this chapter with a masochistic question by Vijay Prashad, who, invoking W. E. B. DuBois, famously and provocatively asked the South Asian American community, "How does it feel to be the solution?" It is a question, applied across Asian Americans generally, that is painstakingly negotiated in the work of acclaimed Japanese American playwright Philip Kan Gotanda, whose work bears exceptional relevance in contemporary Asian American cultural politics as it contends with model minority discourse and the relationship of Asian Americanness to Blackness in the U.S. racial system. Through a comparative reading of two of Gotanda's plays, *After the War* (2007) and *I Dream of Chang and Eng* (2011), this chapter analyzes the role of Black characters in signifying longing for a politically redemptive Asian American subject position while simultaneously demonstrating the limits of Asian American radicality within an antiblack hegemony. This chapter argues that Gotanda positions Blackness as a moral center of unambiguous oppression, conjuring what I call the "Afro-Asian superego," and considers the Asian American political choice of either solidarity or complicity, ambivalent about agency as the Asian American subject is positioned as both victim and perpetrator of epistemic violence. Thus, I consider how Blackness operates as a racial superego for the Asian American masculine political imagination, subjecting Asian American identity to masochistic punishment by an ideal of Black resistance. Ultimately, this chapter ends gesturing toward the pleasure of failure, of the morally masochistic punishment for failing political responsibility.

Building upon the exploration of a coalitional, self-punishing Asian American anti–model minority masochism, Chapter 4 turns to the 2006–2007 run of Marvel Comics' *Incredible Hulk*, penned by Korean American writer and filmmaker Greg Pak. Also an acclaimed independent filmmaker of such Asian American works as *Robot Stories* and *Asian Pride Porn*, Pak authored a now-celebrated run of *The Incredible Hulk* from 2006 to 2007 entitled *Planet Hulk* and *World War Hulk*. In these two sequential storylines of superhero comics, Pak reinterprets the Hulk—a Jekyll-and-Hyde-inspired beast whose strength grows proportional to his anger and sense of hurt—as a racialized tragic hero/messiah who becomes a utopian revolutionary leader of other fellow abjected monsters, only for his own rage to be the hamartia that ironically brings everything to ruin. Whereas Chapter 3 dwells upon the psychic landscape of idealized Blackness, Chapter 4 interrogates the logics of cultural politics that allow such idealizations to occur in the first place: that is, a politics of ressentiment. I argue that Pak reinterprets the iconic superhero as a loose allegory of racial ressentiment, deftly utilizing the graphic novel as a form to stage the limits of racial ressentiment itself. As a creature who literally feeds on ressentiment, the Hulk requires more pain (both emotional and physical) to actualize and become legible to himself. I read Pak's run with *Hulk* as an Asian Americanist and techno-orientalist reclamation of a classic superhero figure as the boundless rage embodied within the body of a meek scientist (and doubly emphasized by Pak's introduction of Asian American sidekick Amadeus Cho, as well as his own tacit acknowledgment of the fact in the Asian American superhero anthology *Secret Identities*). Yet, in Pak's 2006–2007 run, the Hulk opens greater political possibilities not through the moral economy of ressentiment, but through the embrace of his penetrability and pleasurable desubjectification, that is to say, masochism. Pak's *Hulk* demonstrates the crucial differences between ressentiment's "politics of woundedness" and the pleasures of masochism, ultimately offering a contentiously optimistic vision of masochism as a potential dialectical corrective to contemporary Asian American cultural politics.

The final two chapters return to the techno-orientalization, becoming-machine, and model minority embrace of the opening Vincent Chin chapters. In Chapter 5, I ask: How does one *feel* when becoming-machine? Chapter 5 follows the encounter between techno-orientalism and masochism initiated with Vincent Chin into the realm of literature, focusing on the becoming-car and other becoming-objects and tying this techno-orientalist move to affective coldness, one of the two primary affective facets of Deleuzian masochism. As Stephen Sohn writes regarding techno-orientalism, "Alien/Asians conduct themselves with superb technological efficiency and capitalist expertise, their *affectual absence* resonates as undeveloped or, worse still, a retrograde humanism" (2008, 8, emphasis mine). Such an observation is striking alongside Fredric Jameson's (in)famous declaration that, in late capitalism,

> The end of the bourgeois ego, or monad, no doubt brings with it the end of the psychopathologies of that ego—what I have been calling *the waning of affect*. But it means the end of much more—the end, for example, of style, in the sense of the unique and the personal, *the end of the distinctive individual brush stroke* (as symbolized by the emergent primacy of mechanical reproduction). (1991, 15, emphasis mine)

Within techno-orientalist cultural production, the "waning of affect" is perhaps best embodied by the racialized Asian figure; affectively, the techno-oriental is the postmodern subject par excellence whose hordelike presence also signifies "the end of the distinctive individual brush stroke." Furthermore, affective flatness seems to signify the absence of an interiority, an "interior milieu" in Bernard Stiegler's terms, as the techno-orientalized figure is affectively rendered as only exterior, as only tool.

Thus, I turn to works of contemporary alternative literature written by Asian American men. I analyze Tao Lin's semiautobiographical novel *Taipei* (2013) and

Tan Lin's fictional memoir *Insomnia and the Aunt* (2011) as texts that conceptualize Asianness itself as affective flatness accessible through technological mediation. In the ostensibly postracial *Taipei*, Tan Lin produces an aesthetic of flatness to demonstrate the Asian male protagonist's interface with high technology and new media, although close examination of the text reveals a considerable preoccupation with racialization, a means of accessing Asianness precisely through becoming-machine. As the protagonist Paul moves through the mundane minutiae of his digitized life, his phenomenological experience with the world becomes indistinguishable from technological interface, which also, in turn, is the central means by which he accesses a sense of race, all while the text attempts to performatively position itself as having achieved model minority inclusion. Meanwhile, Tan Lin's *Insomnia*, described as an "ambient" text, situates its narrator reflecting on his childhood with his Chinese aunt, with whom he watches television late into the night. *Insomnia* effectively demonstrates explicitly what *Taipei* does implicitly: a relationship between affective flatness, becoming-machine, and Asian American subjectification. Together, these texts express a racial phenomenology inherited by the techno-orientalization elaborated in the previous chapter, suggesting that Asian American masculinity retains masochistic attachment to machineness.

Finally, all threads of inquiry converge in Chapter 6, which concludes with a critical playing of the 2011 cyberpunk video game *Deus Ex: Human Revolution* (*DX:HR*) by Eidos Montreal. This chapter delves into new media analysis of an explicitly techno-orientalist video game in order to provocatively explore masochistic self-annihilation. As a medium, the video game particularly emphasizes the presence of the gamer—who is part reader, writer, and actor—and places them directly into a masochistic relationship with the game itself. The potential for technologization of Asian bodies explodes exponentially in the medium of video gaming, in which the player immerses and empathizes with the environment and procedural logics of the gameworld. *DX:HR* deploys an interplay of cyberpunk content and an immersive first-person gaming interface to generate a cyber-racial erotics of violence. The 2011 video game, widely touted for its agentic gameplay, "cyberrenaissance" aesthetics, and posthumanist themes, stars a white male "supercrip" cyborg detective named Adam Jensen as he unravels a transnational corporate conspiracy to control the world through cybernetic augmentation. As the player assumes the body of Jensen to explore the near-future world of *DX:HR*, they encounter classic, sexually mediated orientalist tropes in the Chinese dystopia Hengsha, such as China doll prostitutes, dragon ladies, dirty streets, and (cybernetic) Asians who "all look the same," all of which serve as signifiers of a cyberpunk, techno-orientalist ethos.

As a game, a medium governed predominantly by active and direct interactivity, *DX:HR* satisfies the desire for masochistic self-annihilation, providing an opportunity for the Asian American gamer to experience not only their own body-as-stereotype, but also their own body-as-other. I argue that this is precisely how *DX:HR* presents generative potential for the Asian subject who plays it and engages its deeply problematic gameworld. I thus suggest that by playing and performing within the techno-orientalist gameworld of *DX:HR*, the Asian American subject may exercise a mode of what Elizabeth Freeman terms "erotohistoriography," a deployment of violent erotics to contend with one's own subject formation. Through a reading of *DX:HR* , this concluding chapter gestures to an Asian American cultural politics that locates itself in slippages, role reversals, and unintuitive affects. *DX:HR* is a private theater for the racially depressed, presenting a virtual world of self-annihilation for the Asian American gamer to reflectively interrogate their own racialization.

Thus, across multiple media, *Model Minority Masochism* aims to provoke, flirt, and lacerate in the manner of its objects of study. Through these instantiations of self-objectification and self-annihilation, *Model Minority Masochism* subjects Asian Americanist critique to the masochistic operations that have long lurked beneath as a dominant cultural logic. It aims to capture a portrait of contemporary panethnic Asian American masculinity: bound up, haptically pliable, endlessly reproducible, a conduit of racial power relations whose future remains uncertain.

1
Vincent Chin's Wedding
Techno-Orientalist Becoming and Asian American Liberalism

So long as it has been the home of the "Big Three" automakers—General Motors, Ford, and Chrysler—Detroit has been called "Motor City." There is something of an automobile phenomenology to Detroit, which I felt as I took to the freeway. As Jack Katz wrote,

> [T]he driver, as part of the praxis of driving, dwells in the car, feeling the bumps on the road as it contacts with his or her body not as assaults on the tires, swaying around curves as if the shifting of his or her weight will make a difference in the car's trajectory, loosening and tightening the grip on the steering wheel as a way of interacting with other cars. (2000, 32)

In driving, one "becomes" the car one drives, and Detroit feels as if it were built with this fundamental truth in mind. When I drove to visit them, Vincent and Lily, I did so down I-94 East from Ann Arbor in a Chevy Impala, which felt something like the bulky plate mail of sedans, hurling down long, wide lanes of asphalt like a unidirectional joust. Baudrillard once wrote of the Southern California freeway, "Driving is a spectacular form of amnesia. Everything is to be discovered, everything to be obliterated" (2020, 9), referring to the visuality of Californian deserts continuously unfolding as one cuts across them, but driving in Detroit feels more like an act of remembrance of a once-thriving futurity, of hugging the husks of industrialism amid a postindustrial sprawl. On the radio, Tupac Shakur's "Dear Mama" came on:

> When I was low you was there for me
> And never left me alone because you cared for me
> And I could see you coming home after work late
> You're in the kitchen trying to fix us a hot plate
> Ya just working with the scraps you was given
> And mama made miracles every Thanksgiving
> But now the road got rough, you're alone
> You're trying to raise two bad kids on your own
> And there's no way I can pay you back
> But my plan is to show you that I understand
> You are appreciated (1995, 2:18-2:46)

2 Model Minority Masochism

It was curious, listening 2Pac's tough-love ode to his mother, a rap by a legendary young man of color who died prematurely, on my way to the gravesites of the murdered son and grieving mother, both of whom would instantiate a key moment of Asian American history. Following a map I'd found in the archives the day before, I pulled into Forest Lawn Cemetery, taking the map's turns until I arrived at my destination: the Chin headstones. Lily Chin and her husband C. W. Hing Chin were memorialized in front, a red standing headstone emblazoned with Chinese characters and two lions. And behind them was their son, Vincent J. Chin. "Forever in our hearts / Beloved Son," it read. May 18, 1955 – June 23, 1983.

After I laid sunflowers at the sites, I found it difficult to leave, standing alone at the plots, the air utterly still. That this son and mother, whose lives would become narrativized and iconized in ways far beyond their control, were people who were just trying to live their lives. If the Asian American condition is one of melancholia, as Anne Cheng, David Eng, and Shinhee Han have argued, then one need look no further than these two grassy plots for proof. Affect is not only a sticky thing; it is a radiant one: the headstones were warm from the sunlight, and I wondered who else had knelt here before. Words can grasp at the violence inflicted on him—whole communities, marches, even identities formed in the discursive placenta of slogans and banners—and yet at the end of it all, the stillness can only barely allude to what had unfolded to shape our present.

One of the most iconic, haunting images in Asian American history is a portrait of Mrs. Lily Chin taken by Helen Zia, which first appeared in the Chinese American periodical *East West Journal*. Middle-aged and conservatively dressed, Mrs. Chin is seated in a cropped, humble room, her torso facing the camera but her head tilted a few degrees away, her face betraying a solemn sadness. But most importantly, a photo of her son Vincent sits on her lap, which she cradles intimately. It is a portrait of mourning, bespeaking a silent, exhausted rage, the photo-within-the-photo portraying a man tragically young for his life to be cut short, his mother's grim stoicism undergirded not only by calamity, but by injustice.

In the 2009 documentary *Vincent Who?*, activist Stewart Kwoh states, "We don't have a lot of Jesse Jacksons in our community, but we do have a number of Lily Chins." As a prominent figure throughout the campaign for redress, Lily Chin was a deeply influential, earnest voice for her murdered son, and her grief was a public spectacle, bringing her a level of minor celebrity through her passionate appearances at a multitude of rallies, press conferences, and news articles from 1983 through the mid-1980s. The image of the bereaved Lily Chin, accompanied always by a reminder of her son, has a peculiar symbolic value within the study of Asian American history and politics. But her possession of the image of Vincent Chin itself would become the means by which she would be visually identifiable. Lily Chin would become the Bearer of Vincent's Portrait, emphasized even more strongly by Joe Mortis' photograph—in this shot, the portrait of Vincent, held at a slight tilt, occupies the majority of the shot, with Lily Chin's hands, sweater, and bracelet being the only visible parts of her. The photograph of Vincent Chin would become the fetish substitute of melancholia that would forever haunt the imagery of Lily Chin, or perhaps, more accurately, the sign of Vincent Chin's photograph is enough to signify the presence of Lily Chin, she who mourns.

The photograph of Vincent is not only a substitute for his brutal murder, but for Lily Chin, as well, demonstrating the completion of Vincent Chin's conversion into fetish-object, temporally suspending both Chins. This abstraction functions on the level of mythological signification, effectively completing the conversion of the murdered Chinese American man into an object. Here, the photograph of Vincent Chin—and perhaps Chin himself—becomes what Joseph Jonghyun Jeon has called a "racial thing," a materialization of "uncanny phenomena" at the intersection between "reification and racialization" (2012, xxiv). The melancholic haunting of the racial thing, amplified by the political deployment of its visual rhetoric, furthermore, produces a masochistic moral economy around which Asian American subjectivity would come to congregate. Rebecca Comay argues that such fetishistic substitution, when placed within the melancholic schema, produces a masochistic relationship with the lost object:

> The incorporation of the object requires [melancholia]'s abbreviation as a frozen attribute and thereby inflicts upon it a kind of second death ... a violence which will in turn reverberate within *the sadomasochistic theater of grief* wherein, famously, *it is the lost object itself which is being whipped by the subject's most intimate self-flagellations.* (2006, 94–95, my emphasis)

With every dramatic retelling of Vincent Chin's story, from speeches and press releases by American Citizens for Justice (ACJ) members or by Lily Chin herself, there is necessarily a re-invocation of the incipient violence, a movement toward "intimate self-flagellation," a paradoxical reiteration of death, "a kind of second death" in order to seek its redress.

Lily's son's death was a story that would be publicly recounted again and again, almost gaining the iconicity of a folkloric fable. I am, of course, obliged to recount it yet again here. On June 19, 1982, Vincent Chin was celebrating his upcoming wedding to his fiancée Vickie Wong at the Fancy Pants Club, a strip club with three of his friends (Kresnak 1983, 6A). Two white men in the bar, Ronald Ebens and his son-in-law Michael Nitz, both of whom were autoworkers, the former a Chrysler foreman, the latter recently laid off from Chrysler. The two dancers—white woman Racine Colwell and Black woman Angela Rudolph (also known as "Starlene") were performing. Reportedly, Ebens and Nitz watched Chin and his group gossip about the dancers, speaking disparagingly about Rudolph in favor of Colwell, whom they tipped generously. Colwell would later recall that the two white men blurted statements like "nip" and "chink." After Chin tipped Colwell generously, Ebens reportedly got agitated, telling Rudolph, "Don't pay any attention those little fuckers, they wouldn't know a good dancer if they'd seen one" (qtd. in Moore 1987, 14). Chin rose to confront Ebens, punching him, and then a fight ensued. Rudolph would recall that Ebens or Nitz shouted, "It's because of you motherfuckers that we're out of work." Vincent and his friends departed the space. According to eyewitness reports, Ebens and Nitz drove their car in the surrounding area for 20 or 30 minutes and found Vincent Chin and his friend Jimmy Choi in front of a nearby McDonald's. Nitz held Chin from behind as Ebens swung a baseball bat repeatedly against Vincent Chin's body, first his legs, then his ribs, and finally his head, bashing his skull open, until police arrived on the scene, guns drawn. As Vincent lay dying, Ebens pointed to Jimmy Choi and said, "I did it, and if they hadn't stopped me, I'd get you next." Vincent, on the other hand, moaned, "It's not fair." Vincent Chin went brain dead after eight hours of emergency surgery and was released from life support four days afterward. "His four hundred wedding guests," writes Helen Zia, "attended his funeral instead" (2000, 60).

However, it was not so much the slaying itself but, rather, the light sentencing of perpetrators Ebens and Nitz that would facilitate the galvanization of Asian American political organizing in the 1980s on his posthumous behalf. Nine months after his death, on March 18, 1983, Ebens and Nitz appeared for their sentencing in the Wayne County Circuit Court, facing a plea bargain from second-degree murder to manslaughter—the district attorney's office did not send representation to the sentencing. Edward Khoury, Nitz's defense attorney, portrayed Nitz as a law-abiding citizen "making a contribution to the community" who acted "in the heat of passion." Ebens' defense attorney Bruce Saperstein stated that Ebens' background is "impeccable," but "normal people act strange when loved-ones appear to be seriously injured," referring to the notion that it was Vincent Chin who provoked the attack,[1] and the fact that Michael Nitz received a head injury from the brawl that required eleven stitches (although investigation revealed that it was actually Ebens who inflicted that wound). When Judge Charles Kaufman asked, "Did the victim have a criminal record?," Saperstein replied, "I don't have any background on him either way, Your Honor." Shortly afterward, the sentence was dealt: Ebens and Nitz were given probation and fined $3780 each—$3000 for the killing and $780 for court costs. Judge Kaufman would infamously remark in a later interview that Ebens and Nitz "aren't the kind of people you send to jail" (Waldemeir 1983).

The 1982 murder of Vincent Chin was without a doubt a watershed moment in mainstream U.S. Asian American identity. There is, in fact, a popular narrative that Asian America emerged from Vincent Chin's bludgeoned skull. From Ronald Ebens' two-handed swing of a baseball bat—that quintessentially American object of play and violence—in Detroit 1982 came a movement for redress, for justice, which for the first time on a national scale coalesced the otherwise disparate Asian ethnic groups in America into one singular Asian American political constituency. The story of Vincent Chin's murder—a Chinese man slain for being mistaken as Japanese in a period of virulent Japanophobia—is something of a linchpin in the canon of Asian American studies, a subject of multiple books and documentaries,[2] framed as a hate crime and the tragically predictable absence of justice.

Compellingly, legal scholar Frank Wu even ventures to say,

> Before the Vincent Chin case, it's fair to say there weren't Asian Americans. There were Chinese Americans; there were Japanese Americans; there had been briefly in

the 1960s a student movement on the West Coast. But there wasn't a meaningful, abiding Asian American *Movement*. It faltered. It didn't have an icon, a symbol. It didn't have a narrative that people could identify with. (*Vincent Who?*, 2009)

Wu's characterization of the early articulations of Asian American identity as a "brief ... student movement" is reductive; on the contrary, the Asian American movement was *definitively* the "brief student movement" that Wu mentions, particularly as it defined Asian Americanness in principally left-wing, anti-imperialist, and solidarity-driven terms (I will expand upon this later in the chapter). Yet, Wu is not altogether incorrect in a sense; while the Justice for Vincent Chin movement wasn't the birth of the Asian American movement or Asian America per se (both of which were largely leftist formations), I *would* argue that it was a turning point for a *liberalized* Asian American panethnicity with widespread, mainstream appeal. As David Eng describes, this is a liberal personhood premised upon "the right to self-possession: of body, interiority, mind, and spirit" (2010, 44). But whereas Eng critiques queer liberalism "as one incarnation of liberal freedom and progress constituted by the racialization of intimacy and forgetting of race," the Asian American liberalism consolidated in the wake of the Chin case inverts this dynamic, inaugurating a self-possessive Asian American subject constituted by the disavowal of sexuality. In any event, Wu's characterization underscores the weight of signification endowed to the Chin case, particularly in relationship to the once-fledgling panethnic political formation that was, and now is, "Asian America." Indeed, as Ronald Takaki noted in 1989, "all Asian Americans—Chinese, Japanese, Koreans, Filipinos, Asian Indians, and Southeast Asians—are standing up this time" (1989, 484). Moreover, sociologist Yến Lê Espiritu noted in 1992 that "as a result of the Chin case, Asian Americans today are much more willing to speak out on the issue of anti-Asianism; they are also much better organized than they were at the time of Chin's death" (1992, 153).

It is historically inaccurate to say that Asian American panethnicity was truly "born" in the aftermath of Chin's murder, but I cite these examples of eventualization to illustrate its narrative weight and its paradigmatic role in coagulating a contemporary panethnic Asian American identity. In other words, Asian America may not have been "born" in the Chin murder, but we can ask what *version* of Asian America emerged from the resulting organizing and cultural responses. For Wu, the death of Chin and the organized community response to Ebens' and Nitz's light sentencing formed the event that birthed a particular mainstream iteration of "Asian America." Methodologically speaking, I analyze the cultural politics of the Vincent Chin affair as a social drama, a broader performance event itself whose multiple pulls of signification, from the beating to the civil rights organizing by the American Citizens for Justice, created the conditions for an Asian American cultural politics premised upon a masochistic becoming-machine. Indeed, the eventualization of Chin in the aftermath of his death and trial inaugurated a moral-masochistic liberal "Asian Americanness," one that would enable Chin to function as a figure of masochism upon which both pleasure and subjectification would concur.

In addition, this masochistic figuration is both a response to and redeployment of Asiatic racialization that pushes Asiatic racial form outside of the boundaries of the human in unsettling ways in 1980s Detroit. That Chin was "mistaken" as Japanese is misleading; it is perhaps more accurate to say that the bludgeoning *made* Chin Japanese. More generally, the Chin case has carried particular rhetorical clarity in demonstrating the superseding of racial over ethnic marking within the U.S. social system; Asianness,[3] and by extension Asian Americanness, arose as the determining factor of Chin's death rather than any specific ethnic marker. But even to say that Chin "became" Japanese is insufficient: I argue that, metonymically speaking, Chin *became* the Japanese car itself. But in this "becoming"—a term drawn from the work of Deleuze and Guattari—a contemporary iteration of Asian America formed masochistically, drawing both pleasure and meaning from the fusion of flesh with machine. Thus, this opening chapter asks: What does the social drama of Vincent Chin teach us about Asian American relationships to objecthood and machineness, and how does this inform the consolidation of Asian American liberalism? How can we think of racial "becoming-machine" simultaneously as a technology for Asian American subjectification, masochistic desubjectification, and crystallization of the contemporary model minority?

Moreover, in this objectification of Chin, we see the convergence of three intertwining but conflicting cultural logics: ressentiment, melancholia, and masochism. To simplify, ressentiment is a politics of woundedness for moral authority; melancholia, the perpetual grief that feeds endlessly upon the lost object; and masochism, the suspenseful derivation of pleasure from pain. Chin's becoming-machine establishes the conditions for all three of these cultural logics to sometimes harmonize over, and sometimes contest, the narrativization of Chin. The Vincent Chin case and its performative aftermath gesture toward a complexly masochistic relationship between the racialized subject and the racial form of that subject, establishing a diffusion of morally masochistic economies through which Asian America has ethico-politically defined itself since the Chin event. The social drama surrounding the 1982 murder of Vincent Chin, which transpired just days before his scheduled wedding, was itself a wedding of the contemporary liberal masculine Asian American subject to techno-orientalism, one whose ongoing signification would result in a masochistic attachment to Chin's murder and the techno-oriental objectification it performed.

This chapter and the following one analyze Chin's murder and its responses as an ongoing performance event that intervenes into the discourse of Asian American subject formation and political organizing. This first chapter examines the techno-orientalization of Chin and the immediate Asian American response as performance nodes, focusing on the documentary *Who Killed Vincent Chin?* (1987) and the activist organizing documents of the American Citizens for Justice, while the second chapter examines theatrical reckonings of the Chin murder several decades later.

Becoming-Machine and Metonymic Racialization in Motor City

> In 36 years, I barely spared a word
> About my days in Ypsilanti,
> Known chiefly for giving us Iggy Pop
> And an obscure pioneer in continental drift.
>
> I was watching the 9 o'clock news
> With my father in the living room,
> As was the family habit. I was 9,
>
> Eating a Baby Ruth in June
> When a picture of Vincent Chin
> Flashed onscreen with a discussion
> Of murder, Japan and the Motor City.
>
> My father said not to take it personally.
> We were going to have a barbecue with
> Our blue collar neighbor on Saturday,
> Once he was done at the Ford Factory.
>
> Our other neighbor across the way
> With the tall bottle-blonde daughters
> Was a Baptist preacher, fond of discussing
> Pearl Harbor with me every other day,
> Because I couldn't tell him a thing about Laos.
> —"Ypsilanti, 1982" by Bryan Thao Worra

Vincent Chin's murder is inextricable from a context of heightened Japanophobia, in which Japan represented an economic-technological threat, specifically due to Detroit's historical association with its auto industry throughout the 20th century, a history that began less than a century after the state of Michigan dispossessed the Anishinaabe of their land. Throughout Detroit's longtime status as "Motor City USA," industrial mechanization has been a persistent component of its corporate manufacturing infrastructure. The city is the birthplace of Henry Ford's first moving assembly line at the Ford Highland Park Plant, which opened in 1910, and its prestige as "a symbol of itself" (Galster 2012, 6) in the U.S. national consciousness fluctuated according to the U.S. relationship to industrialization at large at various historical moments. With the Second World War and the postwar industrial boom, thanks to robust labor activism, Detroit became an American model for prosperity and high standard of living for decades. However, as Scott Kurashige has aptly described, in the wake of the 1967 revolts by Black people combating police brutality and unemployment, Detroit would become patient zero for the deindustrialization, automation, and neoliberal financialization that have become the contemporary American norm. As historian George Galster elaborates, Detroit shifted from being a site of technological ingenuity and "industrial unionism" to that of "postindustrial apocalypse" in the early 1970s, a "murder capital," "a place of unbridled crime, violence, and racial strife that could be patrolled successfully only by robocops" (2012, 6–7). In other words, what was once a beacon of cutting-edge 20th-century industrialism became a site associated with deterioration within the American imagination. Thus, Detroit of the 1970s and 1980s was a space of anachronism, of uneven modernity, an industrial symbol of material futurity decaying into a symbol of quixotic futility in the face of corporate globalization. However, it was also, notably, a site of radical organizing, for autoworkers and Black activists, the site of operations of Grace Lee and James Boggs. Nevertheless, whether conceptualized as innovative or antiquated, as a boon to productivity or as a threat to labor, industrial technology has been a nucleus of Detroit's identity in cultural production and the U.S. public imagination.[4]

Consequently, automation was a considerable terrain of contestation within early-1980s Detroit. This has been a particularly threatening preoccupation among Detroit's labor unions, most notably the United Auto Workers (UAW), especially when increased levels of automation spanning throughout the 20th century would result in unemployment and displacement. Moreover, according to Galster, the proletariat of the Detroit auto industry "found that the devilish font of their physical resources extracted considerably more sacrifices of psychological resources than anticipated. Four core characteristics of the Detroit auto industry—assembly line production, draconian management, cyclical instability, and long-term employment declines—ally to forge an economic engine of anxiety" (Galster 2012, 243). Such conditions, paired with the transnational tensions of the auto industry in the 1980s, resulted in the racial scapegoating of Japanese, which then came to apply to all Asians, international and domestic, in Detroit. The rise of fuel-efficient Japanese automakers in the late 1970s and early 1980s inculcated U.S. resentment toward racialized "competition," in this case, toward orientalized subjects.

The UAW, which notably boasted a proud history of supporting civil rights for African Americans, ironically became an institutional player in the production of this discourse, developing nationalist "Buy an American Car" bumper stickers as early as 1975 (Frank 1999, 168). The November 14, 1983, issue of the *Baltimore Sun* reported that

> The guard shack at the parking lot entrance to Solidarity House, the international headquarters of the United Auto Workers, has a sign declaring "300,000 laid-off UAW members don't like your import. Please park it in Tokyo." A bumper sticker on the window says, "Toyota, Datsun, Honda and Pearl Harbor."

Writing in 1983, Ronald Takaki additionally noted other bumper stickers, in the spirit of the American automakers' "buy American" campaigns, stating phrases like "unemployment—made in Japan." To the credit of the leadership of the UAW, many within the organization strongly cautioned against the economic nationalism spilling into racist vitriol, with research department staff member Lee Price cautioning the organization to draw the line before the rise of racist remarks, physical features, or World War II (Frank 1999, 169). Nevertheless, what may superficially have begun as a critique of globalized capitalism transformed primarily into an expression of nationalism, and, by extension, racialization. To a certain degree, as Japan became increasingly associated with an orientalized, faceless mass of automobiles, racialization and mechanization began to blend together. That is, affectively speaking, the yellow peril threat and the threat of automation came to draw from the same symbolic well: the brawn of American labor being replaced by the affectless, soulless horde, robots as orientals by other means (or vice versa).

Detroit in 1980 was majority people of color, boasting a white population of 34%, a Black population of 63%, but a comparatively tiny Asian American population, with barely over a thousand Chinese Americans and five hundred Japanese Americans among the 1.2 million total Detroiters. As is almost a given for small-population minoritized groups, Asian Americans had the dual distinction of being both invisible and conspicuous at once, according to Scott Kurashige, tending toward more modest political and civic influence prior to the Chin movement.[5] This positionality made Asians in the Detroit area particularly susceptible to the perpetual foreignization that has marked Asian racialization in the United States for centuries. Labor-based Japanophobia, produced at the precipice of increasingly transnational flows of immigration, capital, and production, echoed a long-standing tendency within American orientalism since the 19th century that ties racial form to material class relations. To recall Colleen Lye's study of orientalism in U.S. naturalism cited in the Introduction, Asiatic racial form does not necessarily remain constrained within the boundaries of the human, particularly given how Asianness has easily become associated with increased industrial automation, in being perceived as similarly competitive with white American labor.

Within the visual regime of Asiatic racial form, the Asian subject can be thought of as undergoing a techno-oriental becoming-machine. To recall Deleuze and Guattari's formulation, becoming is not a metaphorical relationship, but one effectively of "reality," one in which the very constructions of the subject and the endpoint of becoming blur together. That is, becoming is a mode by which the particles of an assemblage[6] enters the territory of another, and the nature of both are altered, and both units are deterritorialized (1987, 237–238). In Deleuze and Guattari's schema, becoming is not unidirectional but, rather, informs the two forms themselves such that they bleed into one another. Through becoming, it becomes possible conceptualize the relationship of Asiatic racial form to the machine, producing a techno-orientalism at the core of this central event of Asian American history.

In the case of becoming-machine, Asianness and machineness develop a coterminous metonymic relationship. As Kaja Silverman states, whereas metaphor "exploits relationships of similarity" (1984, 110), metonymy "exploits relationships of contiguity between things, not words: between a thing and its attributes, its environment and its adjuncts" (1984, 111). The events of Vincent Chin's murder and its aftermath suggest that Asiatic racial form does not operate merely on the level of representational similarity (the Oriental is *like* a machine, the machine is *like* an Oriental) but, rather, on the level of continuity (the machine *is an extension of* the Oriental, the Oriental *is an extension of* the machine). Yet, insofar as there is contiguity within metonym, there is also asymmetry. It is this asymmetry, paired with continuity, that gives metonym both a peculiar performative power, and a potential for resignification. As Peggy Phelan writes, "In performance, the body is metonymic of self, of character, of voice, of 'presence'" (1993, 150), and as a consequence,

> Performance uses the performer's body to pose a question about the inability to secure the relation between subjectivity and the body *per se*; performance uses the body to frame the lack of Being promised by and through the body—that which cannot appear without a supplement. (1993, 150–151)

The Toyota, then, becomes not only a *symbol for* and an *extension of* the imagined Japanese threat in in early 1980s Detroit, but also potentially a site of contestation.

The unstable metonymy of techno-orientalist becoming-machine would be the affective terrain upon which Asian American activists and cultural producers would perform; they would project or negotiate the trajectory of their racialization, securing various racial masochisms premised upon correspondingly various forms of objecthood. Insofar as we consider self-objectification as central to masochism, the performative responses to Vincent Chin's death are spectacular examples in which Asian American objecthood and subjectivity converge. For the clearest instantiation of becoming-machine, I first turn to the work that has rightfully been considered the definitive account of the Vincent Chin affair, the 1987 documentary *Who Killed Vincent Chin?*

Clinging to the Chrome: Becoming-Car and Chin as the Detroit Android

> "Real Americans Buy American" continues to be one of the more popular sayings gracing the large chrome bumpers of cars in Detroit. The case of Vincent Chin has peeled back those slogans, showing that what makes them cling to the chrome is a powerful and ugly undercurrent of racism. It's a revelation that we Detroiters will not soon forget.
> —Matt Beer, *The Detroit Times*, June 2, 1983

Christine Choy and Renee Tajima-Pena's 1987 documentary *Who Killed Vincent Chin?*, widely and rightfully acknowledged as the definitive work documenting Vincent Chin's story, won an Emmy and an Academy Award nomination for compellingly covering Chin's murder through a thorough and powerful editing of news clips and interviews, intimately covering a wide range of individuals from Vincent's mother Lily Chin, Robert Ebens, his defense attorney Bruce Saperstein, Helen Zia, and Fancy Pants dancers Angela Rudolph and Racine Colwell, among a number of others. As a documentary, it is immensely successful at exploring the question of its title, which seems to be a rhetorical question with a self-evident answer, but instead properly examines the social context in which the murder occurs. Writing in 1988, Vincent Canby of the *New York Times* praised the film, noting aptly, "There would also seem to be no doubt about who did it. Yet, by the end of their film, Ms. Choy and Ms. Tajima have so successfully analyzed this sudden, sad, fatal confrontation that almost everything except the Big Mac becomes implicated in the events." Indeed, Ebens and Nitz are undoubtedly the literal perpetrators, but through its panoramic exploration of Detroit as a social context, *Who Killed Vincent Chin?* effectively points to larger discursive factors as being equally guilty parties, putting society on trial equally alongside the two men in question.

In saying this, I depart from Linda Williams, who critiques *Who Killed Vincent Chin?* as focused too much on the certainty of culpability of Ronald Ebens. She writes,

> [T]he singlemindedness of *Vincent Chin*'s pursuit of the singular truth of Ebans' *[sic]* guilt, and his culture's resentment of Asians, limits the film. Since Ebans *[sic]* never does show himself in the present to be a blatant racist, but only an insensitive working-class guy, the film interestingly fails on its own terms. (1993, 21)

Williams' assessment, I would argue, misreads the film, suggesting that *Who Killed Vincent Chin?* attempts to be a specific indictment of individual racist actors, as opposed to offering a more "complex" view of the events that took place. On the contrary, *Who Killed Vincent Chin?* does not propagandistically aim to paint Ebens as an individual racist who was influenced by "his culture's resentment of Asians" but, rather, demonstrates the complex flows of racial power that evade the liberal-individualist conceptualizations of racism altogether.

In a retrospective, Renee Tajima-Peña has written that *Who Killed Vincent Chin?* was reflective specifically of a politics that emerged from the Asian American movement in which she was politicized. "It was tailor-made for the ideological construct 'Asian American'" (2002, 8), writes Tajima-Peña.

> The construction of an Asian American political identity ... went beyond good feelings and ethnic belonging. It had to do with our livelihoods and fair access to the resources of society.... When I began making the film, I saw myself as an *Asian American* filmmaker—a cultural worker. (Tajima-Peña 2002, 9, emphasis in original)

Thus, in contrast with the actual movement that she powerfully documents (as I will describe in the next section), Tajima-Peña's conceptualization of Asian America is not identitarian but solidarity driven, focused more on the actional, political production of Asian Americanness rather than a static ethnic essentialism. *Who Killed Vincent Chin?*, while remaining Asian American focused, reflects this orientation, less invested in the production of Asian American identity (nationalist-essentialist or otherwise) as it is in interrogating the libidinal investments of whiteness and the mutual racial becomings that emerge from the fissures it leaves behind.

With all of this in mind, I focus on a segment in the first third of the documentary, explaining the social context in which the Chin murder occurred in terms of what I have described as techno-orientalist violence. The exquisitely directed and edited *Who Killed Vincent Chin?* is not primarily a text that explores techno-orientalism; rather, it is primarily concerned with providing a panoramic portrait of the event and the multiple social forces at work: Detroit unemployment, the sense of entitlement from white privilege, and the colorblind denial of racism. However, one of the most crucial early segments of the documentary profiles the racialization of the Japanese automobile, which the film aptly covers through a display of anti-Asian propaganda developed by the Detroit auto industry. Approximately 31 minutes in, the film features a fear-mongering American cartoon of dark-eyed "foreign" cars surfing across the ocean to reach American shores, creeping past the Statue of Liberty like cockroaches, eventually constituting a faceless dark horde that overtakes the heterosexual white couple kissing on the screen of the Americana-suffused drive-in theater, all to a menacing horror soundtrack. The voice-over narrates: "When it started, America was unprepared. From across the ocean they came, little cars determined to change the buying habits of a nation. And for a while, there was no stopping them." A few minutes later, the documentary displays a still of a Japanese car with buck teeth, flying overhead Detroit, releasing a bomb, an imperial Japanese flag shadowed underneath—a cartoon that had been originally displayed at Flint, Michigan's, Six Flags Auto World Theme Park in 1984 (Darden and Thomas 2013, 170). In these propaganda pieces, there is, as Lye suggests about Asiatic racial form in general, a white anxiety of oriental threat that is leveraged on the specific visuality of the Asiaticized body. In the former example of U.S. auto industry propaganda, the surfing horde of cars are legibly Asiatic in their hordeness; their empty eyes and uniformity providing a primarily affective contrast with the white couple, performatively exhibiting a capacity for (heteronormative) love and expression. The couple's extradiegetic awareness of the cars exhibits furthermore a threat to sexual normativity, their palpable fear at this interruption bespeaking an economic threat that is not only material, but libidinal. Meanwhile, in the latter example, phenotypic Asian features are located onto the bodies of the car itself. The second image, a still rather than an animation, is less focused on the performativity of relentless swarming, and more premised upon the anatomy of the car itself (see Figure 1.1).

Within these cartoons, the boundary between car and Asian blurs dramatically; not only is Asianness ascribed to the vehicles, but also the mechanical is ascribed to

Figure 1.1 Stills collected from *Who Killed Vincent Chin?* by Christine Choy and Renee Tajima-Peña. Top Left and Right: Japanese cars surf across the ocean to assault the American heteronormative way of life. Bottom: Buck-toothed Japanese car releases bomb with the backdrop of the Japanese Imperial flag.

Asianness. There is, in these cartoons, a mutual becoming. The movement of machine to the hyper-racialized human as we see in the cartoons—such as in the "Pearl Harbor" bombing still, which depicts a Japanese car with stereotypically Japanese *facial* features, as opposed to features of the Japanese Zero, the plane to which the car is clearly being analogized—paradoxically moves the automobile *further* from a humanity circumscribed by white normativity; the vehicles are anthropomorphized only enough to be orientalized, revealing this mode of techno-orientalism as a discursive technology of dehumanizing abjection. In other words, the car's becoming-Asian is *not* a becoming-human, but quite the opposite; the Asian car is fully abject,[7] abjection both physically and psychically cathected upon the body of the Japanese machine itself.

To reinforce the body of the car as the site of contestation, *Who Killed Vincent Chin?* next cuts to a (literally) striking scene: actual news clips from a public lynching of Japanese cars. In early 1980s Detroit, "Japanese cars were vandalized and their owners were shot at on the freeways" (Zia 2000, 58), and car dealers "held raffles for the honor of taking a baseball bat to a Toyota to bash it to pieces" (Wu 2002, 71). An early scene of *Who Killed Vincent Chin?* captures such an event: a large crowd of white Americans takes turns swinging a sledgehammer—multiple two-handed swings—against the bodies of ownerless Japanese cars. Children are present, waving flags. Police officers stand nearby but do not interfere, assuming relaxed poses. The news caption reads, "Striking Back" (Figure 1.2).

"Striking back" implies a righteous resentment, of fighting against that which has wronged them. Indeed, the news media captured by *Who Killed Vincent Chin?* exposes a logic of ressentiment, of developing a moral economy equating righteousness with having suffered injury.[8] Under ressentiment, revenge is individuated upon particular objects of fury. The crowd in question is not just striking back at the economic downturn, at having lost their jobs; the specific targeting of Japanese cars means that they "strike back" against a machine, colored and exaggerated by racial logics. They "strike back" against a machine built by a machinelike people, a society of simulacra who can perform the American industry better than the Americans themselves. It is a foreign machine that they rage against; rather than direct proletarian rage toward the exploitative bourgeoisie that disenfranchises them domestically, they perform the nationalist ideology that enframes the entire corporate entity, from CEO to workers, as a single unit against a foreign power. Here, *Who Killed Vincent Chin?* reveals a feedback loop between social drama and stage drama, a choreographic spectacle of violence predicated upon the annihilation of foreign metal bodies. It is embodied rehearsal, the destruction of things made doubly things by virtue of racialization; their

Figure 1.2 Channel 4 Southfield news report of public lynchings of Japanese cars with sledgehammers, sanctioned by the police, the report reading "Striking Back." Still from *Who Killed Vincent Chin?*

Asianness, their uncanny signification as possessing a race, heightens their threat. And in turn, the discursive logic leads equally to its inverse, that the race itself is monstrous from its mechanization, from its oriental, machinelike quality.

But above all, the underlying violence committed upon the automobiles reveals an intriguing masochistic operation of the Detroit labor force itself. As the participants of the Detroit car lynchings were the perpetrators of violence, this may seem counterintuitive or perhaps points to a *sadistic* relation instead. However, the crucial dimension of this interaction between Detroiters and cars is that there is no mistake that the participants are the former victims in the theater of Detroit techno-orientalism, hence the headline "striking back." The propaganda cartoons of the cars and the performative spectacle of the car destruction equally contain the self-victimization of ressentiment, presupposing the Japanese as an omnipotent villain. The omnipotence ascribed to the other within the resentful fantasy is augmented precisely by this techno-orientalization, as the figure of the oriental-machine is at once soulless and all-powerful, an ascription that provides moral validation to the public car destruction. The car destruction, then, is immediately understood as a carnivalesque and thus merely temporary reversal of a status quo in which the oriental-machine remains sovereign.[9] But in any event, *Who Killed Vincent Chin?* establishes that both the cartoon car propaganda and even the physical car destruction produce a compensatory fantasy structure that is, first and foremost, fantasy, that the violence is somehow unreal and mythological, the realm of the masochistic imagination.

Regardless of whether Ebens and Nitz "actually" participated in such prior activities, *Who Killed Vincent Chin?* clearly implies that such liminal performances of violence upon a racially marked vehicle were choreographic rehearsals for the two-handed baseball bat swings of Ronald Ebens upon Vincent Chin's racialized body—or perhaps, vice versa. These Bakhtinian carnivalesque public performances produced a topsy-turvy world of transgression,[10] but the stage for such techno-lynchings transcended the lots of the auto dealers. In a constellation of anti-Asian hostility in early-1980s Detroit already described, the car slayings were one node among many, but of particular note was the means by which they were embodied. Unlike the anti-Japanese bumper stickers and the racialized propaganda, the car bludgeoning provided a corporeal momentum. To recall Karl Marx's oft-cited words from his 1844 essay on Estranged Labour, "[T]he worker sinks to the level of a commodity and becomes indeed the most wretched of commodities" (1844, XXII). For Ebens and Nitz, white workers disenfranchised by global capitalism, it is the transference of their own dehumanized status as commodified laborers onto an abjected externalized Other, their expressive rage a performative enunciation of their (white) humanity relative to the (Asiatic) machine they have broken, rather than the person they have killed. In the context of such violence, Vincent Chin *became* automobile, at least within the frame of *Who Killed Vincent Chin?* Moreover, Chin's becoming-car is the opposing Janus head of the becoming produced in the Japanophobic cartoons and original choreographic spectacles of the destruction of Japanese cars documented in *Who Killed Vincent Chin?*: the automobile's becoming-Asian.

Intriguingly, Ebens and Nitz were positioned as the wronged subjects of their own social drama. With Ebens' "It's because of you motherfuckers we're out of work," Chin, having become-automobile, is attached to the specter of the omnipotent techno-oriental machine, seen as perpetrator within the moral economy of Detroit. Like the public car destruction, the murder of Chin is a fantasy of ressentiment, understood as mere fantasy by the techno-oriental imagination. The unsurprising irony is that, between competing dramaturgical grids of intelligibility, Ebens and Chin compete for the position of wronged subject, and *Who Killed Vincent Chin?* brilliantly demonstrates this dialectic through its thorough and persistent survey of all of the players involved. The emotionally devastating climax of *Who Killed Vincent Chin?* shows the reactions of Ebens and his legal team to the press when he has learned that he was won his appeal in the civil rights trial. The film cuts away to an interview with Ebens and his wife, in which Ebens states, "Detroit. It's got the reputation for murder capital in the world. It's like," he pauses for a moment, then says indignantly, "and—and I didn't even do it on purpose! You know, I didn't just walk up and shoot somebody!" Then, cutting back to the trial aftermath, the documentary shows Ebens' lawyer Khoury telling the assembled reporters, "The press has always reported this case one-sided since the beginning, and it's really nice to get twelve people who agree with the way we look at this case." Finally, a few minutes later, *Who Killed Vincent Chin?* cuts back to Ebens' interview, wherein Ebens says, "He [presumably a reporter] asked if justice failed somewhere in this case and uh, I don't see anywhere it did fail. I—I think the way the system worked the way it should have worked. Right down the line."

The indignation and apparent remorselessness from Ebens and his legal team within *Who Killed Vincent Chin?* simply provides more evidence for the masochistic fantasy of self-victimization of Ebens and his team, positioning them as the recipients of unfair media attention. Then, in its final shot, the documentary cuts to an inconsolably bereaved Lily Chin, literally trembling in shock. Ebens' fascinatingly absurd insistence that "he didn't just walk up and shoot somebody" to morally soften his actions speaks to the potency resentment, one buttressed by the sense of imagined unreality made at least partly possible by the techno-oriental interpellation carried within each bludgeon.

Ebens would not seem to express remorse until well into the 21st century. In a clinical assessment of Ronald Ebens by Veronica A. Madrigal-Dean, ACSW, and George Czertko, MD, Ebens was psychologically profiled as having borderline personality disorder, but most notably, "bigotry and masochism," as well as, it is implied, misogyny:

> The clinical impression is that of a Borderline Personality Disorder with the potential for manifesting psychotic-like behavior under conditions of severe stress. While this defendant went to every extreme to portray a very positive picture, again, preprogramming that any sharing of negative data could result in a negative picture of his character, it is felt that the façade he presents thinly conceals numerous unresolved problems: Acute and chronic dependency on alcohol which impedes

> his ability to engage in meaningful interpersonal relationships, bigotry and masochism. [...] In addition to all the aforementioned problems, there appear to be deep-seated problems in dealing with females as well as persons in authority.

I include this assessment not to psychologically pathologize Ebens but, rather, to point to a curious overlap—or perhaps a mutually constitutive relationship—of masochism, bigotry, and misogyny in the man who bludgeoned Chin to death. In an astonishing interview with a young Michael Moore in 1987, Ebens boldly declared, "If he (Chin) hadn't started it, he'd still be alive.... I mean, don't get me wrong, I'm not saying it's right that he died. All I'm saying is that if he hadn't started it, he'd still be alive. They were looking for trouble and they got it" (qtd. in Moore 1987, 15). This again points to a moral economy of ressentiment, drawing upon a perceived sense of victimhood to justify retaliatory violence.

Thus, one of the compelling accomplishments of *Who Killed Vincent Chin?* is not so much its formation of an Asian American identity, but its portrait of *white* subject formation, of its capacity to produce both physical and epistemic violence based on its own appeals to victimization, a ressentiment driven by the displacement of class consciousness onto race. The annihilation of Chin, which was equally the *production* of a machine figure, buttresses and secures this whiteness upon the moral economy of white ressentiment. Consequently, the legal battle that would ensue between Ebens and Asian Americans seeking redress was a contest of competing narratives of injury. One of the great accomplishments of *Who Killed Vincent Chin?* is its potent exhibition of Chin's murder as a becoming-machine itself, demonstrating the marriage of Asiatic racial form to the machine (ejected, then, as abject refuse) that served as a prerequisite for both white violence and white self-making. In this regard, it is actually critical of the moral paradigm of liberal identitarianism itself, the ressentiment that allows the "we" in "it's because of you motherfuckers that we're out of work" to cohere.

What, then, of the objects of this racial violence, of the survivors in the wake of becoming-machine? As I will demonstrate next, Asian American responses to this becoming-machine, despite their valorous attempts, did not fully reject this relation outright; rather, they reconfigured it, partly as a consequence of politically strategic necessity.

"It's Not Fair": The American Citizens for Justice and the New Sexless Machine

What was once the Fancy Pants is now in ruins. It is September 2019, and the building sits in shambles on Woodward Avenue, its round marquee covered in rust and fraying at the edges. A long graffiti mural covers its long-abandoned wood walls, something resembling a yellow, anthropomorphized cat—maybe a domesticated Sphinx—with unnervingly detailed eyes, adorning a three-pointed crown on its head, reaching out with a human-like hand, a background of either wave crests or mountain peaks behind it.

There is one loose wooden panel; behind it is utter ruin—scattered wood, candy boxes, tin roofing, rubber tubes, loose bricks—maybe this is the occasional sleeping site for the many unhoused folks, who are the principal denizens of this mostly abandoned stretch of land, walking the summer heat carrying overstuffed plastic bags. Somewhere in these collapsing walls, Ebens told Chin, "it's because of you motherfuckers that we're out of work." And Chin punched him.

I got back into the Chevy Impala and began my drive northward on Woodward. Only a few blocks past the Fancy Pants was a large abandoned factory: the *factory. This was the Ford Highland Park Plant, the first automobile factory with a moving assembly line, the factory where the first Model Ts were made, a plaque commemorating the site. What do I make of the fact that the fight that would result in Chin's murder, in his becoming-car, began a mere stroll away from where the modern American automobile was first mass-produced?*

In the archives, I'd found a report for a panel of mediators, written by Edward Rosenbaum, of the financial losses of Vincent's death. It is always a curious thing to monetize the gap that the dead leave in their wake. It was through this document that I learned that Vincent, apparently, chauffeured his mother Lily considerably and worked meticulously on his car:

> She [his fiancée Vicki Wong] said that Vincent had spent about three hours per week driving his mother around and about two hours per week in working on or washing his auto. She said that he tried to do everything himself and that he tried to repair everything. (Rosenbaum 1986, 13)

The Highland Park Plant has been closed since 1974. Did Vincent, and then Ebens, pass the plant on their way to the McDonald's where it all concluded? The man who built cars, who killed a man who loved cars, for being the race of the wrong cars, broken and bludgeoned like a Toyota at a UAW picnic. Vincent moaned, "It's not fair."

There would be banners of those last words. Decades later, there would be plaques.

On March 31, 1983, 13 days after the notoriously light sentencing of Ebens and Nitz, journalists Helen Zia and Henry Yee, lawyer Lisa Chan, and community leader Kin Yee, in cooperation with Vincent Chin's mother Lily Chin, among others, founded the American Citizens for Justice (ACJ), a civil rights organization with the primary purpose of seeking the justice for Vincent Chin that the first trial denied. Their preamble reads as follows:

> We, as citizens of the United States of America and members of the Detroit, Michigan Asian American community, in order to seek fair and equal treatment for all individuals, regardless of their race, creed, color, sex, or national origin; to support just enforcement of our laws; to promote understanding between all groups of people; to educate the public on human rights issues; to bring about greater awareness of the needs and concerns of Americans of Asian ancestry; do hereby establish this constitution for the American Citizens for Justice. (Bridges et al. 1984)

The tone of this document is representative of the ongoing communications of the ACJ throughout their organizing work in the 1980s. Strategically working within juridical frameworks and mobilizing across a broad coalition of community groups, the ACJ consistently appealed to a liberal Americanism in order to achieve its goals. The opening sentence of the preamble, listing "citizens of the United States of America" before "members of the Detroit ... Asian American community," both emphasizes membership within the U.S. nation-state and subtly excludes those members of the Asian American community who may not, in fact, be citizens, not unlike the Japanese American Citizens' League in the period of Japanese American internment. The ACJ was committed to what Evelyn Brooks Higginbotham has termed (referring to Black Baptist activist women from 1880 to 1920) "the politics of respectability" (1993, 14), which aims to "earn their people a measure of esteem from white America" (1993, 14) but has had a tendency to disavow the culture of the "folk"—simply put, the disrespectable.

The Asian American model minority is the telos of Higginbotham's politics of respectability; it is the actualization of the structural position to which respectability aspires. Although the pragmatics of the political strategy of the ACJ required such modes of respectability in order to garner popular support to great support, one paradoxical side effect of some of their efforts was an ideological restructuring of contemporary model minorityism even as they actively tried to oppose its construction and widely educate the public about its harm. In these next several pages, through an examination of their archives, I analyze the organizing work of the ACJ through the lens of performance historiography, considering the means by which their collective process of narrativization performatively enacted a legible grievability for Vincent Chin and, in doing so, resignified the becoming-machine enacted by the murder itself to palatably appeal to a wider audience, sometimes veering into assimilationist rhetorics. Before I continue, however, I cannot stress enough how absolutely vital the ACJ's work was in raising awareness of anti-Asian violence, fighting for redress and justice, and contributing to a more equitable racial landscape in the United States, and its members are rightfully celebrated within the Asian American community as visionaries and role models. Moreover, this modest section barely scratches the surface of the history of their organizing—a definitive historical account this is not. The critiques that follow are not critiques of the ACJ per se, but a description of rhetorics that they had no choice but to take in the Reaganist political milieu within which they worked. The ACJ's historic and absolutely necessary efforts engaged the mise-en-scène of the broader U.S. public, but most especially Asian Americans, tethering the narrative of Vincent Chin to the dramaturgical imagination of liberal justice.

Chin's last words—"It's not fair"—would serve as the crux of the logic of the ACJ's rhetorical strategy, one that would prove to be quite effective in garnering support among many mainstream Asian Americans. As I stated earlier, the invocation of "fairness" is premised upon the notion that, in U.S. racial politics among others, "fair" treatment is something that can be attained or has been historically attained, or, perhaps more accurately, it is premised upon the notion *as if* this were true. In the context of settler-colonial racial capitalism, "it's not fair" is strategically subjunctive, pointing to the contradiction between the nation's presumption of fairness and its actual record, although this can just as easily be interpreted from a place of belief in that "fairness," as well. After all, "fairness" implies an adherence to a tacit U.S. social contract, a sense that the law-abiding subject should be entitled to the benefits of recompense from liberal democracy. Consequently, the ACJ's public relations efforts focused on portraying Chin as a subject deserving of fair treatment.

The ACJ mobilized locally, but the organization would eventually spearhead a movement that would garner nationwide attention, demanding that the Michigan Court of Appeals vacate the sentences and order a retrial (Chan 1991, 177) and eventually pushing for a civil rights investigation by the U.S. Department of Justice. The ACJ was enormously successful in its panethnic mobilization of the Asian American community around the issue and would be reasonably successful in the achievement of its legal objectives. As Sucheng Chan summarizes,

> Sufficient evidence of violation was found and a federal grand jury was convened in September 1983. Two months later the grand jury indicted Ebens and Nitz on two counts. The following year they were tried in a U.S. district court, whose jury convicted Ebens of violating Chin's civil rights but acquitted him of conspiracy, while acquitting Nitz of both charges. Ebens was sentenced to 25 years in jail and was told to undergo treatment for alcoholism, but he was freed after posting a $20,000 bond.
>
> Ebens's attorney appealed the conviction and a federal appeals court overturned it in September 1986 on a technicality: one of the attorneys for American Citizens for Justice, who had interviewed several of the prosecution's witnesses, was said to have "improperly coached" them. The Justice Department ordered a retrial, which took place not in Detroit but in Cincinnati, a city whose residents not only had little exposure to Asian Americans in general but also were unfamiliar with the hostility that people in Detroit harbored against Japanese cars and Japanese-looking people. Much to the dismay of Asian Americans across the country, the Cincinnati jury acquitted Ebens of all charges. Neither he nor his stepson ever spent a day in jail. Lily Chin, Vincent's mother, was so upset by the final outcome that she left the United States—a country where, she felt, no justice existed—to live in China. (1991, 177–178)

It is undeniable, then, that the ACJ played a central role in organizing Asian American legal efforts in the wake of Ebens' and Nitz's sentencing, including the "improper coaching" of a witness (which I will address later in further detail at the end of this chapter). However, I wish to draw particular attention to how the ACJ strategically managed the public perception of Vincent Chin. As legal scholar Robert S. Chang accurately writes, "In order for Vincent Chin to become the focal point of organizing and politicizing people about anti-Asian violence, the unsavory parts of the narrative were suppressed" (1999, 23). An examination of archival documents from the

ACJ makes this clear; for example, in ACJ speeches and press releases, there is rarely any mention that the Fancy Pants Club, where the initial altercation between Chin's party and Ebens and Nitz transpires, is a strip club. Instead, ACJ spokespersons repeatedly refer to "a bar." ACJ spokespersons often emphasize Chin's background as an engineering student, or often heavily emphasize his betrothal. A March 23, 1983, ACJ statement for the Chinese On Leong Association is reflective of these tendencies:

> Vicent [sic] Chin was well-known and well-liked among Detroit's Chinese .... He worked hard to help support his family, and at the time of his killing, had a promising career with an engineering firm. Chin worked a second job as a waiter at the Golden Star Restaurant, where Monday's [On Leong] meeting was held.
>
> On the night of his death, Chin and his three friends were celebrating his upcoming wedding which was to take place later that week. Chin's father had died only a few months earlier; as an only son, a large wedding had been planned for Chin and his bride, with over 400 guests invited. Instead of celebrating Chin's wedding, his guests attended his funeral.

The On Leong press statement's narrative of Chin magnifies his respectability; both as an "only son" and as the sole male presence in the household, Chin is praised for dutifully supporting his family, even working a second job. His futurity as a guarantor of social reproduction is represented both economically and socially: "a promising career with an engineering firm," and the "large wedding ... planned for Chin and his bride, with over 400 guests invited." Helen Zia's massively influential 2000 memoir *Asian American Dreams* describes Chin in much the same tone as ACJ's documents, as well:

> Vincent grew up into a friendly young man and a devoted only child who helped support his parents financially. He ran on his high school track team, but he also wrote poetry. Vincent was an energetic, take-charge guy who knew how to stand up for himself on the tough streets of Detroit. But friends and co-workers had never seen him angry and were shocked that he had been provoked into a fight ...
>
> Vincent was part of an entire generation for whom the immigrant parents had suffered and sacrificed. Other Asian Americans also found a strong connection to the lives of Vincent, Lily, and David Chin. Theirs was the classic immigrant story of survival: work hard and sacrifice for the family, keep a low profile, don't complain and, perhaps in the next generation, attain the American dream. For Asian Americans, along with the dream came the hope of one day gaining acceptance in America. The injustice surrounding Vincent's slaying shattered the dream.
>
> But most of all, Vincent was everyone's son, brother, boyfriend, husband, father. (2000, 63)

Although aimed at two slightly different audiences—the Chinese American community in the midst of ACJ organizing and a mainstream lay American readership retrospectively, respectively—both the On Leong press statement and Helen Zia's recounting are clear in establishing the respectability of Chin.[11] The former places an emphasis on filial values and scholarship, while the latter is particularly intent on establishing Chin's mainstream Americanness in his investment in the "American dream." Zia's statement particularly invokes a wholesome masculinity, mentioning his work on the "track team" and characterizing him as "an energetic, take-charge guy." Additionally, Zia makes it abundantly clear that he and his family were not a threat; by both of these accounts, Chin and his family were quite literally model minorities, and the violence inflicted upon Chin was doubly unjust by virtue of the fact that he had, in effect, played by the rules. And finally, the most tragic dimension of the narrative is the wedding that does not happen; the promise of what Lee Edelman has called (heteronormative) reproductive futurity is disrupted. The loss of marriage, and with it, the possibility of the Child and of social reproduction, serves as a central narrative fulcrum of Ebens and Nitz's atrocity. Zia's declaration of Chin as "everyone's son, brother, boyfriend, husband, father," furthermore, establishes his symbolic value as legible primarily within this same hetero-familial nexus—the label of "father" especially, particularly since Chin was not a father. In the father, the relatability of Chin is magnified not by a mode of kinship that he embodied, but one that he *potentially* could have. The official Chin narrative thus demonstrates that adherence to Americanness possesses a sexual dimension, that the "successful" integration of Chin and his family depend equally upon their docility to an economy of labor and of normative sexuality.

I must stress again that within the extremely difficult context of working with Asian American communities at this time, leaders such as Zia, Kin Yee, Roland Hwang, and Marisa Chuang had little choice but to take such rhetorical stances, and the ACJ is rightfully celebrated for its critical work. As an unpublished December 1988 essay by David Fukuzawa at Central Michigan University observes, much of the Chinese American community largely perceived the ACJ as a radical organization, simply by virtue of the fact that they were protesting at all (Fukuzawa 1988). This wasn't a universal perception—after all, some of the largest sources of fundraising for the ACJ came from On Leong organizations both in Detroit and throughout the country—but it is worth pointing out that both the political status quo of the community and the very parameters of legal culpability within the liberal justice system profoundly constrained the discursive and political possibilities of an Asian American cultural politics. And from the standpoint of mass community grassroots organization, the ACJ was wildly successful, with a coalition of allies that extended well beyond Asian Americans, including the local NAACP and several African American churches.

Thus, the ACJ—with any markers of Asianness deliberately absent from their title, despite their overwhelmingly Asian American (and principally Chinese American) leadership—assumed the position of patriotic indignation. As Cynthia Lee reports in *The Detroit News*, the ACJ organized a rally of over five hundred people in attendance on May 9, 1983, waving both American flags and "Jail the racist killers" placards (Lee 1983a). Kin Yee, then president of the ACJ and colloquially known as the "mayor of

Detroit's Chinatown," remarked that the rally was "the first by Asian-Americans in Detroit's history," with thirteen thousand Japanese, Chinese, and Koreans living in the metropolitan area. Most of the ACJ's public demonstrations were of a similar nature, with performative displays of U.S. patriotism alongside the indignation over particular actors in power—in this case, the Wayne County prosecutor William Callahan—for failing to live up to the American promise of pluralism.

Ultimately, these rhetorical moves aim to render Chin's life as grievable. Considering the symbolic and epistemic violence that the Ebens and Nitz sentencing inflicted, the project of the ACJ was of imbuing Chin's life with value, emphasizing his dutifulness and normativity while expunging the unsavory. The act of remembering, of memorializing Vincent Chin, is one haunted by the question posed by Judith Butler: "what makes for a grievable life?" (2004, 18). As Butler articulates, grievability is never a given, and its unequal distribution is correlative with global and local inequalities, as well as discursive dehumanization. "On the level of discourse," writes Butler, "certain lives are not considered lives at all, they cannot be humanized; they fit no dominant frame for the human, and their dehumanization occurs first, at this level" (2004, 25). Exclusion from "the human" is exclusion from grievability: "Violence against those who are already not quite lives, who are living in a state of suspension between life and death, leaves a mark that is no mark" (Butler 2004, 25). The establishment of Chin as a moral and economic paragon of respectable-heteronormative Americanness—ensuring that the upcoming wedding, and not the strip club, is remembered—speaks to this strategic need to ensure that Chin is deserving of grief by conforming to normative humanness. However, regarding grievability, Butler insists that attempting to fit normative grievability has severe political limitations, reifying forms of kinship that non-normative lives have problematized and disrupted as long as they have existed. Speaking of gay and lesbian lives in particular, Butler writes,

> [I]t is one thing to assert the reality of lesbian and gay lives as a reality, and to insist that these are lives worthy of protection in their specificity and commonality; but it is quite another to insist that the very public assertion of gayness calls into question what counts as reality and what counts as a human life.... [T]o be called unreal and to have that call, as it were, institutionalized as a form of differential treatment, is to become the other against whom (or against which) the human is made. It is the inhuman, the beyond the human, the less than human, the border that secures the human in its ostensible reality.... To be oppressed you first must become intelligible. To find that you are fundamentally unintelligible ... is to find that you have not yet achieved access to the human, to find yourself speaking only and always *as if you were* human, but with the sense that you are not. (Butler 2004, 29–30)

Butler thus asserts that to argue that a life is "worth protection," that a life matters, is a comparatively unambitious one compared with the profound restructuring of reality itself that comes from publicly embracing the non-normative. For Butler, then, the "human" is an ambivalent category, defined (as all identifying groups are) by what it excludes, often violently, and on the basis of grievability.

The becoming-machine of Vincent Chin is what the ACJ's rhetoric toward grievability attempts to combat; closer proximity to both sexual and economic normativity also means closer proximity to the "human," insofar as "the human" is in fact constituted by such normativities. Yet, I would argue that the becoming-machine is not truly undone; rather, it is reconfigured within a melancholic masochistic apparatus. The insistence on Chin's grievability recalls Anne Cheng's racial melancholia in a literal sense, describing the racialized object-turned-subject who becomes dependent on mourning—in this case, a single figure in Chin. The racial melancholy of the ACJ is, in fact, a dominant affect of its rhetoric. However, as I have alluded earlier, melancholia bleeds into masochism by way of pleasure through self-annihilation. Notably, pleasure—specifically, Chin's pleasure—is disavowed. Whereas in melancholia, there is a disavowal of the normative timeline of grief (grief is perpetual), in (Deleuzian) masochism, pleasure is disavowed in order to effectuate the ideal of coldness. Melancholically, Chin is frozen in time, like the photograph in the opening of this chapter, but the disavowal of the sexual Chin, the Chin who threw the first punch, the Chin who was civilization's discontent, is the necessary prerequisite.

Chin's excessive heteromasculinity and pursuit of pleasure—indeed, his *organicity*—are purged from the official narrative. Given the valorization of pleasure within queer theory as "a rallying point of the counterattack against the deployment of sexuality" (Foucault 1978, 157), I do not mean that Chin was a "queer" or even "feminist" figure; the Fancy Pants Club was by all means a site of heterosexist objectification of women, and on the eve of his wedding, Chin was reportedly a very active and enthusiastic participant. Chin furthermore did little to de-escalate the fight, throwing the first punch and shouting at Ebens and Nitz in the parking lot "Come on, you chickenshits, let's fight some more" (qtd. in Chang 1999, 23). Robert S. Chang hypothesizes that the initial animosity from Ebens and Nitz arises from a libidinal conflict of heteromasculine competition:

> Chin was displacing [Ebens and Nitz] as (the rightful) consumers of sexual attention. Here we have economics, race, gender, and sexuality coming together…. Loss of jobs entails a loss of masculinity. The loss of masculinity was caused by a racial and foreign Other, an Asian man who in many ways was just like them. (1999, 23–24)

Considering the multiple levels of emasculation occurring in this context, Chang's reading deepens the implications of Chin's murder, suggesting that the racialized battle between Chin and Ebens ultimately transpires on the territory of patriarchy, and their shared attachment to dominant manhood ultimately provides the conceptual currency of value for the conflict. Moreover, there is something unsettling and curious about the fact that Chin and his friends allegedly disparaged Rudolph, the

Black dancer, elevating Colwell's white femininity at Rudolph's expense, and Ebens came to Rudolph's defense.

Nevertheless, the sanitization of Chin, whose sexual expressiveness (even hetero expression) is strategically suppressed, whose moment of irrationality and violence is minimized and normalized ("an energetic, take-charge guy"), deliberately frames him as a model minority whose capacities for assimilation and complicity within a postindustrial capitalist market make him an aspirational American capitalist subject—and, even more tellingly, as an *engineer*, a job emphasizing his technological prowess. Insofar as it is premised upon utility and a degree of predictable fungibility, model minorityism is in fact coterminous with techno-oriental becoming-machine, and one that is buttressed by Asian American communities themselves, including the ACJ. In the case of Vincent Chin, Butler's argument that the inhuman forms the boundary of the grievable requires a degree more specificity, when there are forms of "inhumanity" that are acceptable (the machine-like) and others that are not (the undisciplined and chaotically desiring). The promise of heteronormative futurity, the disavowal of pleasure with the excesses it typically entails, and the fidelity to the capitalist market (and moreover, a STEM field, as an engineer) converge to secure Chin's status as a grievable model minority and, I would suggest further, a cyborg. Chin's conversion into model minority is thus *also* a becoming-machine, only of a different, more palatable order, one that both liberalizes and domesticates the excessive masculinity that dominated his narrative. Unlike the threatening and grotesque becoming-machine of the Japanese car, the becoming-machine of the official ACJ narrative suggests a model minority that would serve domestic interests and help secure heteronormative futurity.

Yet, the ACJ organizers positioned the murder of Vincent Chin as a *repudiation* of the model minority. The capacity for Chin to be targeted, after all, demonstrates the perpetually foreign racialization of Asians. And yet their critique of model minoritarianism was premised principally on one dimension: that Asians are not succeeding, economically or socially, to the extent that popular opinion seems to suggest, or as much as Asian Americans *deserve*. Although the critique of model minoritarianism varied within the organization, it was often not so much ideological as it was aspirational on an identitarian basis. As the ACJ began to expand its advocacy beyond the Vincent Chin case, it would become more vocal at critiquing the model minority paradigm in this same register. This was especially true of Dr. Marisa Chuang, one of the key organizers of the ACJ, who prepared remarks for Detroit resident Bonlap Chan to the Detroit City Council on July 7, 1983, in order to argue for Asian Americans to be counted as "minority contractors":

> Contrary to the myth of the "model minority," the Chinese Americans do have our share of problems facing all minorities. We have high suicide rates, illiteracy rates and unemployment rates. We are grossly underemployed, too. Many of us are still discouraged by the inaccessibility of existing social programs or full economic opportunity.... After seeing that the Asian groups were not recognized by the

Department as part of 'minority contractors' and observing that the Asians stood very slim chances of being awarded contracts by the City, I gave up.

Chuang thus repudiates the "model minority" on the basis of a lack of economic advance and assimilation relative to popular perception, but for the aim of attaining precisely the economic advance that has been denied. Chuang and Chan thus leverage the critique of the model minority in order to hasten Asian American inclusion into the market.

In this and other cases, the ACJ's organizing not only sought out justice for Chin but, in the process, participated in an iteration of Asian American subject formation itself. In strong contrast with the articulations of Asian America that emerged in the rise and wake of the Third World Liberation Front strike in 1968, the ACJ often wedded justice for Chin to a form of ethnonational pride. This is also evident in some of the other writings and documents of Dr. Marisa Chuang. In a an educational frequently asked questions pamphlet entitled "A Dialogue with Dr. Marisa Chuang: The HOW, WHO, and WHAT'S of the American Citizens for Justice Committee," the question "What can I do to help the cause?" is answered with: "There are plenty [sic] you can do to fight injustice and to gain ethnic pride. Contact any of the coordinators of various subcommittees listed below and volunteer your time and efforts." According to Chuang, to participate in the efforts for Chin is to "gain ethnic pride," firmly suturing both ressentiment and melancholic idealization to a static, strategic-essentialist formation of ethnic heritage.

Again, this stands in stark contrast with the radicalism of the earlier, left-wing Asian American movement that Frank Wu minimizes in his account of the Chin movement. Instead, it is closer, in fact, to the paradigm of ressentiment held by Ronald Ebens himself. Echoing a similar sentiment as Tajima-Peña's quote earlier in this chapter, Chris Iijima—folk singer, critical race law scholar, and cofounder of I Wor Kuen—writes in the *Columbia Human Rights Law Review*,

> In essence, the recognition and proclamation of racial identity—at least in the contemporary context of Asian Americans—was originally a means to a political end and not the end itself. Asian American "identity" was not meant to be a synonym for "heritage." It was a means to identify with others who shared the experience of subordination. (1997, 54)

He would later write, in no uncertain terms, "That [Asian American identity] has now become synonymous with 'pride in one's ethnic heritage' is a complete evisceration of what it was originally and what it was meant to be" (2001, 7).

As the Vincent Chin case shows, there is a political and psychic toll attached to the politics of inclusion, one that perhaps necessarily operates from a logic of masochistic disavowal. As Deleuze writes,

> Disavowal should perhaps be understood as the point of departure of an operation that consists neither in negating nor even destroying, but rather in radically contesting the validity of that which is: it suspends belief in and neutralizes the given in such a way that a new horizon opens up beyond the given and in place of it. (1989, 31)

Taking Deleuze's definition, the disavowal of the desiring and violent creature, the disavowal of the scene of Chin's pleasure, is one that "opens up" a new horizon, instantiating Chin's status as model minority. Disavowal also produces a mechanized, non-desiring figure, what Deleuze calls "a new sexless man," a figure who transcends sensuality and the need for it:

> The masochistic process of disavowal is so extensive that it affects sexual pleasure itself; pleasure is postponed for as long as possible and is thus disavowed. The masochist is therefore able to deny the reality of pleasure at the very point of experiencing it, in order to identify with the "new sexless man." (1989, 33)

Bourgeoning Asian American subjecthood in 1983 disavowed Chin's pleasure, even if Chin's pleasure seems to have been a lubricating catalyst for the racial violence stemming from Ebens and Nitz's castrated masculinity (horrifically recuperated by the phallus of the Louisville slugger). But additionally, Deleuze's masochistic disavowal is one of temporal postponement, of suspension, of the denial of pleasure even "at the very point of experiencing it" (1989, 33). According to Deleuze, Masoch, and by extension the masochist,

> does not believe in negating or destroying the world nor in idealizing it: what he does is to disavow and thus to suspend it, in order to secure an ideal which is itself suspended in fantasy. He questions the validity of existing reality in order to create a pure ideal reality, an operation which is perfectly in line with the judicial spirit of masochism. (Deleuze 1989, 32–33)

The vicarious disavowal of Chin's pleasure by Asian American narrativization results in that pleasure's postponement and resubstantiation in the repeated re-narrativization of Chin, symbolically transforming him into this masochistic "new sexless man"—or rather, a new sexless *machine*—by way of repetitive signification.

Indispensable to this melancholic masochism was the tireless figure of Lily Chin.[12] If the Japanese car was the endpoint of the becoming-machine of Chin's murder, the photograph of his photograph was the endpoint of this model minority idealization: proper, static, and neatly fit within the boundary of the frame. Recalling Rebecca Comay's argument that there exists an underlying masochism within melancholia wherein the subject is whipped in "the sadomasochistic theater of grief," the ACJ's deployment of Lily Chin throughout its campaign nevertheless produced a fetishized visual spectacle of suffering, playing into the fantasy that an "infinitely sympathetic rescuer" (Kucich 2007, 24)—namely, the U.S. justice system—may intervene and end the social drama with reconciliatory justice. Indeed, in Deleuze's interpretation of masochism, the mother figures prominently in masochistic fantasy, both idealized and disavowed as a representative of the law. The presence of what John Kucich terms as "the two interdependent elements of masochism" (2007, 33)—that is, "cherished suffering and fantasies of omnipotence" (2007, 33), or melancholy and magic, respectively—helps consolidate the Lily Chin photos as vivid props in the masochistic theater of grief. Kucich explains that these phases operate in sequence to produce masochistic fantasy: "The melancholic phase revolves around instances of self-sacrifice or self-punishment, in which exclusion, dependence, or abjection are cherished; the magical phase, by contrast, exaggerates autonomy, inclusion, and self-esteem. In masochistic fantasy, these two phases logically reinforce one another" (2007, 33). Furthermore, masochism serves to produce a "morally simplified" world, the brutal flagellation of Chin-as-martyr[13] establishing clear character lines of protagonist and antagonist within the Asian American social drama. While the ACJ's organizing tactics disavowed the unrespectable pleasure of the strip club, it masochistically deployed the pain of melancholy represented by the respectable, grieving mother to summon the fantasy of the omnipotent savior of justice. That is to say, the ACJ disavowed the scene of sexuality for scenes of the wounding of the heteronormative telos—the mother mourning the son, the wedding that became a funeral—to follow a masochistic script of compensatory fantasy. Thus, what begins as a reaction to techno-oriental violence becomes an appropriation of techno-orientalism through model minoritarianism, within a masochistic fantasy structure tethered to a politics of respectability in order to galvanize its narrative antagonisms.

Here, techno-orientalism becomes repurposed as a masochistic technology of subjectification in order to resist the mode of abject otherness. It is also a masochism that may, on some level despite itself, urge toward its own death. After all, the later Freud (breaking from his initial argument that masochism was merely sadism turned upon one's own ego) suggested that the death instinct, the "inherent" urge to return to inorganicity, runs within hypothetical, primary masochism: "Masochism, the turning round of the instinct upon the subject's own ego, would in that case be a return to an earlier phase of the instinct's history, a regression" (1989, 48–49). In becoming an organization committed to providing redress to wrongful, racialized death, the ACJ sought out that moment again and again, masochistically repeating the wound within the limited confines of an American legal system that would ultimately fail them.

Once again, the official Chin narrative demonstrates that model minority adherence to Americanness possesses a sexual dimension, that the "successful" assimilation of Chin and his family depend equally upon their docility to an economy of labor and of normative sexuality. That is, Chin is obedient to the econo-sexual mores of his home. He was the right, not the wrong, kind of machine. Not unlike how the model minority is in actuality the reverse mirror image of the yellow peril, Chin is configured from repository of neo-Luddite fear to a helpful cog in the U.S. sexual-economic order.

In the decades to come, as Vincent Chin grew to crystallize as a symbol for Asian American organizing and self-making, there would be a number of performances that rearticulated configured Chin vis-à-vis model minoritarian ideology. The following chapter concludes the discussion of Vincent Chin with an examination of historiographic theater that redeploys and shifts masochism toward multiple political aims.

2
Bludgeons and Becomings
Vincent Chin, Suspenseful Reveal, and the Limits of the Legal

I drove only a few minutes up Woodward into Ferndale. The contrast between here and the Woodward of the Fancy Pants and the Highland Park Plant was stark. The Golden Star Chinese Restaurant, where Vincent worked, once stood here at the corner of Woodward and West Nine Mile Road. Now, commercial gentrification has struck, taking the form of gastropubs and artisanal stores selling hipster T-shirts. Highland Park was predominantly Black, but here, white shoppers and merchants dominated this street corner in Ferndale. I even had to pay a parking meter.

There, settled among some greenery between the roadways, was Vincent Chin's memorial plaque, dedicated in 2009 on the anniversary of the attack that killed him on June 19, 1982. It's easy to miss, situated precariously on a raised island interrupting a crosswalk at the dead center of an intersection between two main thoroughfares. "From a Whisper to a Rallying Cry," the title reads. " 'It's not fair.' These were the last anguished words whispered by Vincent Chin as he lay dying, the victim of a hate crime on June 19, 1982. His words became a rallying cry for the Asian American community outraged at the lenient sentences his assailants received and they spawned a civil rights movement."

What of the ephemera commemorated by monuments adjacent to shopping centers? Narratives of racialized working-class death engraved by bar associations? Protrusions of melancholic affects approximating liberation through the inevitably inadequate nomenclature of "justice," a cruel optimism that is destined to fail by design, remembered decades later generically as "civil rights"? The plaque is not a becoming, but a paradox, a precious public archive of a repertoire of rage, yet also an understatement, bronze letters in the corner of shoppers' eyes as they dash to make the green light.

Perhaps the most uncanny contradiction is that the Asian American demand for legibility has produced new genres of inscrutability. And perhaps it is through masochism that we can peel back the layers of respectability and become seen. With all the perils and pleasures that such revealing entails.

On a dark, minimally set stage, the twenty-first scene of Ping Chong's 1995 experimental play *Chinoiserie* plays out: a projection stating "From a Chinese-English Phrasebook of 1875" is displayed overhead. Three of the performers conduct a range of choreographic movements corresponding to the lines stated by Ping Chong and Aleta Hayes, who alternate statements. Starting with phrases that are from the actual 1875 phrasebook—"He took it from me by violence / He claimed my gold mine. / He cheated me out of my wages," the statements quickly become anachronistic, forming a pastiche of esoteric statements that meanderingly approach a foreboding of exclusion and anti-Chinese sentiment. Chong and Hayes say such lines as "Was *Coolie High* a film about inner-city Chinese youth?," to a string of racial epithets, to "The Chinese immigration will soon be stopped," to "Everybody was kung-fu fighting—huh!," and then one of the last, and longest of the lines: "The Vincent Chin murder case united the Chinese community in ways never seen before." Even among the seeming randomness of the phrases, the line about Vincent Chin stands out as serious and expository, a jarringly prosaic climax to the litany of phrases.

In a sense, this scene serves as a synecdoche of the larger play: an escalating rhythm of short phrases and movements with a masochistic climax of racial injury. It is a move that is simultaneously erotic and historiographic—in short, what Elizabeth Freeman calls an "eroto-historiography." It is one of several performative interpretations of the murder of Vincent Chin, assembling new masochistic signification to the event. This chapter concludes the discussion begun in Chapter 1, comparing *Chinoiserie* with the 2013 UC Hastings Vincent Chin trial re-enactment by Frank Wu, Denny Chin, and Philip Kan Gotanda. Taken together, these staged representations of the Vincent Chin event illustrate Walter Benjamin's famous assertation that "To articulate the past historically does not mean to recognize it 'the way it really was.' [...] It means to seize hold of a memory as it flashes up at a moment of danger" (1968, 255). Whereas *Chinoiserie* suspends the murder of Chin like a narrative reward and engages the audience in a masochistic erotics of violence, the Hastings re-enactment deploys masochism as an analytic, deploying self-criticism in order to demonstrate the inability for individualist legal frameworks of racism to adequately confer redress.

Suspense and Masochistic Reparation: Ping Chong's *Chinoiserie*

Commissioned by the Lied Center for Performing Arts in Lincoln, Nebraska, in 1995, *Chinoiserie* is the second of what would be known as dramatist Ping Chong's "East/West Quartet." As a multimedia queer theater maker and artist who began work in 1972, Chong's oeuvre is massive, spanning more than 50 plays across three continents, and having earned two Obie awards, a Guggenheim Fellowship, and a spread of many others. His *East/West Quartet* remains quite influential within Asian American theater studies.[1]

Chong describes *Chinoiserie* as "a documentary concert theatre work" and "meta-theatre" (2004, xxiv). Taking as its departure point the 1793 first contact between Chinese Emperor Qianlong and the trade emissary of King George III, the play fluidly moves between various historical moments, all engaged with the encounter of China or Chinese people by Anglo-Americans. Blending an international array of instrumentation, vocal song, elaborate choreography, and overhead projection with a non-linear pastiche of historic flashes, *Chinoiserie* is a multimedia production requiring particular attention to the audio and visual registers. But one of the central theatrical thrusts of *Chinoiserie* is that of Vincent Chin and the grief of his mother Lily Chin. The Chin narrative haunts the whole of *Chinoiserie*, serving as a slow, masochistic reveal, displaying an aesthetics of suspension. As Deleuze notes, suspension (along with disavowal) is a central aspect of sexual, Oedipal masochism, writing "It is no exaggeration to say that Masoch was the first novelist to make use of suspense as an essential ingredient of romantic fiction" (1989, 33). Suspense functions to draw the reader or audience into the masochistic fantasy, for "the art of suspense always places us on the side of the victim and forces us to identify with him" (Deleuze 1989, 34). The torturer's whip, after all, must suspend and produce anticipatory tension before its strike, in order to fulfill its erotic potential. Similarly, *Chinoiserie* flirts with the audience, teasing toward its climax of horror, dangling Chin's death before the audience as its terrible narrative reward.

Chinoiserie relies highly on its nonverbal stage elements to propel its dramatic action, such as its overhead projection, which provides a combination of historical exegesis, character context, and poetry. Most crucially, the overhead projection provides a slow count, numbering each scene from 1 to 40, each number accompanied by the entire cast in unison stating the number. With the passing of each number, the play visually projects a built-in rhythm, hurtling its audience forward and instilling a lingering tension, unclear which number would be the last, or whether the numbering would alter or cease. The scenes vary greatly in length and in context, portraying moments including but not limited to Ping Chong's contemporary autobiographical anecdotes, historical narrations, historical re-enactments, and a restaging of Sinophobic theater.

However, there are two crucial sound cues that reappear repeatedly throughout the performance. The first is the sound of a baseball being hit and an accompanying roar by the crowd, which first appears in the middle of Scene 9, following a meditation on Chinese-derived gunpowder tea and immediately after one of the ensemble actors asks the audience, "Whose history is this anyway?" (Chong 2004, 75). The second is the sound of a loud cannonball, appearing first at the top of Scene 10 to initiate a scene covering the 1792 confrontation of Great Britain with China, forcibly demanding China open its doors to trade. After this latter sound, as the actors collectively narrate the story, alternating stating in chorus the onomatopoeia "Boom boom boom," indexing the cannonball sound with their percussive voices.

Both the baseball and the cannonball sounds are repeated several times throughout the play as the scene numbers steadily increase one by one; the former is enshrouded in a degree of mystery due to its apparent decontextualization, whereas the latter begins in context and becomes resignified repeatedly. Still, despite the relative lack of characterization and linear narrative structure, both sounds seem to suspensefully build toward a linear climax. It is only with the first vague reference to Vincent Chin in Scene 16, followed by Lily Chin's first appearance—played by noted African American dancer and performer Aleta Hayes—in Scene 17, that it becomes apparent how these sounds are destined to resolve. At the beginning of Scene 16, Hayes states a line quoted directly from a scene of *Who Killed Vincent Chin?*: "Boom. Boom. Boom.

/ All I heard was boom boom boom. / Men fighting, ya know" (Chong 2004, 83). Notably, this line is from the Fancy Pants dancer Angela Rudolph, who is named by her pseudonym "Starlene" and given exposure in *Who Killed Vincent Chin?*, but *Chinoiserie* does not do so, leaving her role and name ambiguous and unmarked. This transitions surreally to the baseball bat sound, a sports announcer gleefully announcing the Detroit Tigers' defeat of the Toronto Blue Jays, and then the shift to Scene 17 showcasing Hayes as Lily Chin, who tells the story of adopting a young Vincent from China. Unlike her role as Rudolph, Hayes' role as Lily Chin is explicit, her name displayed as white text on a blue background via overhead projector.

Both Lily Chin's and the Starlene's accounts would appear in segments at a time, hinting at the final bludgeoning of Vincent interwoven with the historical political narrative of Anglo-American Sinophobia, but Lily Chin as a character would be named, while Rudolph would not. Many of Lily Chin's lines—written by Michael Matthews and largely derived from *Who Killed Vincent Chin?*—establish the Chins as law abiding, respectable U.S. subjects. For example, in Scene 22, Mrs. Chin recalls:

> My husband serves in the American army
> we were happy to come to America
> my father say America hard
> my husband say America good
> and I think so, too.
>
> And lots of Chinese
> lots of Chinese
> my husband say all American good
> he get job in a factory
> we go to baseball game
> very American
> but they kick and curse at us.
> I ask my husband
> why they do this?
> Why they do this?
> *(Sound of baseball being hit. A crowd roars.)*
> (Chong 2004, 96)

This two-stanza monologue establishes the immigrants' hyper-Americanness, a willingness to participate in the armed forces,[2] participate productively in the economy, and even attempt to partake in the quintessentially American pastime of baseball. In other scenes, Hayes-as-Lily Chin describes her son as "an American boy," assuming the pose of a baseball player with each repetition of the phrase. It demonstrates the same enthusiasm for assimilation in the previous section, a continuation of the same political-rhetorical strategy. Then, the final violence inflicted upon Chin serves as the dramatic apogee of the play, revealing furthermore the baseball bat as the instrument of Chin's death. Following Scene 35—an eerie rendition of the cast singing "Take Me Out to the Ball Game" first in Chinese, then in English, followed by the baseball hit sound—Scene 36 gruesomely describes the murder itself by three of the male actors in ensemble:

MICHAEL: Nitz
RIC: Ebens
MICHAEL: Two big white *guys*
RIC: One with a *mustache*
MICHAEL: Two big white *guys*
RIC: One holding a *bat*
MICHAEL: A bear hug from *behind*
RIC: A full swing to the *head*
MICHAEL: A bear hug from *behind*
RIC: A full swing to the *head*
MICHAEL: He held the bat with both *hands*
RIC: A full swing to the *head*
MICHAEL: Again
RIC: Again
SHI-ZHENG: *Again*
CAST: Boom boom boom
MICHAEL: All I heard *was*
CAST: Boom boom boom
MICHAEL: Doubles, triples, and *home runs*
CAST: Boom boom boom
MICHAEL: His skull was *crushed*
RIC: Pieces of brain bleed into *tar*
MICHAEL: The body released turns and *falls*
RIC: He was wearing white *socks*
MICHAEL: The body released turns and falls
RIC: Not a speck of blood on white *socks*
MICHAEL: A black man standing on the corner *says*:
PING: Ebens swung the bat as if a baseball player was swinging for a home run, full contact, full swing.
　　　(Sound of baseball being hit.) (Chong 2004, 114–115, original emphasis)

Within this frenzied, climactic retelling, the dramatic crescendo of violence reaches its peak; furthermore, it mirrors the usage of repetition seen throughout the play prior. "A bear hug from *behind*" and "A full swing to the *head*" are repeated for dramatic emphasis, but they also invoke the rhythmic echoes throughout the play of "boom boom boom" and the baseball bat strikes. Ric, Michael, and Shi-Zhen stand in a triad in that order, all dressed in black, with Ric and Shi-Zhen dipping to their respective sides with each emphasized phrase. This final annihilation of Chin in the play, followed by

Aleta Hayes' sobbing (and later, singing) Lily Chin in Scene 37, functions as the ultimate fruition of masochistic suspense until this point, a suspense including not only the selective details of Chin's murder, but also an entire history of Chinese contact with Britain and the United States.

Moreover, the usage of repetition, the slow numbered count that leads to the climax, also infuses the play with industrial relentlessness. *Chinoiserie* produces masochistic suspense through an aesthetic of industrial erotics in which the components of narrative are assembled to produce a final product. In a very literal sense, *Chinoiserie* stages what Elizabeth Freeman has termed "erotohistoriography," an erotic mode of not only presenting the past, but also existing within it through sensation:

> Erotohistoriography admits that contact with historical materials can be precipitated by particular bodily dispositions, and that these connections may elicit bodily responses, even pleasurable ones, that are themselves a form of understanding. It sees the body as a method, and historical consciousness as something intimately involved with corporeal sensations. (2010, 95–96)

But of course, given that this is eroto*historiography* rather than eroto*history*, *Chinoiserie* is a particular interpretation of the (at that point, decade-old) history of Chin, a sensory memorialization that treats the death as a narrative reward. Moreover, the "boom boom boom" of the cannonballs and the baseball bat swings place Chin into a continuity of the modern, an age of mass reproduction, and equally, mechanical racialization. The erotohistoriographic aesthetic of masochism grafts onto the mechanical and symbiotically shares its affective logics. In this sense, *Chinoiserie* treats the murder of Vincent Chin as the masochistic climax of the entire play, erupting not only from a history of anti-Chinese rhetorics and violence, but also an avant-garde theatrical structure whose postmodern timekeeping and poetics parallel the assembly line. The projection at the end of Scene 37, immediately following Lily Chin's lament, reads: "Vincent Chin's murderers never served any jail term. They were fined $3780 and released on probation" (Chong 2004, 117), silently providing the emotional fulcrum upon which the metahistorical narrative rests. However, on this theatrical assembly line, the assembly of meaning comes with the disassembly of the Chinese body once aural smoke of the "boom boom booms" is clear. Through the staging of self-annihilation, *Chinoiserie* embraces a masochistic fantasy of reparation. The play spectacularizes historical wounding as self-wounding through its strategic deterritorialization of the Chin murder, Anglo–Chinese relations more broadly, and Ping Chong's personal life experience.

Chinoiserie, echoing the prior Asian American responses to the Chin murder, reflects a racial masochism of the machine, one that would fantasize and spectacularize self-annihilation. In this sense, *Chinoiserie* reveals racial masochism's entwining with a poetics of modern machinery, suggesting that self-annihilation is to be found in the staccato of the cannonball and the baseball bat, American rhythms into which Asian Americans try to enter. Chin's inclusion into the rhythm of Scene 36 is only possible via his dismantling, his techno-lynching, and his becoming-machine, for the postmodern catharsis of the witnessing audience. The theatrical masochism of *Chinoiserie*'s quasi-narrative arc depends on a techno-orientalist onslaught to the senses and presents a Chinese American subjectivity based upon Chin's disintegration itself.

The play seems to seek reparation, although the shape of such reparation is necessarily vague;[3] regarding the end of *Chinoiserie*, Joshua Takano Chambers-Letson writes that the play uses

> the stage to imagine the kinds of collective, social acts that are required in order to make reparative justice possible. This occurs through an excavation, confrontation, and reconciliation with the past. Using the imaginative space of the stage, *Chinoiserie* models a reparative practice to create conditions of possibility in which justice might finally make itself known. (Chambers-Letson 2013, 95)

The play's deployment of Vincent and Lily Chin also echoes what Anne Cheng has described as the move from grief to grievance:

> public grievance is a social forum and luxury to which the racially melancholic minorities have little or no access. If the move from grief to grievance, for example, aims to provide previously denied agency, then it stands as a double-edged solution, since to play the plaintiff is to cultivate, for critics, a cult of victimization. So the gesture of granting agency through grievance confers agency on the one hand and rescinds it on the other. (2000, 174–175)

Such theatrical melancholia, then, allows grief to become political, although it also risks undercutting the temporal space for grief itself. However, I must pessimistically add the caveat that within the boundaries of respectability, the potential reach of the borders of grievability are shortened even as they are actually widened to include a Chinese American man. This is because, in regard to the Vincent Chin case, *Chinoiserie* represents an unintentional aesthetic materialization of the American Citizens for Justice's (ACJ's) organizing strategies. Like the ACJ organizing material—and notably, *unlike* the 1987 *Who Killed Vincent Chin?*—*Chinoiserie* omits the desiring Chin, the angry Chin, retreating to a logic of American universalism even as it ostensibly critiques it. The melancholia of the ACJ's rhetoric, reflected again in *Chinoiserie*, temporally disrupts the normative timeline of grief and confers melancholic racial subjects a capacity to grieve that the state juridical apparatus denied. Yet, it nevertheless validates the preexisting boundaries of grievability, thus thwarting the "pathological" potential that melancholia often seems to afford. Although it intriguingly attaches the Chin narrative to a transnational history of Chinese–Anglo interaction, *Chinoiserie* ultimately aspires to a universal humanism that (rightfully) seems largely impossible given the racial-political strife exhibited throughout the rest of the play: the final overhead projections of *Chinoiserie* read "You believe in the goodness of mankind" and "To be continued into the 21st century" (Chong 2004, 122). There is, as in masochism, a kind of faith in the contract; in this case, a liberal social contract in which "the goodness of mankind"—unraced, color-blind, and for that matter, gendered—may be able to overcome social difference and social disparity.

Moreover, the naming of Lily Chin, alongside the *unnaming* of Rudolph, even as both women's words are quoted from *Who Killed Vincent Chin?*, further demonstrates this point; the mother, and not the stripper, is given acknowledgment, even though both of their testimonials are crucial for its intended dramatic effect. Whereas *Who Killed Vincent Chin?* is open about Fancy Pants' status as a strip club, and Vincent Chin's interaction with its employees, *Chinoiserie* re-obscures Fancy Pants and returns to the official strategically respectable ACJ narrative, even as the play quotes directly from Rudolph. Paradoxically, even as it narratively eroticizes the techno-oriental lynching of Vincent Chin, *Chinoiserie* adheres to the model minoritarianism of the ACJ in order to streamline its narrative.

Ironically, the dismantling of the model minoritarianism of Vincent Chin would occur on a different stage, one more pedagogical than rarefied. While *Chinoiserie* would deploy masochism as an aesthetic, the 2013 Vincent Chin Trial Reenactment would deploy moral masochism as an *analytic*, one that dislodges the oft-overdetermined affects and narratives ossified within the Vincent Chin affair.

The UC Hastings Re-enactment and Masochistic Reconfiguration

The Vincent Chin Trial Reenactment was staged at the University of California, Hastings Law School, in San Francisco, California, on January 30 and February 1, 2013, free and open to the public. While also a masochistic performance, the UC Hastings re-enactment reconfigures masochism itself as a mode of self-interrogation. Crucially, the Hastings re-enactment deploys masochism not as fantasy, but, as in Amber Jamilla Musser's sense, an *analytic*. The re-enactment was cowritten by UC Hastings Dean Frank Wu, Judge of the U.S. Court of Appeals Denny Chin, and the Asian American Bar Association of New York and was directed by famed playwright Philip Kan Gotanda, an alumnus of Hastings himself. Having a clear legal emphasis, the hour-long re-enactment consists primarily of the staging of select transcripts from the series of trials involving Ebens and Nitz, including examinations, cross-examinations, and arguments from the prosecution and defense. The various figures in the Chin legal drama—including Saperstein, Kaufman, Liza Chan, and others—are predominantly performed not by trained actors but by Hastings law faculty and alumni in the Baxter Appellate Law Center. Throughout, Frank Wu and Denny Chin stand at either side, narrating, providing commentary, and providing contextual walkthroughs between excerpts. A PowerPoint display provides photos of and other additional material and information on the various figures who appear in the narration.

Although performed with minimal theatrical production apparatus, I examine the UC Hastings re-enactment as a work of documentary theater.[4] Thus, being mindful to the form, I find it particularly curious that the UC Hastings re-enactment, contrary to *Chinoiserie*, elects to provide a multifaceted account that problematizes its own moral thrust, within a structure that has been traditionally read as didactic or even non-aesthetic. Although the re-enactment ends with a melancholic nostalgia for death—Denny Chin closes, "The death of a man was the birth of a movement"— the piece overall resists the normative idealization as in the ACJ propaganda (Wu 2018). The UC Hastings re-enactment could have been entirely propagandistic in its account of Chin yet nevertheless chooses to provide a multifaceted picture of the various arguments of both the prosecuting and defending sides of the trials.

Beginning with the original sentencing of Ebens and Nitz, the re-enactment transitions to the federal civil rights trial that begins on June 5, 1984, which is prefaced by Denny Chin's explanation that the primary point of contention was not Ebens and Nitz's violence (which was undisputed) but, rather, that of motivation: "The government had to prove that Ebens and Nitz acted *because* of Chin's race" (Wu 2018). The re-enactment spends the plurality of its time on this particular trial, beginning with the opening statements, followed by two witness testimonies (both examinations and cross-examinations), and closing statements. Far from obscuring the fact of the strip show, the first witness portrayed is Racine Colwell, an exotic dancer at the Fancy Pants Club who testifies that Ebens states, "It's because of you little motherfuckers that we're out of work" (Wu 2018). The cross-examination of Colwell by defense attorney David Lawson attempts to cast doubt on her objectivity, emphasizing that Vincent Chin was a regular patron of the club and that perhaps Colwell enjoyed his company.

The presence of Colwell's testimony in this curated re-enactment not only serves as strong evidence in favor of the prosecution but also undeniably acknowledges the unrespectable strip club scene in which the initial fight occurs. Furthermore, Lawson's cross-examination displays a curious irony that would persist throughout this segment of the re-enactment: unlike the dismissiveness of Saperstein in the first trial, the defense rhetorically aims to *humanize* Chin. The re-enactment performs Lawson's closing remarks, in which he states,

> Vincent Chin was the same as Ronald Ebens: a human being. He was not a person who had only great virtues and no faults. Vincent Chin got drunk and he went to nude bars and he started a fight and then he wanted to finish the fight. And Mr. Ebens, like Mr. Chin, became full of rage, and Mr. Ebens wanted revenge. Vincent Chin wanted to finish the fight. Does this make him a hero or a martyr? (Wu 2018)

Although this can certainly be read as a cynically color-blind and reactionary move— that Chin occupies the space of universal humanity only insofar as it aids the case of the white perpetrator—it is nevertheless noteworthy that the re-enactment de-sanitizes Chin and restores missing pieces from the "official" ACJ narrative detailed in the previous chapter.

Moreover, the re-enactment curiously chooses to hold ACJ lawyer Lisa Chan accountable for improper witness preparation, which would be cited as the primary justification for overturning Ebens' guilty civil rights verdict in 1986, a point that is typically minimized in accounts of the Chin narrative: *Chinoiserie* and even the commendably balanced *Who Killed Vincent Chin?* all overlook this point entirely, while historian Sucheng Chan mentions it only briefly without further elaboration. The UC Hastings re-enactment makes the narrative choice to depict Chan's improper coaching at length based on her interview of Chin's friends Jimmy Choi, Robert Siroskey, and Gary Koivu on May 17, 1983; Chan coaches all of the witnesses together to ensure that there is continuity in their testimonies, despite the fact that several of them express uncertainty with the exact details of the event. Chan's opening to the meeting is particularly problematic (the following is quoted directly from Appendix A of 800 F2d 1422 *United States v. Ebens*, which is performed in the re-enactment):

> We will agree this is the story, this is it. When it's a federal prosecution, h'm, we're all going to have to be agreeing on this is what happened. Now, if you don't agree, like I explained to them earlier, you definitely remembered certain things happened, say, it's a black car and you definitely remembered it's a white car and we kind of (inaudible), okay, other than that, let's all have it sort of down, have it down pat, is it five minutes or is it ten minutes. Is it more like eight minutes, let's all agree. Otherwise, you all look funny on the stand. You all supposedly were there. But one says two minutes, the other says eight and that's what robbed me before. (Wu 2018)

Throughout the following interview, Chan is also particularly insistent on finding verbal examples of racist hate speech from Ebens and Nitz, hard evidence of Ebens and Nitz's inherent racism that would aid the government's civil rights argument. Choi (played, amusingly, by Gotanda in the re-enactment), Siroskey, and Koivu have difficulty deciding exactly what it was that Ebens or Nitz said and its racist content, and Chan guides their preparation throughout.

Technically, defense attorney Lawson's closing remarks are not altogether incorrect when he states, "we have three different racial allegations by three different people surfacing at three different times. People worked hard with each other and their attorneys searching the dark recesses of their minds to find something. Anything that could make this a racial murder" (Wu 2018). The UC Hastings re-enactment acknowledges that the prosecuting legal team pushed insistently to find evidence of overt racism from Ebens and Nitz in order to consolidate Chin's racial victimhood, when, on the basis of the presence of ethnic slurs, such evidence was ambiguous. Furthermore, the ACJ's success in community mobilization was ironically counted against the prosecution, accused of influencing the jurors in the initial civil rights trial.

Yet, given the broader context of all that occurred surrounding Chin's death and the punishment that was dealt in the wake of his death as I have explored throughout these first two chapters, it would be absurd to say that race and racism were altogether absent. The failure, rather, is in the law itself, and the utter incapacity of the U.S. juridical system to have an adequate vocabulary or grasp of racism beyond the liberal paradigm of overt racial injury by individual perpetrators. That is, the very field of liberal intelligibility cannot properly account for something approaching "justice," or perhaps, that we must reconceptualize anti-racist reparation beyond what the parameters of "justice" allow. In its multidimensional portrayal of the players on both sides, the UC Hastings re-enactment displays the very cognitive limits of the legal apparatus to grasp the operation of racist discourse. As Frank Wu concludes in the re-enactment,

> Was race a factor? Ebens steadfastly denied that he was motivated by Chin's race and in post-trial interviews even to this day he continues to deny that he is a racist. Perhaps Ebens is not a hardcore racist, but perhaps too, racism may be more ambiguous and complex and subtle. Clearly, the mix of the recession, alcohol, testosterone, and tempers was a lethal combination. Ebens was not a racist in the conventional, simple sense, but he may have well been motivated by racial impulses that he may have only been dimly aware of, if at all. (2018)

Here, Wu gestures toward an understanding of race that is "more ambiguous and complex and subtle," an operation of racism that operates more deeply and systemically than the "injurious performatives" of hate speech described and problematized by Judith Butler. Moreover, by portraying the Chin trials from a multitude of vantage points, displaying how Ebens eventually but perhaps fairly "won" by the rules of the legal game, the UC Hastings re-enactment implies the absurd incapacity of the legal apparatus to even provide adequate terms by which injustice was committed.

The 2013 UC Hastings re-enactment masochistically subjects its own political protagonist—the Vincent Chin justice legal team—to punishment and furthermore demonstrates the potency of masochism, in the analytical mode, to demonstrate the absurdity of the rights-based liberal law of American possessive individualism. Thus, the ACJ, rather than Chin, becomes the focus of masochistic punishment. Deleuze argues that masochism aims to subvert the law by embracing and pushing it to its furthest extremes through the deployment of the contract, which consists of promises to torture and punish according to the desires of the masochist:

> By scrupulously applying the law we are able to demonstrate its absurdity and provoke the very disorder that it is intended to prevent or to conjure.... A close examination of masochistic fantasies or rites reveals that while they bring into play the strictest application of the law, the result in every case is the opposite of what might be expected (thus whipping, far from punishing or preventing an erection, provokes and ensures it). It is a demonstration of the law's absurdity. (Deleuze 1989, 88)

The UC Hastings re-enactment displays a literal scrupulous application of the law, and doing so demonstrates its very limit, not just in procuring justice, but in limiting and codifying racist violence within the bounds of overt performative "hate speech."

Through this masochistic performance of legal implementation, the UC Hastings re-enactment does not foreclose all conclusions but one (ressentiment and outrage) but, rather, opens up a more compelling conclusion: that Lisa Chan and the ACJ's misstep was not so much in breaking "the rules" but, rather, in following too closely the terms in which racism (and by extension, "fairness" and equal treatment) is defined in juridical discourse, that is, as words of overt injury. After all, it was not so much the overtly racist motives of killing Chin as the light sentence of Ebens and Nitz given by Judge Kaufman that was of greatest violence to Asian Americans. It was the epistemic violence from the sovereign juridical power, more than the bludgeoning itself, that loudly declared that Asian lives did not matter. The masochistic UC Hastings re-enactment ironically demonstrates the futility to achieve "justice" insofar as the terms of injustice remain as they are, bounded in narrow terms of epithets and overtly discriminatory intentions. As Butler writes,

> the court's speech carries with it its *own* violence, and ... the very institution that is invested with the authority to adjudicate the problem of hate speech recirculates and redirects that hatred in and as its own highly consequential speech, often coopting the very language that it seeks to adjudicate. (Butler 1997a, 54)

And although the UC Hastings re-enactment falls short of demonstrating this, one can infer from it that the greatest culprit is not Ebens or Nitz, but systemic racism itself, from the courts to techno-orientalist discourse of Detroit automakers. Thus, the UC Hastings re-enactment offers a different deployment of Asian American masochistic historiography as it looks toward the future, masochistically engaging its own movement to demonstrate a need for a more radical politics.

Judge Kaufman once stated in 1983, "the Asian community owes me some gratitude, for bringing their community together under one cause." If we are to examine only the masochistic cultural politics deployed by the ACJ, Kaufman would, distastefully, have a point. For better or for worse, despite the radical potential of masochism, it is that former masochism that characterizes the Asian American liberalism that was, at least on some level, interpellated in Chin's murder. The identity itself owes its contemporary life to this double bind, this marriage that Vincent Chin officiated before his own actual wedding, between the technological and the oriental, in which he becomes both the object of violence and the object of history, with Asian America itself gaining liberal legibility in his wake.

3
An Asian Is Being Whipped

The Afro-Asian Superego in the Theater of Philip Kan Gotanda

> "You are not White and that is what matters to some men."
> —Learned Jack, from Philip Gotanda's *I Dream of Chang and Eng*

> "Three years they lock you up. And now you're standin' there defendin' that White boy over me."
> —Earl, from Philip Gotanda's *After the War*

> "How does it feel to be a solution?"
> —Vijay Prashad, *The Karma of Brown Folk*

In the introduction to her 2012 text *Samurai among Panthers: Richard Aoki on Race, Resistance, and a Paradoxical Life*, Diane Fujino describes her subject, Richard Aoki, as "the most iconic figure of the Asian American Movement" (2012, xiii). Fujino's intricate, vital biography of Aoki is admiring of the "Che-esque" (2012, xi) figure who was both one of the leaders of the Asian American Political Alliance (AAPA) and the Third World Liberation Front (TWLF), as well as one of the most prominent and visible personifications of Afro-Asian solidarity. As a gun runner, Aoki was the highest-ranking nonblack member of the Black Panthers, and his agitational work in the TWLF contributed to the foundation of the academic field that has enabled me to write this very book. The emblematic photo of a young Aoki strikingly embodies this dual importance: his expression nonchalant, hidden behind sunglasses, a light mustache above his neutral lips, but most importantly, atop his head, a Black Panther beret affixed with a button of the AAPA. The photo characterized much of what would become Aoki's public persona and image for decades until his suicide in 2009, a revolutionary swagger that would effortlessly draw from Black masculinity and early Asian American self-formation alike.

It was thus no wonder that the left-wing community of Asian American activists and scholars was devastated by the allegation, on August 20, 2012, that Richard Aoki was an FBI informant. Journalist Seth Rosenfeld, as part of his upcoming 2013 manuscript *Subversives: The FBI's War on Student Radicals and Reagan's Rise to Power*, released hundreds of pages of redacted FBI files that seemed to indicate that Aoki had been recruited by the FBI in the 1950s and continued to inform the Bureau of various radical groups' activities throughout the '60s for a total of 16 years. Rosenfeld's account was damning, including an interview with Aoki's handler Burney Threadgill, who claimed that he had "developed" Aoki, and said of him, "Very pleasant little guy. He always wore dark glasses. I got to know him.... The activities he got involved in ... was because of us using him as an informant" (2013, 421). Rosenfeld then cites how Threadgill exploited Aoki's contempt of the Communist Party of the United States' support of Japanese American internment to easily recruit him, and Aoki, a war veteran, was more than happy to undermine domestic communists' causes. Although he is unable to definitively tie Aoki to specific informant actions in the FBI files due to considerable redactions, Rosenfeld implies that Aoki continued to spy on and undermine both Black Panther and TWLF causes, including through his arming of the Panthers (which, Rosenfeld argues, resulted in police shoot-outs that would undermine the Panthers' popularity and boost the support of Reagan and the police), and his violent tactics during the 1969 strike that included the rejection of compromise, the kidnapping and interrogation of a fellow activist, and *perhaps* even committing arson on the UC Berkeley campus.

Activists and Asian American studies scholars—most notably Diane Fujino, Scott Kurashige, artist Fred Ho, and even Black Panther Party cofounder Bobby Seale—sprang to action to defend Aoki's record and reputation against the accusation. Many prominent Asian Americans refused to acknowledge the possibility that he might have been, or insist that perhaps he was, a double-agent who came around to believing in the causes he was associated with, well until his suicide at age 70 in 2009 (which occurred shortly after his potentially damning interview with Rosenfeld). Kurashige pondered shortly after Rosenfeld's allegations:

> My best guess based on the available evidence is that Aoki—like other young people of all races and especially people of color—developed a new identity during the mid-to-late 1960s, renouncing earlier attempts to fit into America and moving instead to be a Third World revolutionary. (Kurashige 2012)

Given the expansive account in Diane Fujino's biography, and Aoki's decades-long commitment to leftist politics and racial justice that continued well after the 16-year period that Rosenfeld marks, this is a fair if nearly unverifiable hypothesis.

Ultimately, however, this chapter is not about Richard Aoki; I do not intend to defend or excoriate Rosenfeld's claims regarding Aoki's complicity. Aoki is one example among many demonstrating the Asian American political attachment to Blackness; I invoke the Aoki controversy in order to draw attention to the symbolic capital that Aoki accrued as a figure within the Asian American consciousness, which has in turn impelled his defense, the antithesis of the model minority, proof positive of the possibility of Asian American solidarity with the cause of the Black freedom struggle. Aoki-as-symbol has been canonized through his performance of solidarity with the politicized Black masculinity of the Panthers, offering a model contrast to the standard Asian American model minority, in addition to the "emasculated" Asian

American male. Although Aoki the person died in 2009, 2012 witnessed his tragic symbolic death, the demise of one of the most visible personifications of Black/Asian solidarity in the United States.

The destruction of Aoki-as-myth is incidentally symbolic of the demographic, and indeed epistemic, shift of Asian America from its radical conceptual birth as the Asian American movement in the 1960s (Wei, Espiritu) for which Aoki himself was present, to its mainstream political consolidation as "an institutional (academic and governmental) sociological category" (Lye 2008b, 95) in the 1980s, and finally to the contemporary moment in which the "Asian American" is figured as "the ideal subject of neoliberal ideologies under global capitalism" (Jun 2011, 129). With high median incomes, broad access to education, and deepening ties to transnational capital and prestige—that is, with the actualization of the model minority stereotype—it is becoming increasingly clear that theorists of Asian America, at least to some degree, require a shift away from the politics of ressentiment. Yet, for radical Asian American activists, scholars, and artists still oriented toward an antiracist praxis, there remains the question of how to formulate a radical Asian American positionality within such a multidimensional milieu, a task that was dealt a moral blow by the revelations surrounding Richard Aoki. Members of the Asian American movement in the late 1960s and '70s aligned themselves with a broader Third Worldist politic that positioned themselves as fellow nonwhite, colonized peoples, taking a particular affinity toward Blackness. Aoki served as a potent symbol of this, and his fall most clearly exposes the political importance that he served, although he is not alone in this symbolism: consider, for example, the Asian American iconography of Grace Lee Boggs and Yuri Kochiyama, whose importance within Asian American activist communities is earned principally through their proximity to the Black freedom struggle. However, in the landscape of the neoliberal present, such expressions may read as idealistic at best, or quixotic at worst, particularly given the heightened absurdity of equating Asian racialization with that of Blackness. The desire for a contemporary Asian American radicality opposed to whiteness is thus complicated by a cruel pragmatism that bespeaks of the possibility of the model minority as an achieved material reality. Figuratively, it is haunted by the possibility that Aoki has been an informant all along, and that perhaps, metaphorically, so have we all, and that even the nostalgic Third Worldist Asian America of the 1960s was compromised by an allegiance to the white surveillance state since the very beginning, bringing a chilling new valence to Tina Chen's compelling claim that Asian Americanness is instantiated "through a politics of impersonation" (2005, xvi).

This chapter considers the means by which Blackness has operated as both a psychic haunting and a disciplinary apparatus for the production of Asian American masculine subjection. Here, I engage with earlier Asian Americanist preoccupations with Blackness and conclude by examining two contemporary works of playwright Philip Kan Gotanda, *I Dream of Chang and Eng* and *After the War (Blues)*. As a Japanese American Sansei[1] artist who has personally engaged with the Asian American movement since its formative years, Gotanda offers insights into the struggles surrounding

Asian America through his cultural production, presenting a critical glimpse into the Asian American literary and political imagination. I argue that in *I Dream of Chang and Eng* and *After the War*, Gotanda positions Blackness as a moral center of racial subjugation, offering Asian Americans the political choice of either aligning in solidarity with Blackness, or seizing upon the opportunity for model minoritarianism aligned with whiteness. Although both plays are historical—*I Dream of Chang and Eng* in the 19th century and *After the War* in the late 1940s—they both euphemistically dramatize post-1990s Asian American concerns over Afro-Asian solidarity and the broader definitions of Asian American(ist) sociopolitical formation more broadly. Blackness, not unproblematically, offers a utopian alternative to the model minority, but one that remains masochistically out of reach. Gotanda's plays stage and variously contend with the Afro-Asian superego as a framework for an Asian American anti-racist ethics.

The Afro-Asian Superego

In truth, Asian American preoccupations with Afro-Asian solidarity have existed since the foundation of Asian American panethnicity in general. To find a clear example, one need only turn to Amy Uyematsu's 1969 essay, "The Emergence of Yellow Power in America," published in the Japanese American journal *Gidra* and reprinted in the monumental if largely overlooked 1971 anthology *Roots: An Asian American Reader*. Crediting the rise of the "yellow power" movement to inspiration from Black power, Uyematsu makes observations about late-1960s Asian American model minoritarianism that have become even more heightened at the time of this writing, noting that

> Precisely because Asian Americans have become economically secure, do they face serious identity problems. Fully committed to a system that subordinates them on the basis of non-whiteness, Asian Americans still try to gain complete acceptance by denying their yellowness. They have become white in every respect but color. (1971, 9)

Uyematsu ties complicity to capitalist economic norms to an allegiance to racial hierarchy, whiteness achieved not only through the denial of "yellowness" but also through class embourgeoisement. The net result of this, argues Uyematsu, is also a de facto allegiance to antiblackness:

> Today the Asian Americans are still scared. Their passive behavior serves to keep national attention on the black people. By being as inconspicuous as possible, they keep pressure off of themselves at the expense of the blacks. Asian Americans have formed an uneasy alliance with white Americans to keep the blacks down.

They close their eyes to the latent white racism toward them which has never changed. (1971, 11)

Thus, according to Uyematsu, Asian American complicity is necessarily antiblack, and part of the impetus of "yellow power" is to develop an identity around an antiracist, anticapitalist militancy. In a sense, this vision would be most rigorously sustained not necessarily through the decades of Asian American cultural politics, but through the rise of women of color feminism, most emblematically symbolized by Gloría Anzaldúa and Cherríe Moraga's *This Bridge Called My Back* in 1981.

Then, the last several decades of post-1992[2] Asian Americanist scholarship have seen a revival of Afro-Asian academic solidarity work, much of it ultimately concerned with broader politico-ethical projects of Asian American Studies at large, exemplified by such works as Vijay Prashad's *The Karma of Brown Folk* and *Everybody Was Kung-Fu Fighting*, Bill Mullen's *Afro-Orientalism*, Daryl Maeda's *Chains of Babylon*, and Ho and Mullen's *Afro-Asia*. As Colleen Lye observed in 2008, the "neo-Bandung allegiance of this Afro-Asianism" (2008a, 1732) may be reflective of Asian American Left's growing anxiety about its potentially reactionary positioning within the U.S. racial order. Lye writes,

> Despite this Afro-Asianist project's more open recognition of the relevance of Asian embourgeoisement to its own desire for a renewed resistance politics, however, it is not yet clear whether the retrieval of Third Worldist genealogies accomplishes something more than a nostalgic response to the rise of Asian capitalism on a world scale and to the thinning claim of Asian American intellectuals to any representative function. (2008a, 1732)

That is, much of the optimistic Afro-Asian solidarity work produced in the last few decades speak to the yearnings for a radical, resistant Asian American positionality that was much more visibly and clearly articulated as an anti-imperial, anti-racist project in the late 1960s and throughout the 1970s. In many ways, as Asian American studies underwent its so-called "transnational turn" (or "denationalization") in the 1990s, heralded by Pacific Rim discourse and diaspora-focused works, there was growing anxiety within Asian Americanist scholarship that the field would cease its radical orientations.

This anxiety is best captured by Sau-Ling Wong's highly contentious 1995 essay "Denationalization Reconsidered: Asian American Cultural Criticism at a Theoretical Crossroads," in which she affirms the value of performatively "claiming America," which she loosely defines as "establishing the Asian American presence in the context of the United States' national cultural legacy and contemporary cultural production" (1995, 17). In effect, Wong's insistence is largely to keep the focus on the presence of Asians in the United States (and, by extension, the Americas at large) precisely because exclusion—both material and epistemic—has been a hallmark of anti-Asianism since the early chapters of Asian American historical narrative (beginning most blatantly with the 1882 Chinese Exclusion Act). To retain the Americanist focus on Asian America, then, is to claim space in U.S. history and to counteract the pervasive perpetual foreignness that stems from both yellow peril and orientalist optics.

It is noteworthy, however, that Wong draws upon an Afro-Asian comparison in order to illustrate her point, drawing a comparative racialization between Asianness and Blackness in relation to foreignness. Noting that Black studies was also moving toward a transnational diasporic frame—Paul Gilroy's *The Black Atlantic* (1995) being most emblematic of this shift—Wong asserts that the differing racializations of Asianness and Blackness attach different valances to denationalization: "A shift from an African-American domestic to an African diaspora perspective might be more politicizing for African-Americans, while a corresponding move might be depoliticizing for Asian Americans" (1995, 18). African origins, Wong writes, can offer "a powerful means of undoing the cultural amnesia white society attempted to impose" (1995, 18), while denationalization with Asian America "may exacerbate liberal pluralism's already oppressive tendency to 'disembody,' leaving America's racialized power structure intact" (1995, 18–19). This is largely because Blackness in the United States has long been associated with a kind of "culturelessness," characterized by deficiency and lack, whereas Asianness has been not so much "cultureless" as inscrutably foreign, a perverse mirror image of occidental modernity rather than a "zone of nonbeing," as Frantz Fanon has described Blackness in *Black Skin, White Masks*.

Additionally, Wong also invokes Elliott Butler-Evans' argument that "Rodney King was beaten [in Los Angeles in 1991] as a member of an American minority, not as a member of the black diaspora" (1995, 18), in order to demonstrate that local minoritarianism—in this case, racialization within the specific national context of the United States—is the impetus of racial violence, rather than a sense of diasporic origin. Thus, argues Wong, even in the case of antiblack violence, it is local racial otherness—that is to say, nonwhiteness—that should be of the highest political and analytic priority, rather than diaspora, which is in Wong's view at most a secondary impetus for racial violence. Consequently, argues Wong, "coalitions of Asian American and other racial/ethnic minorities within the U.S. should take precedence over those formed with Asian peoples in the diaspora" (1995, 18). The primary line of political and analytical alliance, according to Wong, should then coalesce around shared marginalization, rather than shared origin.

Wong's argument against denationalization, then, contains not only an anxiety over the potential loss of Asian American studies' anti-racist critique, but also an anxiety over the loss of alliance with Blackness. I would furthermore infer that within Asian American anti-racist critique, these two are largely intertwined. That is, Asian Americanist critiques of racism have historically entailed an alliance with Blackness, or alternately, an imitation of Blackness. Wong's argument is much in the same spirit of earlier Asian Americanist adaptations of Black masculine militancy, in which the performance of Blackness is a necessary component of the performance of anti-racism. Uyehara's "yellow power," for example, is in direct homage to "black power"—the articulation of Black liberation is a necessary prerequisite to

Asian American cultural nationalism. And certainly, Black masculinity has held a particular importance, especially in its association with militancy and confrontation. Moreover, to reinterpret Frantz Fanon's description of Blackness as the "zone of non-being," Blackness becomes the social position of absolute racialization. This interpretation is entrenched in Afro-pessimism, an emergent school of contemporary Black Studies scholarship—officially inaugurated by scholars Frank Wilderson III and Jared Sexton—operating from the postulate of Blackness as a mode of social death, and essentially inextricable from slaveness (Wilderson 2010, 10–11). Also prevalent in Afro-pessimism is a tendency toward Black exceptionalism, insisting that race relations best be understood not from a white/nonwhite binary, but a Black/nonblack one; Jared Sexton, in his essay aptly titled "People of Color Blindness," argues that the latter half of the enslaved/free binary is "better termed *all nonblacks* (or, less economically, the unequally arrayed category of nonblackness), because it is racial blackness as a necessary condition for enslavement that matters most, rather than whiteness as a sufficient condition for freedom" (Sexton 2010, 36). The result of Sexton's argument is ultimately an anti-coalitional stance, one that centers antiblackness as the locus of racial subjugation at large.

Although a number of scholars have critiqued the Afro-pessimism of Wilderson and Sexton,[3] the foundationalism of Black antiracism persists, including within some strands of Asian American thought, especially of the masculinist variety, in which the politicized Black man figures as the "ideal type" of racial resistance. Daniel Y. Kim illustrates this dynamic in his superb reading of Frank Chin's masculine cultural nationalist project, which we can cautiously regard as representative of a dominant strain of Asian American masculinity.[4] Noting that Chin lambasts Chinese Americans as occupying an "Uncle Tom" role within the racial drama of liberation—that is, "as being just like *certain* kinds of blacks" (Kim 2005, 34), Kim asserts that "[t]o be an Asian American is to be like an African American who wants to be white—it is to be trapped in the perpetual motion of a failed racial mimesis" (2005, 34–35). As Kim insightfully argues, Frank Chin's masculinist assertion is simultaneously homophobic and homoerotic, violently rejecting the heteronormatively understood emasculation of Asian men produced by the white optic, while simultaneously homoerotically investing in the aesthetics of Black masculinity:

> Lacking an ethnically distinct ideal of virility of "their own" with which they can identify, Asian American men are left imitating "styles" of masculinity that belong, properly speaking, to men of other races.... But the "solution" that Chin prescribes for this problematic interracial mimetic desire that threatens to homosexualize Asian American men ... is not the eradication of this desire, but rather its melancholic intensification via the aesthetic. (2005, 36)

For Chin, there is an imperative not to sidestep the mimesis of Black masculinity but, rather, to loathe oneself for the impossibility of attaining it.

Within the antiracist paradigm upon which Asian American studies and the Asian American movement were founded, we can characterize Blackness as occupying the position of racial superego, an Afro-Asian superego, the disciplinary apparatus of the Asian American psyche, counterposed to the id of assimilation and the fulfillment of the model minority. I thus offer Sigmund Freud's well-known tripartite model of the ego, superego, and id as a loose analogy for the Asian American masculine political consciousness, which regulates the moral-ethical orientation of panethnic Asian American identity. The superego, according to Freud, is the ego ideal, which works primarily to suppress the pleasure principle sought by the id and substitute the Oedipal complex. However, the superego is not merely a clone of the disciplinary apparatus of the Father; according to Freud, the superego's

> relation to the ego is not exhausted by the precept: "You *ought to be* like this (like your father)." It also comprises the prohibition: "You *may not be* like this (like your father)—that is, you may not do all that he does; some things are his prerogative." (1989, 641–642, emphasis in original)

The superego is thus a kind of inverted disidentification, one that simultaneously produces an aspirational ideal and the moral boundaries to achieving that ideal (in psychoanalytic terms, the Oedipal sexual objectification of the mother). Similarly, as Freud notes, the superego "answers to everything that is expected of the higher nature of man" and thus "contains the germ from which all religions have evolved" (1989, 643).

In a similar sense, the antiracist Asian American masculine political project has positioned Blackness as the Father figure idealized by the superego, as that which one "ought to be like" while simultaneously placing prohibitions on that mimesis. This is, in effect, an inversion of the logic of assimilationist model minoritarianism, which positions white respectability as a kind of superego. Blackness—and Black masculinity in particular for the Asian American masculine subject—becomes the antiracist ideal to be approximated but not appropriated. However, as David Eng insightfully observes in *The Feeling of Kinship*, the ego ideal "is brought about through the sublimation of homosexual libido into a collective social conscience and through the affective charge of guilt. The disavowal and management of homosexual desire emerges precisely of custodial dread in relation to a judgmental ego-ideal" (2010, 51). The masculine superego develops from a masochistic disavowal of a queer longing. Again, Daniel Y. Kim's analysis of Frank Chin is indispensable here. Chin's now-canonical *Chickencoop Chinaman* (which, among other things, presents a Black boxer as a father figure ideal for the Asian male protagonists who eventually fail to live up to the ideal) demonstrates not only the complex dynamics of the Afro-Asian superego, but also the masochism to which the Afro-Asian superego leads:

> Although [*Chickencoop Chinaman*] insists that the Asian American artist will never be able to stand shoulder to shoulder ... with his African American brothers if his

attitude toward them is one of fawning adulation, it also seems to suggest the impossibility of finding another model for an authentic minority tradition. Where the narrative tends, then, is toward a masochistic repetition of the predicament in which Tam finds himself at the opening of the play—that of having no non-white ideal of racialized masculinity to claim as his own other than those that are associated with African American culture. If Asian American men are thus resigned to "faking blackness," as Kenji puts it, then the message that the reading of *The Chickencoop Chinaman* seems to convey is that they should at least fully acknowledge and embrace the self-hatred that is expressed in their abject relationship to black culture (Kim 2005, 201–202).

In Kim's estimation of *Chinaman*, Black masculinity is an ideal that must not be imitated, precisely because that imitation precludes actual fraternity with Blackness, as a consequence of the performative femininity and queerness that such fawning engenders. Yet, since Black masculinity remains the only viable nonwhite ideal, Chin's ideal Asian American masculinity is a masochistic self-flagellation that acknowledges the failure and impossibility of measuring up to Blackness. Kim then concludes that Chin, in fact, finds something "generative" in this self-punishment; that is to say, "the illusion of virility" (2005, 202) that is ultimately predicated upon an inwardly directed sadism directed toward femininity, queerness, and other "failures" of the ideal masculine Father.

Although Asian Americanist antiracism was obviously not universally committed to the homophobia and misogyny—not to mention the masculine essentialism of Blackness—that subtended the work of Chin, Sau-Ling Wong's essay is evidence that the superego relationship to Blackness nevertheless persisted in the 1990s, and the Asian Americanist responses to the Richard Aoki incident demonstrate its continuation into the second decade of the 21st century, the time of this writing. To clarify, like Lye, I am critical of this turn, and yet, also like Lye, I fully concur with its political necessity. The Afro-Asian superego has the potential to question radically and productively the Asian Americanist paradigm of inclusion, disrupting the Asian American longing for inclusion into U.S. normativity. Yet, the Afro-Asian superego is premised upon an impossibility of mimesis, placing the father as the new masculine ego ideal that the Asian American subject never attains. This is Freudian moral masochism, a shame-driven pursuit of suffering in which the "ego reacts with feelings of anxiety (conscience anxiety) to the perception that it has not come up to the demands made by its ideal, the super-ego" (Freud 1989, 280). In fact, the shame is over failure to achieve the demands of the emblematic "bad subject," the Black ideal, configured in the Asian American gaze as the Father.[5]

By theatricalizing this Afro-Asian superego and the shame it precipitates, the recent 21st-century plays of Philip Kan Gotanda are able to not only present but also actualize the shame of antiblack model minoritarianism while simultaneously and pessimistically demonstrating the structural impossibility of completely disrupting it. Through various deployments of characters that represent the Afro-Asian superego,

Gotanda subtends the paradoxical position of aspiring to a Black ethics outside of white supremacy, while it always necessarily remains out of reach.

"What Would Learned Jack Think?": Black Judgment in *I Dream of Chang & Eng*

The dramatic work of one of the most important Asian American playwrights of the 20th and 21st centuries, Philip Kan Gotanda, spans from 1978 to the present day of this writing. Esther Kim Lee groups Gotanda with David Henry Hwang, Velina Hasu Houston, and Jeannie Barroga as one of the central figures of the "second wave" of Asian American playwrights[6] whose work came to prominence in the 1980s, characterized by their "attitude and preparedness" (2006, 126) and "professional training as actors, playwrights, and designers" (2006, 126). These playwrights also wrote at a time in which the likes of Genny Lim, Frank Chin, Momoko Iko, Mako, and others had already laid the groundwork for Asian American theater, and Asian American theater institutions such as East West Players and the Asian American Theater Workshop had already been established. "With formal training in playwriting and a tradition to follow," writes Lee, "the second wave playwrights found the job title 'Asian American playwright' not at all strange or novel, a contrast to the first wave writers who practically invented the term" (2006, 126). Yet, despite his being one of the most celebrated figures of this "second wave," Gotanda is a slight exception to this characterization, emerging more from a music background than a dramatic one, and was in fact completing his law degree at the University of California, Hastings, at the time he was writing his first play, a musical entitled *The Avocado Kid*. Unlike his peer, friend, and frequent collaborator David Henry Hwang, Gotanda would rise to prominence primarily through Asian American theater institutions. "Whereas Hwang found his big break at the Public Theater and worked mainly in mainstream venues on the East Coast," writes Lee, "Gotanda began and developed his career as a playwright at Asian American theatre companies, especially the Asian American Theater Company in San Francisco" (2006, 139). Through such institutions, Gotanda would go on to write and stage a vast and widely celebrated oeuvre, such as *Yankee Dawg You Die*, *The Wash*, *Fish Head Soup*, *The Ballad of Yachiyo*, *The Wind Cries Mary*, and *The Dream of Kitamura*, among others. Gotanda's work would eventually earn him mainstream recognition that would solidify his place among the greatest U.S. playwrights of the late 20th and early 21st century, including a Guggenheim Fellowship, an award from the Dramatists' Guild, and the Asian American Theater Company's Lifetime Achievement Award. Gotanda's work is formally diverse, although one of his specialties has been the traditional American family drama and the naturalistic, character-driven writing that attends the genre, applying the technique to the particularities of the Japanese American household; this is most notably showcased in such plays as *The Wash*, *Fish Head Soup*, *A Song for a Nisei Fisherman*, and *Sisters Matsumoto*. Interestingly, the play that has arguably garnered the most critical attention within

Asian American studies has been *Yankee Dawg You Die*, a comedic dialogue between an older-generation Asian American actor whose career has consisted of playing a wide range of stereotypical roles, and a newer-generation idealist actor who accuses his predecessor of a racial treason.

What is vital to note is that Gotanda is a writer who strongly embraces the Third-Worldist solidarity politics of the radical late-1960s Asian American movement, a kind of politics that has suffused his writing well into more liberal and neoliberal periods of Asian American structures of feeling from the 1980s onward. Since the turn of the 21st century, Gotanda has been increasingly interested in turning his gaze outward from Asian America and toward other narratives of color, particularly African American ones. His 2006 play *Yohen*, for example, centers around an interracial marriage between a Japanese American woman and an African American man. Many of his plays are implicitly aware of the model minoritarian turn of the Asian American mainstream of his present, but Gotanda sometimes reaches into the distant past in order to critique the Asian American cultural politics of the present. This is absolutely the case in the two plays I examine in the remainder of this chapter: 2011's *I Dream of Chang and Eng*, and the 2007 *After the War*, restaged in 2014 as *After the War Blues*. Both of these historical fictions masochistically critique the present, while also interrogating whether Asian American antiblackness may have been a transhistorical component of Asian Americanness itself.

With its world premiere in 2011 produced through UC Berkeley's Department of Theater, Dance, and Performance Studies, *I Dream of Chang and Eng* is simultaneously one of Gotanda's most recent yet oldest works. The play is an ambitious biographical sketch of Chang and Eng Bunker (b. 1811, d. 1874), the "original Siamese twins" who spectacularly toured the United States in "freak show" fashion until eventually settling down in North Carolina to become "Gentleman Farmers." The twins, who were born in Siam to a mostly ethnically Chinese family in 1811 before being picked up to tour the West, "were so well known as public figures and so ubiquitous as conjoined twins that the term 'Siamese twins' eventually came to describe all such twins even, anachronistically, those who had lived before they did" (Wu 2012, 2). Gotanda has stated that he has worked on this play for over 30 years before finally premiering the version directed by Peter Glazer in the spring of 2011. In an interview in the *San Francisco Chronicle*, Gotanda explains that he had originally aspired to an epic historical fidelity to the Bunkers' lives, conducting extensive research of the twins, but ultimately decided to embrace a fictionalization of their lives,[7] resulting in a play that occasionally suspends realism (such as allowing the twins to at times metaphorically separate by detaching their Velcro cord). Ultimately, the play is a meditative account of the brothers, proto–Asian Americans who capitalize upon their "freak," nonnormatively bodied status to eventually profit from spectacularizing their otherness to white American audiences but also struggle with the ontological paradox of being conjoined, desiring a space for privacy and intimacy especially as they wed the Yates sisters—Southern white Americans—and father a total of 21 children.

Not unlike Suzan-Lori Parks' 1996 play *Venus*, which delves into the signification, exploitation, and complexity of Sarah Baartman (1789–1815), Gotanda's *I Dream of Chang and Eng* locates the intersection of bodily "freakishness" with racial freakishness. Whereas *Venus* focuses on the queerly excessive posterior of Sarah Baartman, which came to function as an eroticized totem for the simultaneous objectification and abjection of Black femininity, *I Dream of Chang and Eng* principally focuses on the twins' status as completely unintelligible abominations "never before seen before by occidental eyes" (Gotanda 2013, 25), and conversely, their own confusion over their identity. Chang and Eng simultaneously suffer from and leverage their complete foreignness from the American field of intelligibility. Being ethnically Chinese but raised in Thailand, the twins struggle over their ethnic location more broadly, especially when brought to the United States. At the beginning of the second act, the Bunkers confer with Afong Moy, who herself was taken from Guangzhou to New York City in 1834 as the "The Chinese Woman," also a paid object of spectacle due to her bound feet. In the encounter, the Bunkers find Moy to be a curiosity as well, due to her authentic "Chineseness," but both Moy and the Bunkers concur that they are not "freaks." Rather, they see themselves as businesspeople and performers who, rather than being passive objects in a cage, actively showcase their bodies as a skill—they performatively enact what Anne Anlin Cheng has recently termed "ornamentalism," taking on a perihuman ontology to constitute oneself as an object of orientalist display.

Baartman herself is referenced during Elizabeth Yates' first encounter with Chang and Eng. Chang and Eng ask Elizabeth about the enlarged bustle in her dress, crudely remarking, "Why are your arses so big?" She responds,

ELIZABETH: It is called a bustle. It is the current fashion.
ENG: I do not understand.
CHANG: (reaching out to touch) Can we?
ELIZABETH: No.
Chang touches her—
ENG: How is this fashion? Explain.
ELIZABETH: The Hotentot Venus? One, Sara Baartman. An exotic, beautiful, full-bodied African lady—brought over, paraded around. Like you, everyone came to see her. Her *posterior* was large.
CHANG: (to Eng) Arse?
ENG: Yes.
ELIZABETH: We all stared but no one would speak it aloud. Instead we went home, closed our bedroom doors and fantasized about this posterior until one day we woke up and voila! We had *big arses*! In a *fashion* of speaking.
CHANG: I do not understand.
ELIZABETH: May you Gentlemen not suffer her fate. (Gotanda 2013, 30)

The exchange between Elizabeth and the Bunkers renders explicit the erotic allure of Baartman, who would serve as a racial bodily template for their own objectification: "Like you, everyone came to see her." Elizabeth narrates the conversion of Baartman from freak show display to masturbatory pornotrope, transmuted into the creation of the bustle itself, a spectral appropriation of Baartman's image while the body of Baartman herself was medically dissected as a dehumanized specimen of scientific curiosity. Elizabeth then bids the brothers hope that they "not suffer her fate," which suggests that she hopes that the Bunkers avoid the transformation into fetish object, a dual thingification as both eroticized aesthetic fashion and object of "rational" knowledge. Thus, the Bunkers' legibility, and indeed fate, is dependent upon the racial formation of Blackness—and in the case of Baartman, Black femininity—which produces the conceptual vocabulary of otherness that brackets the even more illegibly foreign Bunkers. Baartman has helped establish what Diana Taylor has referred to as a *scenario*, which "conjure[s] up past situations" through "reactivation rather than duplication" (2013, 32). The performative objectification of Chang and Eng is thus caught up in the reiterative space of Blackness, but given the agency that they ascribe to their position, their positionality within the U.S. racial system becomes, at least to an extent, a political choice.

This sense of political choice is provided, in part, by Gotanda's choice to add a fictional black masculine critic to the play. In part due to the dramaturgical process at UC Berkeley, Gotanda decided to add a critical supporting character to the narrative, a gay Black sailor named Learned Jack. Throughout the play, Learned Jack assumes various roles across gender, always figuring as the Black character in each scene, but his "core" character of Learned Jack is a free Black crewman of the English vessel Sachem, which transports Chang and Eng to the United States for the first time in Act 1. Chang and Eng board the ship as "precious cargo" and quickly befriend Learned Jack and his white lover and crewmate, Good John. The two sailors are equally inclined toward maritime vernacular as they are toward indexing markers of formal education, swearing and quoting Coleridge (see Figure 3.1). As the banter continues, Chang and Eng begin to ask Learned Jack questions regarding his background. Eng tells Learned Jack, "You do not make sense." When Jack asks for an explanation, Eng continues by saying "Your father was an American slave," and Chang finishes the thought with "You speak the King's English." Learned Jack first compliments the twins on their insight—"You see 'neath the skin of things"—and proceeds to explain that his father, who "never took to being owned," fought as a Tory against his slaveholders and was freed as a reward and brought to London. Consequently, adds Jack, his father raised him "with a keen sense of justice" (Gotanda 2013, 18).

Jack, John, and the twins then have a brief but telling discussion on the respective conditions of their existence, and eventually race (Gotanda 2013, 18–19):

LEARNED JACK: Do you abide by the way you are?
CHANG: We are special.
ENG: The heavens want us together more than not.

Figure 3.1 Learned Jack discusses American racialization with Chang & Eng. From Philip Kan Gotanda's I Dream of Chang & Eng at University of California Berkeley, 2011. Photo by Josh Hesslein / Courtesy of UC Berkeley Theater, Dance, and Performance Studies.

LEARNED JACK: What if the heavens do not give a damn?
ENG: Do you abide by the way you are?
LEARNED JACK: I abide by the way I am. I do not abide by the way others see I am.
ENG: How do others see you?
LEARNED JACK: What comes of you if they cut you apart?
CHANG: The King's physician said we would die.
GOOD JOHN: So would we ...
ENG: How do others see you Mr. Jack?
LEARNED JACK helps GOOD JOHN up—
LEARNED JACK: We make land soon. You will enjoy Boston. As you come into harbor it smells of a spit roasted lamb, spiced with offerings from an Irish Shantee.
CHANG: You show us Boston.
LEARNED JACK: Boston is a free city but my father is in me and I will not abide by a nation that buys and sells men. We will not step onto land there.
ENG: By all accounts you are treated no different than the white sailors. You are paid an equal wage, move freely above and below the decks—
LEARNED JACK: I am a *Black Jack*. Only at sea. You may think America knows you. It does not.
ENG: We are not Black.

LEARNED JACK: You are not White and that is what matters to some men. Come dear John, come awake now—
LEARNED JACK holds GOOD JOHN—
LEARNED JACK: —They have not seen the likes of you in color of skin or shape of body. It is yet to be seen what you are in America's eyes.

The beginning of this exchange opens with a question of "abiding by what you are"—Chang and Eng defer to "the heavens," and thus fate, as the source of their otherness; they are consigned to their position as "freaks." When the question is turned to Learned Jack, however, he makes a critical distinction between exterior reception and interior selfhood, abiding by "who he is" but not by others' perspectives of him. Learned Jack is notably evasive when the twins persist in asking him what that perspective is, but Jack invokes the violence of racism when he refuses to take them to see Boston, making the political decision to not step foot on U.S. soil so long as the slave trade continues. When the twins naively insist on Learned Jack's equal status, Jack clarifies that he is a "Black Jack. Only at sea," pointing to the queer maritime space as the only one in which he can be, to some degree, free.

Then, Learned Jack fatefully warns the twins of racism, stating that America does not "know them." When Eng insists that they are "not Black," Learned Jack immediately responds with "You are not White and that is what matters to some men." The exchange reflects two separate conceptualizations of racism, with Eng pointing to their nonblackness as a potential source of freedom from racial subjugation, and Learned Jack highlighting their nonwhiteness. Symbolically, Learned Jack extends an invitation to solidarity, recognizing commonality in structural positions against a common white hegemony. When Learned Jack adds that "They have not seen the likes of you in color of skin or shape of body. It is yet to be seen what you are in America's eyes," he highlights the foreignness of Chang and Eng, their unknowability, foreshadowing their inevitable orientalization, speaking from his experience as a veteran to racism by virtue of his Blackness; he possesses a "wisdom" surrounding the racist "truth" of America, offering benevolent warning to a fellow nonwhites, extending solidarity. Chang and Eng in turn feel indebted to Jack and, to some degree, responsible to him and what he stands for, especially in later scenes.

Unfortunately, for all of Learned Jack's discussion of interiority and exteriority, Learned Jack lacks a degree of interiority himself, existing primarily as a moral counterpoint to Chang and Eng's trajectory. Paradoxically, he takes on some of the characteristics of the so-called "magical negro," a term popularized by filmmaker Spike Lee and described by Matthew Hughey as

> a lower class, uneducated black person who possesses supernatural or magical powers. These powers are used to save and transform disheveled, uncultured, lost, or broken whites (almost exclusively white men) into competent, successful, and content people within the context of the American myth of redemption and salvation. (2009, 544)

Learned Jack is decidedly not uneducated, and Chang and Eng are decidedly not white, but Learned Jack assumes a similar role as a "magical negro" nonetheless, freely offering wisdom and clarity to the wayward Asian subjects, ironically regarding racism itself. His lack of interiority also allows Chang and Eng, and by virtue the audience, to project an idealization of anti-racist subjectivity, and Learned Jack correspondingly reappears throughout the play in different forms to remind Chang and Eng of this idealization.

Nevertheless, between Sarah Baartman and Learned Jack, the Bunkers find themselves both cautioned by the victimization of Black femininity and offered warning (but also solidarity) by Black (gay) masculinity. Learned Jack is referenced admirably by Chang and Eng throughout as the play continues, especially as Chang and Eng encounter both horrific American racist violence and the privileges associated with being Southern landowners. Nonblackness and nonwhiteness compete as the dominant factors of their racialization. In one scene, shortly after putting on a show in their 1835 nationwide tour, Chang and Eng are captured by a massive lynch mob, mistaken for "Indians" despite their insistence that they are "the famous Siamese twins," saved at the last minute by a white gentleman, Joshua, who vouches for their status as international celebrities. As relief settles over the two of them, they catch a glimpse of two hanged figures who disturbingly match the description of Learned Jack and Good John on the darkened stage. Breaking the realism of the scene, the two victims, metatheatrically doubled by Jack and John, reveal themselves to Chang and Eng. When Chang asks Eng, "Are we colored or abominations?," Learned Jack replies with a familiar "You are not white." When Eng replies that they are now famous, Learned Jack warns them, "Before they had no name for you. Beware. They have seen the likes of you now and America knows what you are" (Gotanda 2013, 43).

Here, the lynched Learned Jack points to the danger of racial subjecthood, of the named subject who remains fixed within the white American gaze, to reference Fanon. In classic Foucauldian fashion, with legibility and knowability comes killability, the quality of being an identifiable target to be abjected from the white supremacist order. Learned Jack thus marks this shift from orientalized inscrutability, of being outside the grid of racial intelligibility altogether, to the state of being "known" by America. They are "known," of course, insofar as "knowing" is itself a technology of otherness and categorization, of which Blackness has been an object par excellence. "Knowing" is not a realization of any material reality but, rather, more reflective of racial objectification, extracting value to reinforce the social supremacy of whiteness. Learned Jack, by invoking this didactic refrain, becomes a sage of racialization, the fact of Blackness that provides him a bare insight into the mechanics of race with which Chang and Eng slowly comprehend. In a sense, the journey of Chang and Eng serves as a euphemism for Asian American subject formation itself as they negotiate between whiteness and Blackness.

Perhaps the most damning moment in Chang and Eng's relationship to Blackness occurs in the scene "Chang and Eng and Slavery." At this point of the play, Chang and Eng begin to settle into their burgeoning role as wealthy landowners in the American

South, a privilege of course foreclosed to Blacks. Chang and Eng's future father-in-law, Father Yates, opens the scene mid-conversation, explaining that "We are in the South. It is how things are done here." He proceeds to extoll the economic benefits of slavery, explaining that a massive investment will lead to a significant payoff as the slave continues to work for free. Chang is clearly somewhat uneasy about this, and a crucial interaction transpires between Chang, Eng, and "Canaan," Father Yates' slave, who is, once again, metatheatrically doubled by Learned Jack:

CHANG: There were slaves in Siam.
ENG: They were indentured workers not slaves.
CHANG: They were Chinese. Chinese slaves.
No response—
CANAAN moves to the other side of the mirror—
CHANG: Just like us.
CHANG and ENG face the mirror, looking at their imagined reflections.
CANAAN stares back at them.
ENG: We are free men.
CHANG: They will figure out what we are. They will have a name for us.
ENG: It is the only way to make a profit. It is what they do here.
Canaan steps through the mirror and hands Eng a *letter*—
CANAAN: (As Learned Jack commenting on his slave character) For you *massa*—
ENG and LEARNED JACK/CANAAN look at each other for a beat—LEARNED JACK exits.

When Eng, after hesitation, replies, "We are free men," Chang responds by invoking Learned Jack's previous line: "They will figure out what we are. They will have a name for us." Eng insists that slavery is the only means to make a profit, but Learned Jack/Canaan, in a bitter moment indexing awareness of their betrayal, addresses Eng as "massa." In this moment, Chang and Eng's nonblackness supersedes their nonwhiteness; they stare into the mirror to imagine themselves occupying the space of whiteness, and such a transition necessitates the betrayal of Learned Jack and of Blackness. Their complicity and perpetuation of slavery facilitates their acceptability, and eventually their marriage to the Yates daughters. Their decision to purchase and exploit enslaved Africans recalls Toni Morrison's indictment of immigrant antiblackness, that new immigrants participate "freely in this most enduring and efficient rite of passage into American culture: negative appraisals of the native-born black population. Only when the lesson of racial estrangement is learned is assimilation complete." Learned Jack's presence in the mirror as subjugated property is the ultimate signifier of Chang and Eng's ascension into American society, but it also highlights the sense of moral failing on the part of the twins, haunting them with guilt, that by participating in slavery, they are by extension enslaving their comrade and former mentor. But also, Chang locates himself and his brother in the "slave" position, pointing out the slavery in Siam to which they themselves had been consigned. Chang's comment also broadens the culpability of slavery beyond whiteness, while Eng's reply ("They were indentured servants") simultaneously distances them from the analogy of enslaved Blackness while (futilely) attempting to redeem Asianness from its complicity with forced labor. Yet, the presence of Canaan / Learned Jack in the mirror suggests that Chang and Eng are indeed somehow analogous to Blackness. They are, to return to Sexton, "masters," just by virtue of their nonblackness, but also nevertheless nonwhite; by being both nonblack and nonwhite, they are also caught between the two binaries of valuation that those negatory categories signify (white/nonwhite, Black/nonblack).

The presence of the mirror in this scene evokes the familiar Lacanian "mirror stage," in which a young child recognizes themselves for the first time in the mirror image; doing so produces an identification. As Lacan writes: "It suffices to understand the mirror stage in this context *as an identification*, in the full sense analysis gives to the term: namely the transformation that takes place in the subject when he assumes [*assume*] an image" (2002, 4). In identifying with the image, the subject understands themselves as self *and* other, that they exist in the social world, and is an *other* relative to their others. The mirror stage, however, does not come seamlessly; Lacan states,

> This development is experienced as a temporal dialectic that decisively projects the individual's formation into history: the mirror stage is a drama whose internal pressure pushes precipitously from insufficiency to anticipation—and, for the subject caught up in the lure of spatial identification, turns out fantasies that proceed from a fragmented image of the body to what I will call an "orthopedic" form of its totality—and to the finally donned armor of an alienating identity that will mark his entire mental development with its rigid structure. (2002, 6)

Thus, Lacan's mirror stage entails a dialectical fracturing caused by the disjuncture between the image in one's mind and the image seen in the mirror. The rise of this fractured subject marks the end of the mirror stage, and the dialectic of this fracture "will henceforth link the *I* to socially elaborated situations" (Lacan 2002, 7). As a consequence, the process of the mirror stage is both crucial to the subject's understanding of herself as a being in a social world and also, as a consequence of the fracture, inculcates in the subject a desire for the other's desire, understanding themself to not just be subject but also object within the scopic regime.

But as the twins see Learned Jack in the mirror, particularly at the point in which they have attained a degree of symbolic whiteness through the act of owning slaves themselves, the play suggests a troubling but productive ambiguity, particularly in the context of contemporary Asian American relations at the time of its writing. There is indeed a Lacanian disjuncture between the image of the conjoined twins who, through unique and fortuitous historical circumstances, have become Southern gentlemen, and the figure of Learned Jack / Canaan. They have achieved "freedom" through the uniquely American paradox of owning slaves, of subjugating Blackness, and yet they still see the image of Blackness in the mirror. The play suggests, then, that the Bunker twins—and perhaps Asian America at large—are existentially more proximal to Blackness than to whiteness even as they perform the most vicious antiblackness possible. And it is this complicity in slavery, paired with their own identification/disidentification with Blackness that is most perverse—in the classic Hegelian sense, by achieving freedom through enslaving, they are also bound up in the object of that slavery, that they are enslaving themselves.

Tellingly, the brothers express a sense of reluctance, a cognitive dissonance. Gotanda's project is not, as stated earlier, to be faithful to the literal history of Chang and Eng, but the incongruence here between history and dramatization is telling. According to *The Two*, a biography on Chang and Eng written in 1978 by Irving and Amy Wallace, Chang and Eng together owned a total of 28 slaves by 1860, and "were rumored to be hard on their slaves, sometimes whipping them" (1978, 189). Wallace and Wallace then continue to cite rather brutal historical anecdotes about the twins' relationship with their slaves, such as exhibiting "a malignant air" when they "saw the negro standing in the front door" rather than entering from the rear and insisting that he "knew his place" (1978, 189). The same person, J. E. Johnson, recalls how, when one of Chang's slaves escaped and was shot dead by a white citizen, Chang and Eng refused the killer's compensation for lost property "and expressed their satisfaction that the negro was out of the way" (Wallace and Wallace 1978, 190). Wallace and Wallace also state that Chang and Eng would fondly tell a story in which they won "a negro" in a game of cards and sold him back at a major profit to the gamblers.

The asymmetry between Chang and Eng, the sympathetic characters who befriend Learned Jack, and Chang and Eng, the brutal overseers who are relieved at the murder of their escaped slave, epitomizes the moral masochism of the Afro-Asian superego, and Gotanda's desire for coalition and solidarity in spite of a material moment in which our protagonists furthered and capitalized upon antiblack exploitation. Of course, this asymmetry also stresses the necessity to read Gotanda's play as a literary rather than historical project, pointing to the underlying political project of *I Dream of Chang and Eng*. The relentless presence of Learned Jack, who haunts the play as Blackness haunts the Asian American political and literary imagination, insists that Asian America find political alliance with fellow racialized peoples, even if it has also benefited from strategic privileges from its oppressors. Learned Jack shames Asian America to ask, as Eng muses upon his decision to start a plantation, "What would Learned Jack think?"

"Orientals Can't Play No Jazz": Yearning for Solidarity in *After the War*

Gotanda's *After the War*, commissioned by and staged at the American Conservatory Theater (ACT) in San Francisco in 2007 and revised and restaged at UC Berkeley in 2014 as *After the War Blues*,[8] is a sweeping drama surrounding life in a Japanese American–owned boarding house in the San Francisco Fillmore district in 1946.

Gotanda tellingly dedicates the play to August Wilson and John Okada, and audiences familiar with the works of Wilson and Okada can immediately pinpoint the influences of both writers. *After the War* echoes the narrative and character structure of Wilson's boardinghouse play *Joe Turner's Come and Gone* and also spends ample time wrestling with the postwar angst of a No No Boy (male Japanese Americans who refused conscription and a loyalty oath while in camp and thus relocated to other, harsher camps), most famously treated by John Okada's novel of the same name. Gotanda's explicit reference to both writers, performing masterful homage through the lyrical style and raw expression of the text, itself performs an Afro/Asian solidarity.

However, *After the War* concerns itself with a key moment of agonizing Black/Asian conflict centered on San Francisco's Fillmore district. Postwar Fillmore reflects a time in which Japanese Americans return to a former Japanesetown that had been resettled by Blacks during their internment. Not only does *After the War* express the challenges faced by two differently oppressed groups competing over limited space and resources, but it also represents a clash of narratives of racialization. The narrative of Japanese American internment comes face to face with the narrative of Black subjugation and slavery, and despite beginning in solidarity, that solidarity eventually proves unsustainable. As I will elaborate later, central protagonist Chet Monkawa ultimately sides with whiteness, insofar as we understand whiteness in this play to be "property," as Cheryl Harris has provocatively argued in her powerful 1993 essay of the same name.

With a large, diverse ensemble cast, the largely naturalistic *After the War* invites a range of analytical angles, but again I focus on the role of Black characters, in particular Earl Worthing, a mid-40s dockworker behind on his rent and one of the most central characters to the narrative, and his sister-in-law Leona Hitchings, an educated woman in her mid-40s who is much more distrustful of Japanese Americans than her brother-in-law. Unlike the quasi-magical Learned Jack, who serves as more of a mystical literary device than a fleshed-out character, treated with comparative thinness as an allegorical symbol, Earl and Leona are full, realist characters and thus not as easily identifiable as racial superegos. Rather than embodying the Afro-Asian superego, they invoke it and conjure it. Yet, Earl and Leona serve a similar function in respect to Asian American agony, raising once again the question of Asian American positionality vis-à-vis Blackness, ending with a tragically pessimistic conclusion that coalition may be structurally impossible, or at least extremely difficult.

The play begins portraying the strong friendship between Earl and the play's central character, Chet Monkawa, a former No-No Boy who manages the boarding house and was once an aspiring jazz musician. In a sense, Chet is ostensibly an "ideal critical subject," having actively resisted the internment rather than rehearsing the model minoritarianism and respectability of the Japanese American Citizens League; he even borders on embodying the Afro-Asian superego itself. The solidarity between the Chet and Earl is both personal and political. In Act 1 Scene 7, Chet and Earl exchange a one-on-one conversation, in which Earl begins complimenting Chet on how effectively he can perform Blackness: "We walk in [to the jazz club], you Japanese.

I turn around, suddenly you a colored man" (Gotanda 2007, 18). As the discussion veers into Chet's incarceration at Tule Lake for his political protest, Earl insists that Chet never deserved to be especially imprisoned, nor Japanese Americans as a whole interned, regardless of the circumstances:

> EARL: Don't matter, don't matter. All you folks shoulda never been took to Camps and you shoulda never been put into that Tule Lake place. I don't even need to know why and I understand. Man don't need to have a reason, he change the rules to suit hisself then say it's for everybody's good, like hell.'Specially when it come to war time. Civil War, my great grandpa fought, hell who wants to be a slave? 'Sides we gonna get 40 acres and a mule. See my 40 acres? See my mule? First World War. 'Course they want the Colored man, who's gonna do all the dirty work. Okay, we go, America gonna finally give us our due. We fight, we do the dirty work and we die. What we got to show for it? Our very own graveyard on the other side of the fence where the weeds growin'. This War? Where my pretty backyard with the swimmin' pool? Where the hell my martini? Ship yards close down 'cause we won the war but guess who the first one lose his job? Over one year now Earl T. Worthing ain't found steady work. All us Colored folks losin' jobs, no wonder the music gettin' meaner. (Gotanda 2007, 19)

In this moment at the beginning of the play, Earl can easily indicate the common villain in the U.S. state for both the Japanese American and African American communities, with the former unnecessarily incarcerated, and the latter repeatedly disenfranchised. Earl is also attentive to the specificity of the No-No Boy narrative, pointing out the futility of wartime service in achieving redress.[9] The friendship of the two men displays the possibility for political empathy, although this also hinges upon Chet's channeling of Black masculinity, symbolized by his musical prowess (jazz in the 2007 *After the War*, blues in the 2014 *After the War Blues*). Chet's acceptance by Earl, in performatively masculine terms, fulfills the yearning for Black acceptance found in the writings of Frank Chin, and it also represents a form of success in relation to the Afro-Asian superego that Chang and Eng spectacularly failed.

However, the ease of solidarity becomes complicated by the entrance of Earl's sister-in-law, Leona. Unlike Earl at the beginning of the play, Leona is Black-centric in her interests, distrusting the Japanese American characters at the Monkawa boarding house. In effect, she serves as the voice of Afro-pessimist critique throughout the play. In Act 1, Scene 10, when Earl urges Leona to be empathetic to the Japanese, given their prior eviction from the Fillmore, Leona retorts,

> And then they come back, after they lose the war and what happens? After *they* lose the war and we won, all us Colored folks get thrown out and all these Japs get to move in. That's just like it always is but that doesn't mean it's right. (Gotanda 2007, 27)

Earl rightfully reminds her of the distinction between Japanese and Japanese Americans, which Leona refuses, given what she considers to be their identical relationship to Black people. When Earl pleads that "They just got back from being locked up," Leona provocatively replies,

> It doesn't matter things like this, everybody got some pain they have to jive with. Lord knows, no one's got more pain than Colored folk. That includes your Jap— "oriental" friends. So they been locked up for 3, 4 years? So what? That ain't pain. I got a life time of pain. 3, 4 years—that's a walk in the woods compared to our pain. Japs don't know nothing about pain. (Gotanda 2007, 27)

Leona's commentary, tainted by overt anti-Asian bigotry such as the usage of "Jap," bluntly belittles Japanese American dispossession relative to the intergenerational atrocity of slavery and its aftermath. Leona's comparative framing of the discussion of racial injury is predicated primarily upon a ressentiment ethos of injury—the legitimacy of sympathy is predicated upon the depths of the trauma. Nevertheless, Leona provides a valuable historical critique of the Japanese American position that within the multi-century context of slavery and mass dispossession, the Japanese American internment is hardly exceptional, and that they are at least partly agents in the furthering of antiblack displacement.

In Act 2, Scene 18, Leona persists in her assertion of the totalizing nature of Black racialization in a later conversation with Lillian, the former fiancée of Chet's brother and Chet's primary love interest in the play:

> You think it just happens to be that way. For Coloreds it can't be like that because when bad stuff happens, you don't just see what's happening to you right then, you see back to your mother, grandmother, great grandmother. You got a memory of things doesn't even belong to you but connected to you. And you know it didn't just happen. What happened before and now is all connected. (Gotanda 2007, 51)

When Leona accuses Lillian of not having any idea of what "Colored" people have been through, Lillian replies that Leona doesn't have any idea of what Japanese Americans have been through, although she cannot counter Leona's point of deeply embedded intergenerational racialized trauma. Leona's commentary establishes Blackness as exceptional among racializations, and that despite the vicious trauma of the internment, Japanese Americans find themselves in structural domination over Blacks, leaving Leona with no incentive to express solidarity.

The climax of the play conveys the tragic disintegration of Earl and Chet's friendship in a catalyzing moment of violence. One of the central character conflicts of *After the War* entails Earl and Chet's complex rivalry for the affections of Mary-Louise, the white Okie taxi hall dancer and sex worker who had once had a relationship with Chet and currently beds Earl (whom she refers to behind his back as a "nigger"), eventually pregnant with his child. Mary-Louise was once Chet's partner, although

Chet eventually comes to favor Lillian by the end of the play, but Earl's detection of their intimacy throws Earl into a rage. However, the climactic confrontation between Earl, Chet, Mary-Louise, and Mary-Louise's brother Benji shatters the possibility of solidarity established at the onset of the play. Earl begins to violently shake Mary-Louise in a jealous rage, which prompts Benji to train a shotgun at Earl. Chet succeeds at pulling the gun away from Benji but then, crucially, points the gun at Earl, whom he perceives to be the biggest threat in the moment. Incredulous, Earl implicates him and ultimately agrees with Leona:

EARL: 3 years they lock you up. And now you standin' there defendin' that White boy over me.
CHET: It's got nothing to do with the boy's race—
EARL: It's all got to do with race. Everything's'bout race. What they done to you they been doin' to us for a long time, can't you see that? We on the same side of the fence. (beat) But maybe you know that. Maybe that's what this all about.
CHET: What are you saying Earl?
EARL: I ask myself what you doin' on that side of the door holdin' a gun in my face and now I think I know, Leona right all along.
CHET: Earl, what's wrong with you? Don't measure me like White folks.
EARL: You got the gun, you the landlord, well?
CHET: If it's not Colored it's gotta be White? Is that it?
EARL: 'Cause that's all there is as far as I know.
CHET: Look at me. Look at me, Earl. I'm standing right here. Can't you see me? Look. Look.
(beat)
EARL: I'm a Colored man, Chester. That's all I know. (Gotanda 2007)

When Chet points the gun at Earl, Earl suddenly realizes that in this moment, Chet's nonblackness outweighs his nonwhiteness, that Chet has symbolically chosen whiteness. Suddenly, the black/white binary becomes reified as a structural paradigm, within which the Japanese American Chet has made a political decision. "Leona," in other words, was "right all along." This is, of course, doubly heightened by the fact that Chet unquestionably holds greater institutional power in this moment, also effectively being Earl's landlord and, spurred on by competition over Mary-Louise, in pursuit of overdue rent. Structurally, as property manager, despite his radicality as a jazz artist and No-No Boy, despite his own history of exclusion, Chet is in effect fated to turn the gun on the Black man. The circumstances of the narrative thus distill the relationship between Chet and Earl to its barest materiality of landlord and tenant.

In this moment, economic hierarchy suddenly becomes a racial one. This should come as no surprise in light of Cheryl Harris' powerful 1993 observation that "American law has recognized a property interest in whiteness" (1993, 1713), "rights in property and contingent on, intertwined with, and conflated with race" (1993, 1714). The confrontation is between Chet, who is propertied and assuming the position typically afforded to whiteness, and Earl, slave descendant, racialized-*as*-property, over the status afforded to the claim over the white woman's whiteness, as well as the debt of rent to stay within *literal* property. And although the narrative places most of the "fault" of the conflict on Earl's actions rather than Chet's, there is nevertheless an overpowering sense of betrayal when Chet aims the gun. The homosocial solidarity between Chet and Earl becomes heteromasculine rivalry through the collision of whiteness and property, and Chet chooses, by and large, to preserve both.

With Earl and Chet's friendship irrevocably dead, *After the War* makes us wonder whether Earl's earlier skepticism of whether "an Oriental can play jazz" was correct, after all. That is to say, Chet is able to *perform* a culture of Blackness without inhabiting its political position; to "play jazz," then, is to do both. Chet Monkawa's approximation of Blackness reveals itself for having been taboo, incestuously imitating the style of Black masculine cool while ultimately finding himself on the side of capital and white property relations, despite all the best intentions. It was the privilege of nonblackness that finds Monkawa trapped in the position of the oppressor.

Nevertheless, Chet's defense of property is ultimately futile; as the final supertitles of the play read, Japanese Town is marked for eminent domain seizure and is effectively razed to the ground by 1960 to make room for transnational Japanese capitalists to build the Kintetsu Mall, which still stands to this day. The play's conclusion implies that Chet is to Earl what the Japanese companies are to the Monkawa Boarding House, that racialization and property's intertwining relies upon eviction or the threat of it. It also, moreover, speaks to precisely the politics embedded within Sau-Ling Wong's skepticism of denationalization 12 years prior, that a lateral, local solidarity with other U.S.-based people of color bears more promise than a transnational one of shared ethnicity.

After the War thus asks the question of whether Asian American advancement and inclusion depends precisely upon antiblackness, and whether an ethico-political choice is in fact possible for the Asian American subject in this regard—it seems to share the pessimism of Sexton and Wilderson, or the critique of the Asian American panethnic political project that we would see in the work of Susan Koshy. In a sense, *After the War* is ironically more fatalistic than *I Dream of Chang and Eng*, despite the latter being based on actual historical events; Learned Jack appears explicitly to the brothers of *Chang and Eng* as if offering a choice between self-interested moves toward identification with whiteness, or solidarity with Blackness. In contrast, *After the War* presents Leona—and eventually Earl—as paranoid interlocutors for an Afro-Asian superego, with Chet reasonable and well intentioned, with the moment of antiblackness presenting an Aristotelian end to his tragedy (although it is the friendship, rather than Chet himself, who dies). While Chang and Eng choose to be oppressors, Chet lands upon the position due to his hamartia, which is nonblackness. Whereas *I Dream of Chang and Eng* implicitly seems to ask "what if" the Bunkers hadn't become complicit in a system of slavery, the fictional *After the War* demonstrates that Chet's structural position as model minority overwhelms his agentic attempts at solidarity.

It is possible to read both of these plays as demonstrations of the Afro-pessimist position, that the Asian American is inevitably the "master" to the Black subject's "slave." *I Dream of Chang and Eng* fits this diagnosis in a literal sense. But *After the War* offers up a complex critique of model minoritarianism and antiblackness while at the same time refusing to offer an "ideal type"—in this case, an Afro-Asian superego *figure*—to emulate. The closest to this "ideal type," if anything, is Chet himself, with his No-No Boy political consciousness and comfortable heteromasculinity. Chet's failure as a figure of solidarity demonstrates that it is the circuitous flow of racial power that determines racial structural positions, more than any intent to oppress, as in the episteme of ressentiment.

Moreover, it is worth considering that while Chet can be read as aspiring to "whiteness as power," Earl and Chet are, in effect, making competing claims to whiteness, albeit in different ways. In this sense, *After the War* works both with and against the exceptionalism of the Afro-pessimist paradigm. While Chet finds himself the beneficiary of whiteness as power through property, Earl seeks whiteness *sexually* through the imperfect (lumpenproletarian) vessel of Mary-Louise. The male competition over the white woman speaks to a kind of colonized desire, made explicit by Leona's accusation to Earl that he desires the white "whore" over her and does not look at Leona with the same desire. However, Earl's claim to whiteness is not assimilationist per se; in a sense, Earl's eroticism and possessiveness of Mary-Louise can be understood as heteromasculine ressentiment. In the context of his early soliloquy ("See my 40 acres? See my mule?"), Mary-Louise is objectified and idealized as recompense within Earl's compensatory logic. In this context, Frantz Fanon's oft-quoted treatise of the subject seems descriptive of Earl's eroticism of Mary-Louise, the "desire to be suddenly *white*.... But ... who better than the white woman to bring this about? By loving me, she proves to me that I am worthy of a white love. I am loved like a white man" (Fanon 2008, 45). And while Earl's perception of Chet's affections for Mary-Louise catalyze the conflict between the two men, Chet ultimately chooses not to couple with Mary-Louise but nevertheless retains the (white) power of property. While *After the War* acknowledges the gravitational pull of the Black racialization in setting the paradigm of race at large and the logics of antiblackness that animate the politics of inclusion, it is critical of all racialized subjects who attempt to pursue redress from whiteness *through* whiteness, including Black ones. Rather than an exceptionalist ontology of Black social death, *After the War* offers a model of variegated traumas and multiple, messy, conflicting attempts at racial rebuilding.

Nevertheless, in both *After the War* and *I Dream of Chang and Eng*, it is the Asian being morally whipped. These plays confront their audiences with shame, hinting at an idealized ressentiment but instead turning in on themselves. They commit to a moral masochism that necessitates self-interrogation, while simultaneously making its subjects intently and uncomfortably aware of their socialities. And although their shapes do not materialize within these performances, the plays necessitate imaginings for new political possibilities, either with the presence of a clear superego against antiblackness (as in *Chang and Eng*), or a diffuse one (as in *After the War*).

Coda: Nurturing the Psychic Life of Coalition

Several years ago, I posed a question to Philip Gotanda, pondering whether or not Asian Americans were, on a multitude of levels, actualizing their "model minority" status. It was an early version of the question that I have explored throughout this chapter, wondering what direction Asian American cultural politics should head in the face of increasing embourgeoisement and material gains.

It was then that he shot me a wryly ironic smile and asked, "Well, isn't that what we wanted all along?"

What have we wanted? In a sense, Asian America itself has principally been an aspiration since its coining by Yuji Ichioka in 1968, one premised on the rejection of "Oriental," seeking something like freedom within its panethnic rallying cry. By asking what Asian America has wanted, we ask what it is, what it always has been.

Gotanda's work makes us question the ethico-political aspirations of Asian American cultural politics altogether. Since 2014, Gotanda has worked on an initiative he has entitled "The American Adaptation Cycle," in which he adapts his celebrated 1985 play *The Wash* to non–Japanese American cultural contexts. For the first leg of the project, Gotanda worked in close collaboration with longtime colleague, actor, and director Steven Anthony Jones to develop "The Jamaican Wash," rewriting the play to fit Jamaican American diasporic mores and historical circumstances. According to Gotanda, this project aims to produce cross-cultural understandings through a solidarity of shared marginality, a collaboration of what Deleuze once called "minor literatures," in order not only to produce solidarities, but also to collectively unseat the universality of the white canon.

In any event, Gotanda's engagement with Blackness as a mode of anti-racist ethics powerfully dramatizes the Asian Americanist anxiety of becoming a model minority. At the time of this writing, an age in which Richard Aoki has been discovered to be a likely informant, when many Chinese Americans rallied to support Peter Liang after he killed unarmed Black man Akai Gurley,[10] when public awareness of the extrajudicial killings of Black people has reached a fevered pitch with the Black Lives Matter movement, the question of Asian American positionality vis-à-vis Blackness becomes all too imperative. Perhaps that is why Earl was initially skeptical that "an Oriental can play jazz." Perhaps Earl was right.

4
Never Stop Making Them Pay

Greg Pak's *Hulk*, Moral Masochism, and Asian American Ressentiment

Prologue: The Hidden Asianness of the Green Goliath

The first major live-action motion picture rendition of Marvel Comics' *Hulk* was played by a Taiwanese American. Although Eric Bana performed the human form of the titular computer-generated protagonist of Ang Lee's *Hulk* (2003), the iconic green superhuman form of the Hulk was, in fact, performed by Ang Lee himself. As demonstrated in the short behind-the-scenes documentary *The Incredible Ang Lee*, Lee decided to don the motion capture suit himself when he decided that it was the most efficient way for him to convey the emotional nuances of the Green Goliath's choreography as he smashed and battled his way through the various obstacles in the superhero's path (see Figure 4.1).

The 145-minute film, although high grossing, was largely disparaged by both critics and audiences alike; the critical consensus was ultimately that the film "had too much talking, not enough smashing" (RottenTomatoes.com), and it was called "leaden and pretentious" by Salon.com and "incredibly long, incredibly tedious, incredibly turgid" by A. O. Scott of the *New York Times*. Part of the film's negative reception drew from a set of asymmetric expectations: the popular conceptualization of Marvel Comics' Incredible Hulk is that of an unthinking, brainless brawn who speaks, in all capital letters, the signature phrase "HULK SMASH." Although Ang Lee's take on the Hulk was widely criticized for being too brooding, his decidedly pensive and earnest treatment of the Green Goliath was perhaps more faithful to the affect of the source material than many audiences and critics have realized. Even in the early stages of the Hulk (inaugurated by Stan Lee and Jack Kirby in 1962), the Hulk had been understood as a fundamentally tragic, tormented figure, combining the fleshy abjection of Mary Shelley's *Frankenstein* with the struggle of multiple identities of Robert Louis Stevenson's *Strange Case of Dr. Jekyll and Mr. Hyde*. The basic premise of the iconic Marvel Comics superhero is that the Hulk is the uncontrollable alter ego of super-genius physicist Bruce Banner, a modern-day Oppenheimer whose exposure to his own bomb would cause him to uncontrollably mutate into the Hulk, an inarticulate muscled monster driven primarily by rage. Central to the mythos of the Hulk is his near-limitless strength, whose power is proportional to his anger. To

Figure 4.1 Director Ang Lee in motion-capture suit performing as the Hulk in his 2003 film of the same title. Screen cap from The Incredible Ang Lee (2003). Courtesy of NBC Universal.

this effect, under the supervision of writers Bill Mantlo and Peter David in the 1980s, the Hulk was established as one of Banner's alternate personalities, the result of developing dissociative identity disorder (DID) from child abuse suffered at the hands of his father. Consequently, the aesthetic of Ang Lee's agonized, somber *Hulk* demonstrates an affective fidelity to this period of the *Hulk* narrative.

This brooding melancholia is a familiar affect to Asian American masculine cultural production, a parallel heightened by Lee's invisible performance of the *Hulk* himself. In both of these regards, Ang Lee's superhero caper is an Asian American movie. By digitally costuming himself as the Hulk—embodying the Hulk while the Hulk is superimposed over his body—Ang Lee reproduces an Asian American masculinity that seeks to undo castration yet disavows its own presence.[1] Although it would be a reach to say that Ang Lee's *Hulk* speaks directly to Asian American cultural politics, I open with this image of Lee to consider an intriguing Asian American male affinity for the Hulk. This is not to say that Lee's racial position was the central factor motivating his donning of the mocap suit, but the image nevertheless visually crystalizes the narrative parallel between the Hulk and Asian American masculine racialization. Banner, not unlike many professional East Asians who immigrated after the 1965 immigration reform and the institution of H-1B visas in the 1990s, is a scientist. As such, he is proximal to technology in much the same way that the techno-orientalized model minority is. However, like such STEM-affiliated Asians, Banner's radical quasi-racial abjection prevents him from full, unmediated entry into American social life and capital, demonstrated quite potently in the '90s by the social drama that was the Wen Ho Lee crisis, in which the Chinese American nuclear physicist at Los Alamos National Laboratory was publicly and falsely accused of espionage for the People's Republic of China.[2]

This masculine Asian American affinity for the Hulk extends to the primary author examined in this chapter, Korean American independent filmmaker and comic artist Greg Pak. Pak is a rare multimedia cultural producer who has held considerable creative sway over a number of mainstream science fictional franchises yet has remained firmly committed to considering issues of race and representation even within these highly commercial media. Born in 1968 in Dallas, TX, trained at NYU's graduate film program, and the recipient of a Rhodes Scholarship in 1991, Pak has produced a corpus of work for both the page and the screen, both explicitly and implicitly engaging with questions of Asian American identity and cultural politics. His first film, *Fighting Grandpa*, dealt with the relationship between his Korean immigrant grandparents, while his short *Asian Pride Porn*, starring playwright David Henry Hwang, satirically imagines a porno laden with politically progressive Asian American gender politics. His highly acclaimed 2003 film *Robot Stories*, starring veteran Japanese American actor Tamlyn Tomita, heavily features Asian Americans in relationship to androids in a post-cyberpunk near future, heavily inflected by techno-orientalist imagery and discourse. But since 2004, Pak has distinguished himself as a comic book writer, beginning at Marvel Comics with the series *Warlock*, authoring a number of titles including *X-Men*, *Iron Man*, and *Hercules*, as well as writing for the relaunch of DC Comics' *Batman/Superman* and Dynamite Entertainment's *Battlestar Galactica* comics. Most recently, as of this writing, he has begun to pen a series for Marvel called "Agents of Atlas," which features a groundbreaking assembly of Asian and Asian American superheroes in one team—a first for a major superhero comic publisher—and in 2019 he donated proceeds from sales on his personal website to support efforts for refugee and immigrant advocacy to combat the Trump administration's mass border detention camps.

It was Pak's run of *Incredible Hulk*, especially in the *Planet Hulk* and *World War Hulk* storylines from 2006 to 2007, that firmly sutured the Green Goliath to Asian American cultural politics through a thematic engagement with racial ressentiment. In the Asian American superhero collection *Secret Identities*, Pak himself explains,

> [I]n a funny way, one of the most obvious expressions of my interest in race and diversity is hiding in plain sight in the *Planet Hulk* epic I wrote for Marvel. In *Planet Hulk*, the Green Goliath fights—and then bonds with—a group of alien gladiators whom everyone else sees as monsters. But all these different aliens end up proving themselves. So behind this crazy sci-fi storyline is an evisceration of racism. (Pak 2009, 55)

Under Pak, the Hulk becomes the figure of radicalized Asian American masculinity par excellence, as well as its philosophical deconstruction, even though the Hulk is not himself literally Asian. Furthermore, as I have already alluded before in the preliminary example of Ang Lee's film, the Hulk has already had a peculiar affinity with what Colleen Lye has called "Asiatic racial form" (2005); Pak's authorship of the Hulk solidifies that attachment through his own identity as author, his long-standing interest in Asian American cultural politics, and he very narrative of his run with the Hulk.

Moreover, Pak does not only provide an Asian Americanist imagining of the Hulk; Pak's Hulk also confronts the affective and discursive logics of Asian American masculinity. Pak's hyper-organic, sinewy Hulk functions as the machine's symbolic opposite, a resentful rejection of the very paradigm of model minoritarianism. Yet, Pak's Hulk offers a deconstructive critique of masculine ressentiment that has persisted throughout Asian American cultural politics and gestures instead toward an ethos of masochistic bottoming. It is through the Hulk, the embodiment of a politics of woundedness, that Pak demonstrates the distinction between ressentiment and masochism, and with it, how both the destructive and recuperative potentials of masochism exceed the political imagination of ressentiment.

Planet Hulk, *World War Hulk*, and the Limits of Ressentiment

Planet Hulk begins with the Hulk's expulsion from Earth by his superhero (and, notably, intellectual) colleagues Reed Richards (Mr. Fantastic), Tony Stark (Iron Man), Black Bolt, and Dr. Stephen Strange, forcibly deporting the Hulk from Earth due to his unpredictable capacity for wanton destruction. The Hulk lands on a planet called Sakaar, which is ruled by a ruthless Roman-inspired empire of humanoid Sakaarans called Imperials, who in turn have enslaved a diverse swath of aliens as laborers, gladiators, and servants, all of whom are treated as racially abject and monstrous. The bulk of *Planet Hulk* consists of a messianic Spartacus narrative: Hulk rises to become the revolutionary leader of the enslaved gladiators, overthrowing the dictatorial Red King, and even becomes king alongside his warrior lover Caiera. In the few days that Hulk reigns as monarch, he brings peace and prosperity to the people of Sakaar, reconciling long-warring factions, his green blood capable of fertilizing the once-barren soil. But his reign horrifically and abruptly ends when the ship that brought Hulk to Sakaar explodes in an apocalyptic blast, massacring the majority of the newly liberated population, including Hulk's wife and unborn son. Once again enraged and grief-stricken, and blaming his superhero-scientist colleagues for planting the bomb on the ship, Hulk mounts an invasion of Earth to avenge his wife and followers, leading immediately to the *World War Hulk* storyline, pitting the Hulk against the rest of Earth's superheroes. The Aristotelian tragedy[3] of *World War Hulk* ends with the revelation that it was not his human colleagues who planted the bomb but, rather,

Hulk's disciple Miek, whom Hulk taught the value of unending retributive rage. Miek, whose hive mother was murdered (thus ending the reproductive futurity of his clan), decided that a Hulk of postwar reconciliation was not true to the Hulk's mission and essence and thus gave Hulk an incentive toward violence once more. At the revelation of Miek's betrayal, Hulk self-loathingly surrenders to the Earth forces, allowing himself to be struck by a focused laser beam from orbit, reverting to his human form to be imprisoned.

Planet Hulk and *World War Hulk*, while not strictly allegorical to Asian American politics, nevertheless share key narrative characteristics with Asian American cultural production besides a self-identified Asian American author explicitly engaged in such themes. Central to this *Hulk* arc is his status as abject—Hulk is literally ejected and deported from Earth by his colleagues—which, as Karen Shimakawa has forcefully argued, alludes to a construction of the Asian subject to a historical regime of exclusion in the United States and "must be radically jettisoned in order to constitute 'Americanness'" (2002, 10), legally codified in such infamous legislation as the 1882 Chinese Exclusion Act, the internment of Japanese Americans through Executive Order 9066 in 1942, and so on. Indeed, the fact that half of the cabal who had plotted to exile him—Stark and Richards—are not just white men but fellow scientists, echoes Asian American anxieties of merely ambivalent acceptance of Asian professionals in STEM fields, again reflected in the aforementioned Wen Ho Lee case. It is, in effect, rage at the deception of the model minority, that the promise of inclusion via adherence to respectable becoming-machine is broken. On Sakaar, Hulk's Asianization is also signified through a new name, "Holku," by his lover Caeira, echoing the Japanese linguistic tendency to add "u" after consonants at the end of English words to adapt to Japanese phonetic norms. To solidify this link between the Hulk and Asian American even further, Pak designed and wrote a new character, super-genius Korean American teenager Amadeus Cho, who becomes a Hulk sympathizer. Cho models the Asian American reader's sympathy with the Hulk, arguing that the Hulk is more victim than perpetrator of violence, and equally accomplished in heroism as his more socially accepted colleagues.

But if we read *Planet Hulk* and *World War Hulk* as Asian American literature as I suggest we do, then the motivation undergirding the Hulk's crusade in *World War Hulk* gains even greater significance. Specifically, the Hulk's impetus throughout the second phase of the interstellar epic is ressentiment, loosely defined as "resentment." In referring to ressentiment, I draw particularly from the Nietzschean tradition of *Genealogy of Morals*, which was most eloquently adapted to contemporary identity politics by Wendy Brown. In the Nietzschean tradition, revenge against oppression becomes the primary motivator of the man of ressentiment, who, for Nietzsche, is troublingly epitomized by "the Jew." Consequently, Nietzsche characterizes ressentiment as a moral logic emergent from "slave morality," premised upon contempt for the privileged oppressor. Crucially, Nietzsche problematizes the logic of ressentiment as imagining unmediated agency on the part of both the oppressed and the noble, that morality assumes goodness in "choosing" to be weak, evil in "choosing" to be strong:

This type of man *needs* to believe in an unbiased 'subject' with freedom of choice, because he has an instinct of self-preservation and self-affirmation in which every lie is sanctified.... [The subject] facilitated that sublime self-deception whereby the majority of the dying, the weak and oppressed of every kind could construe weakness itself as freedom, and their particular mode of existence as an *accomplishment*. (1994, 28–29)

Certainly, the Nietzschean critique of ressentiment appears deeply reactionary, given the theory's implicit devaluation of the subjective position of the marginalized. Frederic Jameson captures the problem within ressentiment, describing ressentiment dismissively in *The Political Unconscious*: "this ostensible 'theory' is itself little more than an expression of annoyance at seemingly gratuitous lower-class agitation, at the apparently quite unnecessary rocking of the social boat" (1981, 202), and the theory itself is autoreferential, its appearance its own expression of ressentiment. Indeed, the most troubling problematic of Nietzsche's original formulation of ressentiment, besides its pernicious anti-Semitism, is its lack of explicit understanding that systematic power relations can or should be altered; Nietzsche concentrates his critique precisely on the marginalized, and Jameson is quite correct in observing that Nietzsche's critique of the "man of ressentiment" paradoxically makes himself a "man of ressentiment," as well.

Yet, Jameson overlooks two crucially productive aspects of Nietzsche's admittedly troubling formulation. First, Nietzsche's discussion of ressentiment focuses not on material disparity (as Jameson implies with "lower-class agitation"), but on categories of social identity that are not necessarily proletarianized. Although, as Rey Chow states in *The Protestant Ethnic and the Spirit of Capitalism*, "The ethnic has, in many ways, been conceived implicitly as a proletarian, a resistant captive engaged in a struggle toward liberation" (Chow 2002, 41), oppressed religio-identity categories, rather than class conflict, are the primary object of Nietzsche's critique. Thus, Nietzsche's theory focuses not on the *dispossessed* and *exploited* per se, but on the *marginalized*, two typically intersecting but not synonymous categories—the former being primarily material in its cultural metrics, and the latter being primarily identitarian. That is not to say that the two cannot inform one another—Marxian theorization of the proletariat deeply informs theories on ethnicity, for example—but, rather, that Nietzschean ressentiment more actively troubles the specificity of identitarian ethnic resentment.

Here, Sianne Ngai's distinction between ressentiment and envy is useful; while both affects importantly target inequality as their locus of contempt, "envy makes no claim whatsoever about the moral superiority of the envier, or about the 'goodness' of his or her state of lacking something that the envied other is perceived to have. Envy is in many ways a naked will to have" (2005, 34). Thus, according to Ngai, envy (rather than ressentiment) possesses a productive deconstructive potential in relation to social inequality, especially when that inequality is materially manifested. Yet, envy has limitations in relation to race; as Ngai states, "'race' names the struggle in which it is most taken for granted that no degree of acquiring what the envied other has—money, education, phallus... will *ever* culminate in the other and one becoming indistinguishable" (2005, 173). Although Ngai does not state this, it is perhaps fair to say that ressentiment, rather than envy, functions as a dominant cultural logic of racial identity politics, given its tendency to moralize the position of the oppressed and its refusal to claim the dominant position of whiteness.

Second, I would argue that the most fruitful dimension of Nietzsche's theory is not so much his condemnation of the oppressed position of "the slave" but, rather, his perhaps-unintentional critique of individualist agency vis-à-vis inequality. The morality of Nietzschean ressentiment depends precisely on agency, on resenting the strong for *choosing* to be strong, and praising the weak for *choosing* to be weak. In the regime of ressentiment, strength and weakness become choices of the fully autonomous liberal individual, as opposed to outcomes of structural exploitation. As Wendy Brown argues through Nietzsche, ressentiment becomes the primary basis of contemporary identity politics, establishing a psychic economy of past victimhood in order to legitimize the moral force of a minoritized subject position. But as Brown aptly observes,

> [I]n its attempt to displace its suffering, identity structured by *ressentiment* at the same time becomes invested in its own subjection. This investment lies not only in its discovery of a site of blame for its hurt will, not only in its acquisition of recognition through its history of subjection (a recognition predicated on injury, now righteously revalued), but also in the satisfactions of revenge, which ceaselessly enact even as they redistribute the injuries of marginalization and subordination in a liberal discursive order that alternately denies the very possibility of these things and blames those who experience them for their own condition. Identity politics by *ressentiment* reverse without subverting this blaming structure: they do not subject to critique the sovereign subject of accountability that liberal individualism presupposes, nor the economy of inclusion and exclusion that liberal universalism establishes. Thus, politicized identity that presents itself as a self-affirmation appears as the opposite, as predicated on and requiring its sustained rejection by a "hostile external world." (1995, 70)

Thus, an identity politics of ressentiment thus *requires* the sustenance of rejection, exclusion, and injury. Accordingly, Nietzschean ressentiment is a critique of a *liberal identitarian* conceptualization of oppression, of a group with a vested interest in retaining its preexisting subject position. But importantly, the identity politics of ressentiment targets the socially privileged for "choosing" to be privileged. Not only does this position moralize power relations; it also does not adequately model the role of power in subjectification, which implicates all of its subjects through fields of power relations. Here, Foucault's well-known description of power bears citation from *A History of Sexuality Vol. 1*: that is, as the multiplicity of force relations immanent in the sphere in which they operate and which constitute their own organization; as the process which, through ceaseless struggles and confrontations, transforms, strengthens, or reverses them; as the support which these force relations find in one another, thus forming a chain or a system. (1978, 92)

That is, power is not simply "owned" by the subjects who are "in power," but, rather, it circulates throughout an entire system, and in fact produces knowledge, meaning, and subjects through establishing its own fields of intelligibility. Sociologist Claire Jean Kim adapts Foucault's models of power to produce a theory of "racial power," and her description is useful to this discussion:

I conceive of racial power not as something that an individual or group exercises directly and intentionally over another individual or group but rather as a systemic property, permeating, circulating throughout, and continuously constituting society. I do not use the phrase "White racial power" because it erroneously suggests that Whites possess and deliberately exercise racial power against others when in fact Whites, too, are constituted *qua* Whites by the operation of racial power. While Whites are undeniably the primary beneficiaries of racial power, they are also its subjects. (2000, 9)

Thus, since Kim asserts that power is primarily a circuit that governs intelligibility, it constitutes subjects themselves, including those who are ostensibly "powerful" or, in contemporary parlance, "privileged"—which is not synonymous but, rather, is descriptive of being principally the beneficiary of power rather than principally its wielder. In contrast, the identity politics of ressentiment is sutured to an ethics of individualist agency, obfuscating the complex relationality of subjectification and relying upon a conceptualization of power in which its wielders fully and agentically come into their own strength. Ressentiment, in fact, merely repeats the logic undergirding individualist accountability that buttresses the moral justification of racism in the first place—a logic that Kim's Foucauldian model of racial power seeks to undo.

Nevertheless, Nietzschean *ressentiment* has suffused itself with Asian American cultural politics, and even the signifier "Asian American" itself. As I have argued in the Introduction, Asian American literary narratives and cultural politics have tended to valorize "resistance" through a glorification of the "bad" (Nguyen) or "ideal critical" (Lee) subject, who arrives upon political consciousness through traumatic encounters with white racism.[4] Rey Chow problematizes the notion of political consciousness as inherited from Lukács, noting that Lukács contradictorily idealizes the subject who labors in what has come to be known more generally as "standpoint theory." The oppressed status of the proletariat both provides the worker with an inherent capacity for resistance and imbues a moralizing sense of "humanity" (the latter of which is strikingly parallel to ressentiment itself). This description of the proletarian has adapted easily to the minoritized ethnic, who is similarly trapped by history (Chow

2002, 40) and thus possesses an inherent nobility by virtue of having been oppressed and excluded—again, as in ressentiment (and, as in ressentiment, gains additional depth by virtue of its identitarian shape). Compellingly, the Lukácsian moralizing essentialism of the oppressed subject, the inner human "soul" that gives the subject the capacity to resist and pursue social justice, is entirely parallel to the "calling" described in Max Weber's description of the Protestant ethic of capitalism (Chow 2002, 43). That is to say, "precisely this narrative of resistance and protest, this moral preoccupation with universal justice, is what constitutes the efficacy of the capitalist spirit. Resistance and protest, when understood historically, are part and parcel of the structure of capitalism; they are the reasons capitalism flourishes" (Chow 2002, 47). The moral idealization of the subject who has become aware of their own oppression—whom we can associate with "the man of ressentiment"—is itself complicit with the moral logics of capitalism. Moreover, despite his dismissal of Nietzsche's ressentiment, even Jameson similarly critiques the emergence of Lukácsian idealization of the standpoint in "History and Class Consciousness as an Unfinished Project," stating that

> "the moment of truth" of group experience—itself negative and positive all at once, an oppressive restriction which turns into a capacity for new kinds of experience and for seeing features and dimensions of the world and of history masked to other social actors—is prolonged by an epistemological articulation that translates such experience into new possibilities of thought and knowledge. (Jameson 1988, 70)

Rather, argues Jameson, the various relativistic standpoints of oppressed groups should instead be situated relative to the broader "common object" of their theorization—that is, late capitalism.

Taking Brown and Chow together, the critique of ressentiment and the narrative of "political consciousness" that accompanies its awakening can remain, in fact, productive. A Nietzschean critique of ressentiment, rather than being an "expression of annoyance" to invalidate demands for redress from the oppressed, can instead be appropriated to demand that a cultural politics of resistance go even *further*.[5] As the following close reading of Greg Pak's Hulk will demonstrate, it is masochism, not ressentiment, that offers such political possibilities.

The Ontology of Hulkness: Ressentiment as Masculine Superpower

Notably, the very ontological basis of the Hulk-as-Hulk is grounded in ressentiment to such an extent that the Hulk is the very embodiment of ressentiment itself. Although Nietzschean ressentiment establishes weakness as proximal to godliness, whereas the Hulk is frequently declared "the strongest there is," the Hulk is a beast of inversion. His physical strength is derived precisely from emotional and physical woundedness: as the Hulk and his associates are fond of repeating, the angrier the Hulk gets, the stronger—indeed, the more Hulk-like—he is. This is codified in one of the Hulk's other names earned on Sakaar: the Green Scar, which draws attention to the Hulk's status as wound itself.

The Hulk's hypermasculine hyper-physicality is thus an expression of the Hulk's (and, additionally, "puny" Banner's) psychic woundedness, exacerbated in Pak's interpretation by an added layer of literal exclusion and racialization. This ressentiment principally manifests itself in masculine terms, with the moral economy of ressentiment expressed through physical violence and contests of dominance between the Hulk and other men. Despite the presence of powerful warrior women such as Caiera and the gladiator Elloe, Pak's *Planet Hulk / World War Hulk* unfortunately does not ultimately challenge the superhero genre's tendency toward male-centrism. Nevertheless, in suturing ressentiment to masculinity, Pak's work opens both to critique. After all, the hyperbolic bulk that is the Hulk's body is so staggeringly male, so excessive, his masculinity approaches drag hyperbole. Banner's scrawny nerdiness—a wiry frame also often stereotypically associated with Asian men—demonstrates the performative dimension of the Hulk, a monstrous hypermasculinity that borders on the absurd. It is analogous to the imagined, aspirational hypermasculinity of straight Asian American men within Asian American cultural nationalism (for which Frank Chin and the *Aiiieeeee!* group are oft-cited as epitomizing), as most thoroughly cataloged and analyzed by David Eng, Daniel Y. Kim, Nguyen Tan Hoang, and Celine Parreñas Shimizu.[6] Of course, as David Eng summarizes, "Paradoxically, this reification of a strident cultural nationalism, with its doctrine of compulsory heterosexuality and cultural authenticity, mirrors at once the dominant heterosexist and racist structures through which the Asian American male is historically feminized and rendered self-hating in the first place" (2001, 21); in other words, that Asian American hypermasculinity validates the very conditions of the racist emasculation to which it responds. Yet, as Ramzi Fawaz argues, despite his hypermasculine presentation, the Hulk paradoxically represents a kind of feminine emotionality: "Banner's vulnerability to science and his subsequent emotional struggles to control his unpredictable abilities indicated a newfound association between the superhero and those traits commonly associated with femininity, including fragility and emotionality" (2016, 12). According to Fawaz's reading, the Hulk's emotionality lacks the self-control of hegemonic masculinity, making him the object of feeling rather than its subject; his monstrosity is thus coded in effeminate and queer terms.

The Hulk's hyperbolically hypermasculine build—visually, a horizontally distinctive shape despite his seven-foot stature—adds to his monstrous abjection, a consistent feature since the beginning of the Hulk comics. His build contrasts with the more normative physicality of his white male peers such as the heavily muscled but legibly attractive Tony Stark and Black Bolt, as well as the wiry, lanky Reed Richards and Stephen Strange. The Hulk's excessive mass, a physicalization of overcompensation, does not earn him assimilation or acceptance into the white masculine order. Of course, this is far from the Hulk's aim; after all, the Hulk is aggressively anti-assimilationist, and his excessive, unruly bulk stands almost as a parody to the normative masculine muscle of the superhero genre. In short, the Hulk embodies muscle drag. More importantly, the Hulk's monstrous hypermasculinity is a symptom of ressentiment, a limitless, revolting strength proportional to his limitless, revolting hurt.

Planet Hulk and *World War Hulk* explicitly demonstrate the (classically) tragic futility of ressentiment, largely through its treatment of the Hulk's protégé Miek. Miek, an insectoid Sakaaran native who matures (and physically metamorphoses) from wide-eyed youngster to embittered adult (complete with a thick, armor-like carapace and pupil-less, inscrutable eyes) through the course of *Planet Hulk*, comes to personify the harsh consequences of Hulk's moral logic. In particular, the discourse between the Hulk and Miek demonstrate that ressentiment is not only an affect, but a definitive dimension of subject formation for both of them. In an early stage of the Hulk's slave revolt, the young Miek discovers the Imperial general who had massacred his hive (but had since defected against the Red King), and he asks Hulk, whom he calls "Two-hands," for moral guidance.

MIEK: Two-hands ... what saying you?
HULK: Why ask me? You know what you want. You brought us here to get it.
MIEK: But what ... what would *you* doing?
HULK: I'd never stop making them pay. (Pak 2013)

This exchange between the Hulk and his protégé reveals the temporality of ressentiment. Miek's present progressive tense merges with the subjunctive ("what would you doing"), inquiring into an action that is both hypothetical and already occurring. This merger of the progressive with the subjunctive implies a unity between the hypothetical future and the action of the present. Then, the final subjunctive line of the Hulk, accompanied by a shadowy, grimacing half-frontal image of the Hulk's face, consolidates the transitive action of revenge into a state of being; to "never stop" implies a permanence, a constant commitment to a masculine economy of violent recompense ("making them pay"). From Miek's perspective, the Hulk is already-revenging because the Hulk is the Hulk, and Miek correspondingly grows into adulthood through his mimesis of the Hulk's moral philosophy.

Yet, although the Hulk effectively occupies the place of the father for Miek in the first half of *Planet Hulk*, it is Miek who in turn comes to embody a violent id of ressentiment for the Hulk, particularly after Miek matures into his massive (and less anthropomorphic) adult form. In the *World War Hulk* edition of *Incredible Hercules*, Miek reflects on his role with the Hulk; in an inner monologue addressed to the Hulk alongside a montage of corresponding events that had occurred throughout *Planet Hulk*, Miek muses,

> Because you need me. Because every once in a while, you start to think that maybe it's time to stop. That all you want is to be left alone. But every time you almost

gave up, Miek was there, reminding you who you are. The humans' shuttle >kiki-kik<[7] killed Crown City, killed your queen and child, and you just wanted to die. But Miek reminded you you were made for vengeance. (Pak 2008)

Here, Miek conceptualizes the Hulk in essentialist, static terms ("who you are," "made for vengeance"), casting himself as a guarantor of that tragic fatalism. In this sense, Miek becomes the masculine ethnic chauvinist; as Miek has learned through the development of his "consciousness," properly oriented and vectored anger toward one's oppressor is a necessary prerequisite for authentic identity. As a consequence, Miek conspires to set the bomb that kills Caiera and the bulk of Sakaar's population at the conclusion of *Planet Hulk*. As Miek explains to Hulk later at the climax of *World War Hulk*,

"Never >kik< stop making them pay." That's what you taught me. That's why I >kik< killed them. That's why you'll kill me.... I always have to remind you, because you always forget. Like when you found your >kik< queen, all you wanted was peace. But that's not who you are. You >kik< conquered Sakaar. >kik< Killed the Red King. We should have slaughtered his people. But you let them live. So I watched them load an old warp core onto that shuttle. They thought it would kill you. But I knew it would just remind you of what you were made for. (Pak 2014)

For Miek, a Hulk who is not angry is not a real Hulk at all; thus, his actions personify the very logic of ressentiment. To a certain degree, Miek is correct; the Hulk's very defining premise, his superhero power, is the proportional relationship between his rage and his power. Moreover, the classically tragic structure of the *Planet Hulk / World War Hulk* narrative demonstrates the self-defeat implicit within ressentiment, the impossibility of achieving a state of thriving livability inasmuch as identity requires a wound. Miek's actions literalize Brown's supposition that ressentiment identity politics require the persistence of woundedness to retain the coherence of the "resistant" subject. But of particular symbolic import here is the misplacement of Hulk's rage: his first instinct is to blame the white male scientist conspirators who were unambiguously behind his initial expulsion. The Hulk attributes the devastation to those who had perpetrated the original act of exclusion. This is demonstrated powerfully at the conclusion of *Planet Hulk*, after the shuttle's bomb explodes and the Hulk melodramatically holds the slain body of Caiera in his arms. Amid the swirling smoke in the ruins, the faces of Reed Richards, Iron Man, Dr. Strange, and Black Bolt gradually form (and gain color) in the background, bringing the clear objects of the Hulk's ire into focus.

The ambiguous attribution of the atrocity speaks to the crisis of ambiguity for model minoritized Asians in America. In the Asian Americanist pursuit of radicality, of the "ideal critical subject," white racism is targeted as primarily a barrier for Asian Americans, and the classic Bildungsroman of Asian American political consciousness occurs through the recognition of the presence of this oft-unseen force.

In *Planet Hulk*, the Hulk and Miek undergo parallel but distinct variations of this Bildungsroman: the Hulk himself transitions from an asocial, misanthropic antipathy to one imbued with political purpose, one in which his monstrousness is no longer just the justification for abjection but, rather, the basis of a revolutionary sociality among his fellow former slaves, which parallels the foundation of Asian American panethnic organization (that is, until the bombing reverts him back to pure ressentiment). As Việt Thanh Nguyễn states, "anti-Asian racism makes us all Asian, rather than singularly ethnic, and that Asian America as a category or identity is effective in a *defensive* posture" (2002, 9). This politicization is reflected in the multiracial nature of the Hulk's revolt; Hulk and his group of former gladiators are all of different species but come to cohere in a coalitional identity—"Warbound"—when confronting a single racial oppressor, reflecting the responsive, defensive nature of a panethnic identity such as Asian Americanness (or, alternately, of the coalitional solidarity of the 1968 Third World Liberation Front, which was again united against a common white opponent). In a sense, the Warbound follows in a longtime superhero tradition of the superhero team, which Ramzi Fawaz describes as a "democratic collective" (2016, 5) that represents a queerly chosen family "who sought to use their powers for shaping a more egalitarian and democratic world" (2016, 11). However, in consisting of various members of oppressed racial groups on Sakaar, the Warbound is more blatantly Third Worldist than other more well-known superhero teams in Marvel and DC Comics that had arisen in the 1960s, such as the Justice League and the Avengers, which focused more on law and order or the defense of humanity from external threats; the Warbound was formed for the overthrow of the Sakaaran ruler and the abolition of slavery. Meanwhile, however, Miek transitions to asociality, idealizing the Hulk, who is at his most powerful, insisting that the Hulk's very identity remain tethered to the violence of ressentiment. Miek embodies the insistence on woundedness and the permanence of revolutionary upheaval; however, I would argue that Miek's most tragic flaw is not his incapacity to forgive (which would be the clearest and most trite conclusion to draw from Pak's *Hulk*) but, rather, his incapacity to grasp the systemic nature of racial subjugation. Miek's conceptualization of racial injury, in accordance with the Hulk's ressentiment, is premised upon an individualist moral economy of justice and punishment, ultimately leaving the actual logics of racialization and slavery unchallenged.

As the narrative shifts from *Planet Hulk* to *World War Hulk*, the racial politic surrounding the Hulk shifts, as well. Ultimately, the slave uprising on Sakaar in *Planet Hulk* draws an unambiguous line between its protagonists and antagonists, given the dominant society's status as a racial dictatorship wherein the pink-skinned Imperials equally enslaved and massacred their racial others. However, the bombing of Crown City results in a shift in this clarity: the Hulk and his Warbound travel to Earth to combat Earth's superheroes—all of whom of course possess their own lore and own long-entrenched histories as primary protagonists—in *World War Hulk*, which taints the moral clarity of the Hulk's crusade. The art style shifts correspondingly, as well: in *Planet Hulk*, primarily penciled by Carlo Pagulayan and Aaron Lopresti, there is a beautifully lush vibrancy of color, brighter palettes, and generally more idealized figurations of the characters; in contrast, John Romita Jr.'s art in *World War Hulk* features darker palettes, and harsher, sharper, angled penciling. Pagulayan and Lopresti's artwork produces an operatic spectacle appropriate to the simpler oppositional delineations of conflict in *Planet Hulk*, while Romita's harsher, less idealized style generates the Brechtian alienating effect of making the reader more aware of the comic-as-comic, of the artifice of cartoon abstraction, within the ambivalent *World War Hulk*. The romantic revolutionary fantasy of *Planet Hulk* is a space where ressentiment is necessary, thriving and sustained by a community of like-oppressed peoples, and its off-world setting allows for an easily manageable and uncontroversial allegory for racial oppression on Earth. However, the transition to Earth correspondingly necessitates the imperfect adaptation of this politic into a politically grayer setting, one in which the (other) white male superheroes of the Marvel Earth are held responsible. The transition from Sakaar to Earth reflects the transition, described by Michael Omi and Howard Winant, from racial despotism to racial hegemony, from naked race relations to more diffuse ones. Accordingly, under racial despotism, resistance could be easily consolidated as oppositional:

> Originally framed by slave revolts and *marronage*, by indigenous resistance, and by nationalisms of various sorts, and later by nationalist and equalitarian racial freedom movements, oppositional racial consciousness and depth as *racial resistance*. Just as racial despotism reinforced white supremacy as the master category of racial domination, so too it forged racial unity among the oppressed. (1994, 131, original emphasis)

However, as domination gives way to hegemony, the discourse of liberal color-blindness comes to neutralize and obfuscate race relations, producing ambiguities for racialized subjects regarding the persisting presence of racial subjugation. In the state of ambiguous hegemony, on Earth in *World War Hulk*, ressentiment serves as a nostalgia for racial despotism, for the subjugated but more obviously legible position of the slave. Utilizing Omi and Winant's terminology, we can loosely associate *Planet Hulk's* Sakaar narrative with that of racial dictatorship, and the Hulk's invasion of the Earth in *World War Hulk* with that of racial hegemony, the former reflecting a historical moment of clearer lines of opposition, and the latter reflecting a setting of dispersed culpability.

Furthermore, this transition from unambiguous to ambiguous status of subjugation is additionally reflective of the shifting of Asian American racialization throughout the twentieth and twenty-first centuries, marked by a transition from violent exclusion to neoliberal model minority inclusion, with the history of the former given primacy in the pedagogical fostering of Asian American "consciousness." The model minority positioning of Asians in America, regardless of how "mythological" or ideological the racial formation, nevertheless retains the discursive capacity to performatively actualize, and yet the anti–model minority narrative of Asian American studies has often dismissed the notion through the historical example of exclusion, even when the Asian American subject in question is not historically contiguous with those early Asian American communities. It is a cultural politics of predetermined culpability by individual white agents. That is, the bomb was, and always had been, set by Tony Stark and Reed Richards.

The metaphor is particularly rich, especially given that the Hulk's colleagues ultimately remain indirectly guilty; although Miek had framed the Hulk's human compatriots, the Hulk's very circumstances on Sakaar—both tragic and triumphant—are ultimately the consequence of the nonconsensual exile enacted by his four colleagues. Thus, exclusion, or abjection, still ultimately frames the *Planet Hulk* narrative and serves as the primary frame of intelligibility for the Hulk. Furthermore, an individualist Asian American cultural politics that locates white racism within white subjects and positioning Asian America as solely a victim under a liberal paradigm of racial injury, rather than articulating racial power as a circuitous flow through which any "subject" can participate regardless of position, all too often ignores its own complicity with, and even reliance on, white racism and capital for its own coherence. In relation to the Hulk, recall that Banner, while the victim of the other scientist superheroes' exclusion due to his green-skinned abjection, is also the creator of a weapon of mass destruction, as heinous a contributor to the military–industrial complex as arms manufacturer Tony Stark (Iron Man) is. Although it was not *his* weapon that incinerated his pregnant wife, Banner was certainly responsible for the creation of weapons like it, the Hulk himself being a direct repercussion of that weapon. Consequently, the Hulk is systemically complicit in an analogous industry as that which killed his loved ones.

Yet, as I will explore, there are two crucial moments in the *Planet Hulk* and *World War Hulk* arcs in which the Hulk shifts from a logic of ressentiment to that of masochism. I begin with the climax of *World War Hulk*, in which the Hulk becomes that which had created him to begin with: a bomb.

Bomb, Bottom, and the Racial Shadow: From Ressentiment to Masochism

As the tragic hero confronted with his hamartia, the Hulk *becomes* a bomb immediately after Miek's confession; John Romita Jr.'s art displays a Hulk who begins to glow and emanate a green science-fictional radioactivity; soon the entire U.S. Eastern Seaboard is awash with his essence. When Richards tells the Hulk, "Bruce. It's—it's all right. We'll help you this time—," the Hulk interrupts with "Stop. Without you, none of this would have happened. I'll hate you forever. Almost as much as I hate myself." The Hulk's transformation into that which had originally created him, and that which killed his wife and unborn child—parallels the moment when his self-contempt and self-punishment reach their apogee. Moreover, in becoming the bomb, he threatens to explode into a male orgasm of violence, a Lacanian *jouissance* stemmed from a torturous psychic pain (see Figure 4.2).

The exquisite exploding Hulk, the orgasmic Hulk of radioactive discharge, only arises when psychic punishment is at its peak and he fully confronts his own complicity in the death of his loved ones. Although the Hulk is at his most pained, he is also at his most powerful when he is self-critical and, moreover, when the culpability of oppression cannot be easily individualized. In including himself as a target of punishment upon the tragic confrontation of his hamartia, the Hulk shifts from ressentiment to moral masochism and in doing so crucially illustrates the differences between the two moral and affective economies. Whereas ressentiment thrives off the perceived injustice inflicted upon the subject, masochism feeds off punishment—such is the case in Sigmund Freud's, Theodor Reik's, and Kaja Silverman's respective traditions of moral masochism. Paradoxically, this distinction furthermore places masochism, not ressentiment, in the social domain; the central flaw of ressentiment is its tendency toward liberal individuation, seeking out individual Others who had agentically "chosen" to be powerful, while the subject of masochism, in Silverman's words, "loudly proclaims that his meaning comes to him from the Other, prostrates himself before the gaze even as he solicits it, exhibits his castration for all to see, and revels in the sacrificial basis of the social contract" (1992, 206). While ressentiment

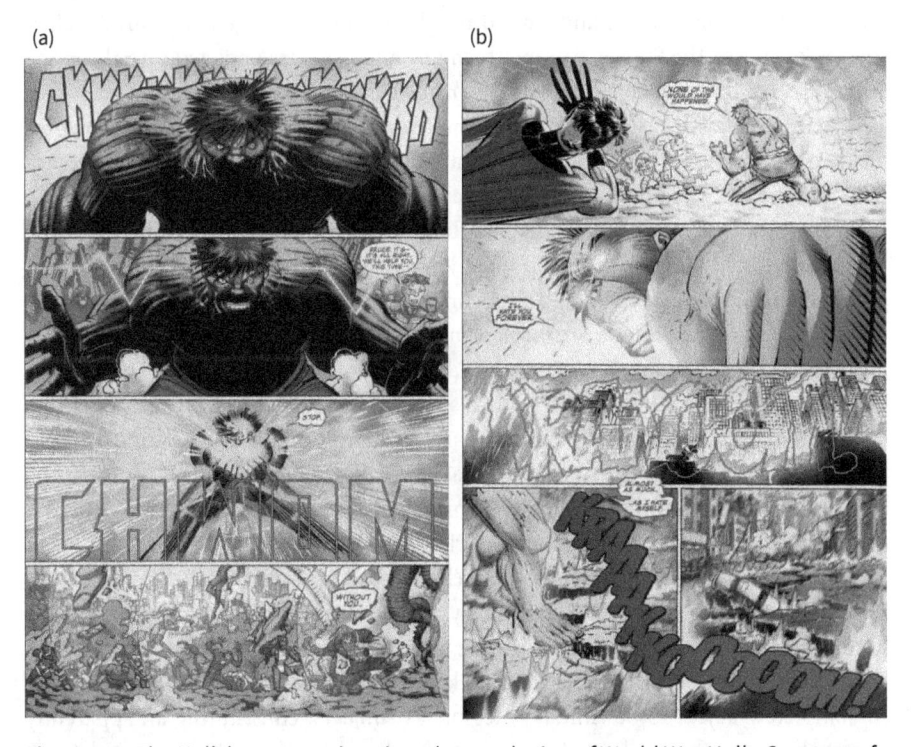

Figure 4.2 The Hulk becomes a bomb at the conclusion of World War Hulk. Courtesy of Marvel Worldwide, Inc.

actively hates the oppressive Other, it implicitly disavows its absolute reliance upon it, thus actually magnifying this relationship; in contrast, moral masochism proclaims this reliance and in doing so possesses the capacity to dismantle it. In the case of the Hulk, masochism both exposes and stages the power relation of racial subjugation; the Hulk's becoming-bomb illustrates the uncomfortable erotics that ressentiment disavows. As a consequence, continues Silverman, "The male masochist magnifies the losses and divisions upon which cultural identity is based, refusing to be sutured or recompensed. In short, he radiates a negativity inimical of the social order" (1992, 206). In effect, this refusal of recompense disrupts the entire moral economy of ressentiment, operating as a form of Foucauldian counter-conduct that pries open the circuits of racial power altogether.[8]

In the conclusion of *World War Hulk*, the Hulk threatens to explode only when it is clear that his superhero colleagues, Miek, and the Hulk himself are all actors within a wider, nebulous flow of racial power. Unlike in ressentiment, the Hulk realizes here that he is not "outside" the province of subjection, but thoroughly enmeshed in it. Correspondingly, as the Hulk becomes-bomb, he begins to radiate, deterritorializing the boundaries of his body. It is this self-punishment, rather than the punishment of the individuated Others, that maximizes the Hulk's reach.

However, in *Planet Hulk*, the Hulk's masochistic tendencies include more than this overt, discharging masculinity. The Hulk demonstrates the recuperative capacity of masochism, and bottoming and pain, through the Hulk's engagement with the alien species known as the Spikes. Among the many alien species depicted on Sakaar, the Spikes are the most abject and horrifying: historically reviled and perceived on Sakaar as a semi-sentient species of pathogen that could transform its victims into zombielike abominations, the Spikes are revealed to be normally benign energy beings who traverse the vacuum of space but have been enthralled as a biological weapon by the Imperials. Once the Hulk learns that the Imperials coerced and manipulated the Spikes into terrorizing the diverse population of Sakaar to serve as a unifying, scapegoated enemy, he enlists their help in the final stages of the slave revolt.

In *Planet Hulk*, the Spikes are faceless, massified, inscrutable, and literally yellow; if the Hulk reflects Asian American masculine ressentiment, then the Spikes are emblematic of the Oriental horde. In some respects, the Spikes are what Sau-Ling Wong has termed the "racial shadow," the figure upon whom undesirable Asianness is projected, thus "render[ing] alien what is, in fact, literally inalienable, thereby disowning and distancing it" (Wong 1993, 78). A consistent trait in Asian American cultural production, the "racial shadow" is the orientalized figure against which the Asian American subject is defined, scorned largely because the racial shadow confirms the stereotypes projected by white supremacy, or because the Asian American subject has internalized such attitudes (a critique famously problematized by David Henry Hwang's first play, *FOB*). Similarly, the Spikes, in their faceless, yellow hordeness, are so completely abject to be (initially) legible as subjects, constituting an apparently chaotic threat to the Hulk's resistance until he discovers the exiled Spike elders. In *Planet Hulk*, however, the relationship between the Hulk and the Spikes is not quite analogous to the trope defined by Wong; although he initially battles them, the Hulk does not exactly disavow or dissociate from the Spikes. Still, the Spikes are a curious member of the alliance, the abject-of-the-abject, the entities who are so utterly beyond legibility as subjects, and whose assistance proves indispensable to the victory of the revolt.

But the most noteworthy moment of the Spikes occurs after the overthrow of the Red King, during the Hulk's short reign as monarch: the Hulk sits upon his throne and spends seven straight hours allowing the Spikes, still insatiably hungry, to feed off his body, so that they are no longer driven to consume the other people of Sakaar. In allowing the Spikes to feed off him, the Hulk enters a self-canceling economy of weakness and strength. The Spikes penetrate his body in multiple points, draining him and inflicting considerable pain, but this pain also paradoxically feeds the rage that sustains his strength and, by extension, his existence as the Hulk. Unlike nearly every other instance in which the Hulk is subjected to hurt, the Hulk instead submits willingly and does not retaliate as in ressentiment. Instead, Hulk is in effect the sexual bottom, the penetrated, his strength demonstrated not through his destructive capacity but his perhaps-feminine capacity to endure, in a Christlike, messianic manner (see Figure 4.3).

Figure 4.3 The Spikes feed off of the Hulk during the Hulk's reign as King of Sakaar in Planet Hulk. Courtesy of Marvel Worldwide, Inc.

Paired together, Hulk's self-sacrifice to the Spikes in *Planet Hulk* and his orgasmic self-destruction in *World War Hulk* gesture toward a cultural-political imagination beyond ressentiment, beyond an idealization of resistance and a contempt for the privileged. Rather, the racial-political imagination of Pak's *Hulk* gestures to something more radical: a bottoming masochism that confronts the omnipresence of racial power itself, presenting even the possibility of healing and reconciliation through the harnessing of its flows. Through the fantasyscape of the *Incredible Hulk*, Pak demonstrates the political limitations of a racialized masculinity premised upon ressentiment while opening the hope for a racial subjecthood founded upon self-critique. The self-punishing masochistic Hulk, the Hulk of Foucauldian counter-conduct, as opposed to the Hulk of outwardly directed ressentiment, enacts what Nguyen Tan Hoang calls "a politics of bottomhood," characterized not by a wielding of power, but a surrendering of it:

> we do not always have to attribute resistance and subversion to gay Asian American bottomhood in order to justify its existence and accord it serious analysis. In certain circumstances, bottoming entails the gleeful surrendering of power; its pleasures do not always depend on resistance and subversion. Even if we ascribe a transgressiveness to bottomhood, as many gay male critics rightly do, part of this transgressiveness involves the very relinquishment of power. (2014, 20)

Thus, a (masochistic) politics of bottomhood reflects not the direct wielding of a power, as in ressentiment, but possibly the abdication of it, or perhaps the reconfiguration of its terms. Bottoming becomes a way of experiencing power while refusing to be its agent. The mode of masochistic bottoming is the *feeling* of power—the Foucauldian calculus of force relations—and thus *awareness* of it, through the body, coupled with its possible deterritorialization. To quote Darieck Scott,

> This is a politics of the bottom, a desire to (a will to) love and live the bottom for its bottomness without surrendering to or ceding the lion's share of the pleasure to the top—indeed, in a way flamboyantly, exuberantly *ignoring* the top except insofar as he dutifully presses on the levers of pleasure. (2010, 254, emphasis in original)

It is a politics that is, according to Scott, "genuinely queer" (2010, 254), upending the normative associations between penetrator/penetrated and empowered/dispossessed. The psychic and physical penetrability of the Hulk can either result in the diffusive if uncontrollable masculine chaos of becoming-bomb, or in the moving gesture to nourish the Spikes, the most racially abject and most traumatizing symbols of historic conflict.

If we understand the Spikes as the "racial shadow" of abject Asianness, the Hulk's willing surrender to their penetration reflects, additionally, a surrendering to the stereotype, to the inconvenient reflection of abjection. The Spikes literally fill the Hulk with their tendrils, their infectious orientalness, and it is only by the Hulk's own superpower, acquired through the violence of self-immolation, that the Hulk can voluntarily withstand and nourish their hunger. Greg Pak's Hulk, in this brief moment of messianic tenderness, reminds us of the possibilities of a reparative ethics, made possible only when the figure of ressentiment becomes a figure of masochism.

Afterword: The Totally Awesome Burden of Representation

> At first I read trailblazing Asian hunk
> then maybe thick, amorous, hung
> and kapow! the punchline
>
> is in the fiction. Because we can't
> be hung, as in my cousin was named
> *Hung*, Vietnamese for manly, brave
>
> and had it legally changed at thirteen
> I'm sure you know why. Imagine:
> forced to forfeit what your mother gave you
>
> because of every person who's made dumb
> jokes about eggrolls, about eyes slanted
> like the eaves of buildings
>
> in the rain. I hope you've never felt that,
> Ammy, I hope you're terrifying, aggressive,
> haughty as I devour in print. Quaking
>
> the world with your steps. I wish
> us your thunderous, amazing haunches.
> Come green man, cousin,
>
> let us be two-faced, ambitious,
> hungry. Tactless Asians.
>
> Toothy, artful, heroic.
> Toxic, angry, hellish.
> —Eric Tran, "Amadeus Cho, Totally Awesome Hulk" (2019)

Greg Pak's *Planet Hulk* and *World War Hulk* offer an important parable for Asian America, but from late 2015 to mid-2018, Greg Pak returned to Marvel Comics to pen the *Hulk* once more. However, this time, the Hulk is not Bruce Banner, but his Korean American supporter, Pak's creation, Amadeus Cho; Cho extracted the Hulk's essence from his mentor Banner with nanites in order to save Banner from an overdose of radiation and then installed the Hulk essence into himself. Following in the footsteps of African Americans Monica Rambeau, Miles Morales, and Sam Wilson donning the roles of Captain Marvel, Spider-Man, and Captain America, respectively, Amadeus Cho serves a groundbreaking nonwhite replacement for a previously white top-tier Marvel superhero.

In Eric Tran's poem, the Hulk explicitly comes to symbolize the figure of Asian American masculine empowerment that I have been discussing throughout the chapter, not only through his physical power, but also through his affective, resentful qualities: "two faced, ambitious, / hungry. Tactless Asians. / Toothy, artful, heroic. / Toxic, angry, hellish." Tran, an award-winning queer Vietnamese American poet as well as a psychiatrist specializing in LGBTQ mental health, establishes a clear affinity with the Green Goliath, attaching the Hulk's spectacular unrespectability to a moral economy of humiliation and racial castration. Greg Pak's conversion of Cho himself into the Hulk makes this affinity between Asian American masculinity and the Hulk even clearer.

Yet, it is immediately apparent from the first issue that *The Totally Awesome Hulk* shares far more tonal commonality with the comics centering around Amadeus Cho than that of the Hulk; Cho-Hulk is both distinctly Asian (and Korean) American and, curiously, considerably less angry. As a consequence, *The Totally Awesome Hulk* is much lighter and more whimsical than the violent epics of *Planet Hulk* and *World War Hulk* and appears to be primarily targeted to a younger audience. The opening sequence, for example, features teenaged Cho eating a series of hamburgers and fries on a beach boardwalk as a two-headed turtle monster emerges from an ocean wave, threatening a young Asian American toddler and his bikini-clad African American babysitter. Cho swiftly transforms into the Hulk (who now sports board shorts and gelled hair) and battles the creature to highly slapstick, comedic effect, all the while flirting with the babysitter. Unlike Banner's Hulk, Cho's Hulk seems to retain all of Cho's character aspects, including his eloquence, humor, and adolescent prurience, and additionally lacks the Hulk's characteristic rage.

However, in the next three issues, the Hulk begins to assume a blatantly masochistic position. Starting in Issue 2, the Hulk begins battling a new foe, Lady Hellbender, an alien Viking-esque warrior woman from the planet Seknarf Nine who has come to Earth to collect monsters. Intriguingly, as Cho-Hulk (at one point, nicknamed "Chulk") battles her, they develop sexual tension, with the Hulk usually finding himself in a compromised, submissive position to her. The covers of issues 2 and 4, drawn by Frank Cho and colored by Sonia Oback, illustrate this masochistic Hulk quite explicitly.

As shown in Figure 4.4, in Issue 2, a muscled, red-headed, and corset-armored Hellbender stands triumphant, wielding a sword in her left hand with a club slung over her right shoulder, her foot resting on the head of the Hulk, who is comically face down and defeated amid rocky debris. In Issue 4, Hellbender is straddling the Hulk and cradling his submissive face, about to kiss, while the Hulk's arms and torso are

Figure 4.4 The covers for issues 2 and 4 of Totally Awesome Hulk. Penciling by Frank Cho, coloring by Sonia Oback. Courtesy of Marvel Worldwide, Inc.

completely bound up in chains, flames dancing in the background. The background text of Issue 4 reads, "Hulk and Lady Hellbender sitting in a tree . . ." with a talk bubble above the Hulk completing the rhyme, "K-I-S-S-I-N-G . . ."

It has not been common for *Hulk* comic covers to depict its hypermasculine protagonist in such compromised and feminized positions, let alone at the mercy of a woman, and eroticized. The images on these covers neatly summarize the relationship between the Hulk and Hellbender as depicted in the comics themselves, one in which the Hulk is more comfortably masochistic and submissive, rather than being driven by the moral economy of ressentiment. And although the opening issues of *The Totally Awesome Hulk* are far more lighthearted and comedic,[9] lacking the angst, epic ambition, and aesthetic virtuosity of *Planet Hulk* and *World War Hulk*, it can be seen as an actualization of masochism's eventual triumph over ressentiment and melancholia, corresponding to the actualization of the Asianness of the Hulk himself. And while placed into a number of masochistic encounters with Lady Hellbender, the Amadeus Cho "Totally Awesome" Hulk does not come close to experiencing the level of self-loathing or anguish of Banner Hulk, especially in the beginning of the *Totally Awesome* run. The mechanics of transformation are different for Amadeus Cho than they were for Bruce Banner: Cho can consciously transform into the Hulk through a control panel on his wrist, rather than the internal force of ressentiment. This is different from the Banner/Hulk dynamic—Banner's transformation into the Hulk is triggered strictly through emotion, and the physical presence of the Hulk also corresponds to the presence of the Hulk's personality (when you see the Hulk, he is the Hulk). In contrast, Amadeus Cho can physically transform into the Hulk but remain, in effect, in control of his own body (when you see the Hulk, he is not necessarily the Hulk), but the injection of the Hulk's essence into him has allowed a Hulk personality of ressentiment to lurk within his psyche anyway, in a repressed form. Pak represents this through an on-the-nose psychic metaphor of Cho driving a car through the desert, with the Hulk locked in the trunk, which is chained shut; Cho remains "in the driver's seat" of their collective personhood through most of these comics.

Over the course of three years of comic series, chiefly in *The Totally Awesome Hulk* but then continuing in the *Civil War II*, *Weapon of Mutant Destruction*, and then the *Return to Planet Hulk* and *World War Hulk II*, Pak takes Amadeus Cho's Hulk through a series of tribulations, including Cho's mournful reactions to the (temporary) death of Bruce Banner in *Civil War #3* in 2016. But even throughout that crisis, Amadeus Cho seems to retain control over the internal force of the increasingly aggressive Hulk in his inner psyche. Cho, even while in Hulk form, remains good-natured and friendly, not overtaken by rage, but the Hulk personality constantly struggles to escape his psychic confines.

This eventually changes when Pak effectively repeats the Planet Hulk narrative: Cho's Hulk is called to Sakaar to liberate its downtrodden once again, this time oppressed by a postapocalyptic tyrant called "the Warlord." Cho wins the Sakaaran people's freedom, but at the cost of allowing the Hulk personality to seize primary control of his body. Much like in the original *World War Hulk*, Cho's Hulk returns to Earth in *World War Hulk II*, while in the metaphorical space that represents Cho's psyche, Amadeus Cho is now locked in the trunk of the car where the Hulk was once trapped. Although he begins as brashly benevolent, the Hulk grows increasingly menacing as his fellow superheroes criticize his brutality to a threatening supervillain, and eventually he lashes out at his former allies. Throughout the battle, Amadeus Cho duels the Hulk in the landscape of their shared psyche—Cho is eventually triumphant over the Hulk, who, cornered, beckons Cho to finish him off:

> Go ahead. Do it. Then you can pretend I never existed. You won't lose much…just your resentment of every kid who ever bullied you…your guilt over your parents' deaths…and that anger you feel whenever you see anyone who's been forgotten and rejected.

Cho hesitates and, rather than killing off the Hulk, reaches out his hand to touch him, merges with him, assimilating him completely into his psyche, their bodies visually melting and blending together at the point of contact, and they form a new, consolidated hero, "Brawn." Thus, Amadeus Cho comes to reconcile with the Hulk, the force of resentment that he had spent most of his time and energy repressing and, as Brawn, more fully integrates fury into his regime of masculine, rational mastery.

Cho's relationship to ressentiment is curious. He had originally felt allyship with the Hulk in the first *World War Hulk* precisely because he identified with the injustice that the Hulk had undergone. But unlike Banner's Hulk, Cho was not strictly governed by ressentiment—he identified it and saw it as a site of common cause while stopping short of allowing it to become the raison d'être of his subjectivity. Upon assimilating Banner's Hulk essence into himself, Cho pledged to repress the vengeful tendencies that were given personification by the Hulk. In this sense, the masochistic Cho Hulk and the integrated Brawn may represent Pak's *prescriptive* Asian American masculinity, while Pak's ressentiment-driven Banner Hulk may represent Pak's *descriptive* Asian American masculinity. In this sense, *The Totally Awesome Hulk* and Brawn provide the positive outcome of my very argument about Pak's earlier Banner Hulks. The trade-off, however, of the positive outcome, the role model, is the disappearance of the productive anguish that produced the conditions of its appearance.

The undermining of ressentiment in *The Totally Awesome Hulk* may also inadvertently produce a cautionary tale—that despite the critique that I have set forth in this chapter, ressentiment remains a necessary component in the dialectic of Asian American masculinity. A Cho without ressentiment may seem more self-actualized, but he is also, paradoxically, an Asian American without history. The repression of ressentiment for an aspirational self-actualization also reflects a yearning for a strand of neoliberal post-racialism in which agency is unbounded by the constraints of social stratification. Through the majority of *The Totally Awesome Hulk*, there is masochism without ressentiment—and this may simply be model minority masochism itself, a masochism of seamless integration. A comparison between the 2006–2007 *Incredible Hulk* and the 2015–2018 *Totally Awesome Hulk* reveals the political necessity for a dialectic between these two moral economies, which resurfaces in the latter run only at the very end with *World War Hulk II*. It is in the final conflict between Cho and the inner Hulk, and the synthesis of Brawn, produced through the total deterritorialization of their selves, that Cho approaches an integration of historicity and futurity.

It may also simply be possible that the comparative thematic depth of *Planet Hulk* and *World War Hulk*'s Asian Americanness—that is, the gripping dialectic between ressentiment and masochism—is perhaps owed ironically to Banner's ostensible whiteness, since Pak is not tethered to any political pressure for Asian American idealization in a continued age of representational scarcity (although again, it is curious that this idealization manifests as masochistic). This suggests one final layer of masochistic dissonance: that is, that Greg Pak's Hulk can be most resonantly Asian when he is not. Or, to be more precise, a disidentificatory Hulk is a more critically engaging Hulk than an identificatory one. Inasmuch as Pak's Hulk *performs* narrative Asian Americanness rather than phenotypically *representing* it, he is freer to critically interrogate the psychic and affective life of racialization. Or, perhaps, it is that Banner-Hulk feels more affectively Asian American precisely because his Asian Americanness requires a degree of imagination, lying just slightly out of reach, like the pleasure that awaits just beyond the torturer's whip.

5

Asians Never Stare into Your Eyes

Affective Flatness and the Techno-Orientalization of the Self in Tao Lin's *Taipei* and Tan Lin's *Insomnia and the Aunt*

In 2011, columnist Wesley Yang published an article entitled "Paper Tigers" in *New York* magazine, a confessional and often-masochistic reflection on Asian masculinity. In the opening pages, Yang writes,

> Here is what I sometimes suspect my face signifies to other Americans: an invisible person, *barely distinguishable from a mass of faces that resemble it*. A conspicuous person standing apart from the crowd and yet devoid of any individuality. An icon of so much that the culture pretends to honor but that it in fact patronizes and exploits. Not just people "who are good at math" and play the violin, but *a mass of stifled, repressed, abused, conformist quasi-robots* who simply do not matter, socially or culturally.
>
> I've always been of two minds about this sequence of stereotypes. On the one hand, it offends me greatly that anyone would think to apply them to me, or to anyone else, simply on the basis of facial characteristics. On the other hand, *it also seems to me that there are a lot of Asian people to whom they apply*. (2011, 1–2, emphasis added)

Here, Yang spells out the terms in which he feels inferiority as an Asian American male—the stereotype by which he is perceived ("a mass of stifled, repressed, abused, conformist quasi-robots"), coupled with the sense that in fact, from his perspective, the stereotype holds at least a modicum (or more) of validity ("it also seems to me that there are a lot of Asian people to whom they apply"). The lived experience of existing under the weight of a dominant stereotype recalls the articulations already well-laid out in Black theories of racial subjectification, notably W. E. B. DuBois' notion of double consciousness, but perhaps even more predominantly, the work of Frantz Fanon in *Black Skin, White Masks*. In his oft-cited chapter, alternately titled "The Fact of Blackness" or "The Lived Experience of the Black Man," Fanon describes the moment of being hailed by a young child on the street, the call of "Look, a negro!" immediately providing Fanon a phenomenological awareness of his own body, via an apparatus that Fanon called the "epidermal racial schema." Importantly, writes Fanon, this schema under the white gaze is a slow construction of my self as body in a spatial and temporal world.... It is not imposed on me; it is rather a definitive structuring of my self and the world—definitive because it creates a genuine dialectic between my body and the world. (2008, 91)

This epidermal racial schema describes the experiential structure of being made aware of one's own raced body, and accordingly, the perceptions and positionalities accompanying that body in a white supremacist order.

Of course, the lived experience of Wesley Yang's Asian American man differs wildly in terms of the historical and racial specificities that accompany Asiatic racial form, as opposed to that of Blackness. Yet, the phenomenological awareness of one's own body as raced, as placed in a grid of racial intelligibility, follows an analogous, if not identical, mechanism. The interpellative hail of the little white child, whether literal, unconscious, or discursive, produces an immediate, insecure consciousness of the misshapen body, and in the case of Asian American maleness, this body takes a machine-like form. Additionally, to Yang's overtly self-loathing dismay, there seems to be a "truth" to the stereotype to which he is being assigned. Not unlike Frank Chin in the 1970s, who bemoaned Asian Americans complicit with white orientalist stereotypes,[1] Yang anguishes over the fact that Asian Americanness may in fact consist of servility to the white racial order; the ultimate irony, then, is that Yang (again, not unlike Frank Chin) responds by performing a kind of masculinist assimilationism, writing: "Let me summarize my feelings toward Asian values: Fuck filial piety, Fuck grade-grubbing. Fuck Ivy League mania. Fuck deference to authority. Fuck humility and hard work. Fuck harmonious relations. Fuck sacrificing for the future. Fuck earnest, striving middle-class servility" (2011, 2). Without problematizing the notion of what "Asian values" are, Yang abjects the castrated racial position to which Asianness has been assigned, but accepting the terms with which orientalist white supremacy has essentialized "Asianness." He is, in effect, attempting to escape the techno-orientalized robotic condition to which he defaults.

Importantly, it is his body that serves as the fulcrum of Yang's angst. As his apparently shirtless, unhappy photo portrait in the "Paper Tigers" article exacerbates, it is the appearance of his body that signifies his apparent roboticism and mindless adherence to "Asian values." The image of Yang's face serves as synecdoche; while it is not the "zone of nonbeing" as Fanon has described Blackness, it is a zone of de-individuation and robotic unfeeling. As problematic as Yang's article is, rife with a reinscription of orientalist tropes and embedded with misogyny, it gestures to the question of what it means to live in an Asian male body in the American racial system. And in Yang's account, that body is, masochistically, inextricable from the techno-oriental mass. Yang represents a recent tendency of masculine East Asian American authors who have become preoccupied with affective flatness in the contemporary moment. Moreover, this affective racialization has a through line to the techno-oriental interpellation of Vincent Chin; as elaborated in the opening two chapters, the murder of Vincent Chin was a material node of techno-orientalism, the discursive optic through which

Asianness and machineness enter a co-constitutive relationship within the U.S. racial imaginary. The Chin case demonstrates a 1980s-era anxiety that racialized a transnational economy that heralded the decline of U.S. industrialism, and how the oriental horde easily maps onto the fear of mechanization in the U.S. labor force at large. The condition of Asian American model minority masochism, then, occurs within this context, the pleasures and pains of racialization, enmeshed in a process of subjectification that is necessarily premised upon the undoing of itself.

When considering Asian American masochism under techno-orientalism, I have thus far concentrated on a psychoanalytically informed discussion of political social drama and its performative aftermath. However, in this chapter, I move more explicitly to the realm of affect: that is to say, in the words of Deleuze and Guattari, "not a personal feeling, nor is it a characteristic; it is the effectuation of a power of the pack that throws the self into upheaval and makes it reel" (1987, 240). Deleuze and Guattari's elaboration of affect[2] gestures to affect as having a social, collective, and outwardly disseminating function, a "stickiness" as Sara Ahmed would come to describe. However, I make the somewhat counterintuitive move to center this discussion of affect in Asian America neither with the work of Deleuze and Guattari, or Tomkins, but the late 20th-century Marxist formulation of Frederic Jameson's *Postmodernism*. Jameson, who of course encapsulates the postmodernity of the sociopolitical moment of the late 1970s and early 1980s, characterizes the condition of postmodernity[3] as having the "waning of affect." Jameson thus points to a kind of affective absence that arrives with postmodern schizophrenia, a blankness and an absence of "feeling." However, this affective flatness bears with it a de-individuating power:

> The end of the bourgeois ego, or monad, no doubt brings with it the end of the psychopathologies of that ego—what I have been calling the waning of affect. But it means the end of much more—the end, for example, of style, in the sense of the unique and the personal, the end of the distinctive individual brush stroke (as symbolized by the emergent primacy of mechanical reproduction). As for expression and feelings or emotions, the liberation, in contemporary society, from the older *anomie* of the centered subject may also mean not merely a liberation from anxiety but a liberation from every other kind of feeling as well, since there is no longer a self present to do the feeling. (Jameson 1991, 15, emphasis in original)

Here, Jameson connects the "waning of affect" with the end of "style," and with it, the "unique," the "personal," the "distinctive individual brush stroke." The affective absence of postmodernity contrasts with Jameson's description of modernity: in modernity, the individual monad struggles and screams under the alienation of industrial urbanity, whereas in postmodernity, the monad's capacity to feel evaporates altogether. The waning of affect, then, bears the capacity to annihilate the individual monad of bourgeois personhood, suggesting a relationality instead premised upon the unfeeling and de-individuated mass.

Jameson's discussion of the "waning of affect" is particularly provocative in a U.S. mainstream moment dominated by smartphones and cyberculture, wherein the loss of analog "personal connection" and a nostalgia for non-mediated sociality run amok within popular culture and critique. Within the contemporary technological milieu, which has witnessed a seeming flatness of affect in the material world, paired with a proliferation and reification of affective states across social media, we are forced to re-interrogate what "affect" and its "waning" mean today. Jameson himself would later revise the "waning of affect" in *The Antinomies of Realism*. The waning of affect that inaugurates the "perpetual present" that he discusses in *Postmodernism* gives way to something else, that is, a "'reduction to the body,' inasmuch as the body is all that remains in any tendential reduction of experience to the present as such" (1991, 28). The body, then, becomes the site that "begins to know more global waves of generalized sensations, and it is these which ... I will here call affect" (1991, 28). Within Jameson's more recent theoretical landscape, affect is not so much waning as it is the primary location of contemporary sensory presence.

And yet, I would argue that Jameson's affective "reduction to the body" is not a refutation of his earlier formulation of affective "waning" but, rather, of the contemporary neoliberal subject's dependence on affect. This is particularly the case in this second decade of the 21st century, this condition of so-called postmodernity that has exponentially grown via the rise of ubiquitous digital technology and cyberculture. In *The Interface Effect*, Alexander Galloway powerfully argues that in such a computation and informatic-driven present, affect in fact explodes:

> Profiles, not personas, drive the computer. Even as a certain kind of modern affect is in recession (following Jameson's famous argument about "the waning of affect" under postmodernity), there seems to be more affect today than ever before. Books are written on the subject. Conferences are devoted to it. The net is nothing if not the grand parade of personality profiles, wants and needs, projected egos, "second" selves and "second" lives. This is all true. So the triumph of affect is also its undoing. The waning of an older affective mode comes at the moment of its absolute rationalization into software. At the moment when something is perfected, it is dead. (2012, 12)

Galloway's description of the proliferation of affect on the Internet also reconciles the earlier Jameson with the later, that is, that the affect of modernity becomes "rationalized" into the computer interface. I suggest that we read Jameson's "waning of affect" not as a reduction of affect—when, in fact, affect is being proliferated and marketed at unprecedented levels—but rather, as an *alienation from* affect, a growing inability to catch it and hold it down as it flies quickly through the air, or as it is quite literally codified. To return to affectual absence, the ostensibly "affectless" figure remains a particularly dystopian and uncanny one; this is a figure who receives but neither digests nor emits affect.

In considering the condition of postmodernity—or alternatively, in Mark Fisher's terms, the current period of "capitalist realism"—some scholars have already critiqued Jameson in not being attendant the dimension of race and gender, and that in fact, the postmodern condition is nothing "new" to the historically marginalized: women, racialized subjects, queer persons, and so on.[4] In any event, the "affect" that Jameson mourns (not unlike the "aura" that Walter Benjamin mourns in "The Work of Art in the Age of Mechanical Reproduction") is itself racialized. As José Muñoz, Fred Moten, Mel Chen, Rachel C. Lee, and many others have argued, affect is not only understood in racial terms, but is itself a racializing apparatus.[5] In this respect, Jameson's "waning of affect" points to a particular racialized figure that haunts the moment of postmodernity: the Asiatic. Whereas, as Muñoz writes, the Latina/o figure is characterized by an "excess" of affect (which is, of course, more reflective of its visual indecipherability by the white gaze than any such "actual" excess), the techno-orientalized subject is characterized by its absence or deficiency. Within the terms established by Jameson, the techno-orientalized subject, associated with mass production and lack of feeling, is perhaps the uncannily cybernetic scion of postmodernity itself. Indeed, Stephen Hong Sohn has already pointed to the affective dimension of techno-oriental racialization:

> In traditional Orientalism, the East often is configured as backwards, anti-progressive, and primitive. In this respect, techno-Orientalism might suggest a different conception of the East, except for the fact that the very inhuman qualities projected onto Asian bodies create a dissonance with these alternative temporalities. Even as these Alien/Asians conduct themselves with superb technological efficiency and capitalist expertise, their *affectual absence* resonates as undeveloped or, worse still, a retrograde humanism. (2008, 8, emphasis mine)

In Sohn's formulation, there is a temporal dissonance between the technologically hyper-advanced techno-oriental and the "retrograde" or "undeveloped" affectual absence associated with Asianness. On this nuance, I disagree slightly—alongside Jameson, I argue that the affective absence associated with Asiatic racial form is not reflective of a temporal retrograde as Sohn does, but a dystopian futurity that postmodernism ominously heralds. I contend that the "affectual absence" of Asianness signals the techno-orientalization described in the previous chapter, the animate but unfeeling body that relentlessly performs a kind of mechanical, uncreative labor long associated with orientalization in the Americas.[6] As I aim to demonstrate through this chapter, affect, or the lack thereof, is itself a technology of racialization.[7]

To this effect, if we consider the racialization of Asian Americans within affective terms, with parameters articulated by a contemporary neoliberal, digitally mediated structure of feeling described by both Jameson and Galloway, then we must consider techno-oriental affect and the particularly unique role that Asiatic racialization plays within this social context. Whether "affectual absence" or "affective flatness," this dimension of Asiatic racialization is attached to a long-standing association of Asian inscrutability, a key cultural and affective characteristic of orientalizing optics that depends on the construction of an opaque, culturally impenetrable other that beckons for Western epistemic mastery. Perhaps unsurprisingly, this Asian inscrutability takes on gendered and often erotically charged dimensions. The construction of East Asian affective flatness was on full display in early-20th-century evaluations of breakthrough Japanese American actor Sessue Hayakawa, whose "cat-like, implacable cruelty, his mysterious brutality" (Miyao 2007, 4) was the inspiration of the French aesthetic concept of *photogenie* (Miyao 2007, 5), in which outer stoicism suggested an inner intensity. But whereas Hayakawa's inscrutability was both a dimension of his sex appeal and an inspiration for modernist cinematic aesthetics, this same affective flatness would become the source of desexualization and alienation for Wesley Yang a century later. In a more contemporary context, Vivian L. Huang adroitly theorizes Asian inscrutability within the domain of Asian American femininity, enabling a "curious relationality ... that allows for possible intimacy and exploitation" (2018, 197). In her reading of Japanese American performance artists Yoko Ono and Laurel Nakadate, Huang argues that inscrutability offers a creative potential for Asian American femmes, that "Inscrutability takes different forms, or it may be more accurate to say that the judgment of something as inscrutable alerts us to the dawning articulation of a new form" (2018, 198). The opaqueness of inscrutability, argues Huang, enables the object of the gaze to become the observer, to look back upon the beholder, and to queer relationality itself, a possibility that evades the masculine heterosexist economy of value implicit in Wesley Yang's essay.

Read together, both the early-20th-century appraisals of Hayakawa's masculine inscrutability and Huang's theorization of feminine inscrutability gesture to a certain sense of productive potential in the potential self-orientalization of inscrutability, although the contemporary rise of digital mass media complicates its associated affectual flatness. After all, Asian Americans are notably "wired"; as early as 2001, the Pew Research Center has noted that "Asian-American Internet users are ... the Net's most active users" (Spooner 2001), utilizing the Internet at a far higher rate than any other ethnic group in the United States. I will not sociologically conjecture here as to the reasons why, but I cite this fact in order to highlight that Internet culture has come to be associated with a large part of Asian American lived experience, and that as a consequence, Asian Americans have a particular investment in the technologically mediated episteme of postmodernity. Asianness itself—that is to say, the racializing apparatus that coheres meaning around the signifier of "Asian"—has become to some degree wedded to this mediation in the contemporary moment.

Like Huang, I am less interested in refuting the notion of the unfeeling, mechanical, techno-orientalized Asian; rather, I am more invested in exploring the lived, embodied experience of the Asian American subject undergoing masochistic subjectification under the regime of techno-orientalized double consciousness. How to paint the interior life of a subject racialized by exterior absence? Furthermore, this chapter asks: Can literal high technology operate as a technology of the self for such subjects, comprising objects of masochistic attachment under a racialized postmodernity? Moreover, this chapter interrogates the psycho-sensory substance of racialization itself: How does race function as the mold for molten experience even when demonstrations of racism (overt, structural, or otherwise) are conspicuously absent? I examine two contemporary works of literature by Asian American authors: the 2013 semi-autobiographical novel *Taipei* by "alt-lit" author Tao Lin, and the 2011 experimental memoir *Insomnia and the Aunt* by multimedia artist Tan Lin. Both *Taipei* and *Insomnia and the Aunt* figure central Asian American characters who ostensibly conform to the "affective flatness" outlined by Jameson, blurring the boundary between the body and technologized mediation in the production of self. Unlike much of the canon of Asian American Bildungsroman prose, these texts do not contain overt moments of racism and othering, yet they provide affective and phenomenological explorations of living in and perceiving a world in which one has long already been racialized. However, both texts treat the subject of race and Asian Americanness differently: whereas *Taipei* attempts postraciality, actively resisting identification of Asian American literature and grasping toward a disembodied whiteness, *Insomnia and the Aunt* explicitly examines the relationship between technological mediation and racial subjectification. Moreover, both *Taipei* and *Insomnia and the Aunt* are equally racially attached to the computer or television *screen*, an object that haunts the techno-orientalized face in that it not only represents affective flatness; it also displays affect flatly.

The Face, the Mass, the Screen: Phenomenological Technoscapes and Masochistic Coldness in Tao Lin's *Taipei*

Tao Lin's 2013 semiautobiographical[8] novel *Taipei* is a nihilistic demonstration of the affective flatness resulting from technological mediation. *Taipei* has garnered a degree of critical attention primarily through this stylistic distinctiveness, and its unerring fidelity to remaining within the haze it constructs. In tracing the story of Paul, the young Taiwanese American alt-lit author (whom we can ostensibly identify as a proxy for Tao Lin himself), Tao Lin sketches Paul's life as unapologetically hollow, consisting of a series of shallow surfaces and emotional alienation for which there is no true outside. Stylistically and topically, *Taipei* can be read as emblematic of Tao Lin's oeuvre, and arguably of the "alt-lit movement" of which Lin became emblematic. A short-lived literary "movement," the term "alt-lit" was coined by author Cory Stephens, according to *The YOLO Pages* poetry anthology, in the summer of 2011 to describe "hipster" literature (Roggenbuck et al. 2014, 6). Central to the alt-lit aesthetic is an all-pervasive irony and enmeshment with Internet culture, embracing the epistemology of its early-21st-century First World moment. The editors of *The YOLO Pages*, for example, note "roughly half of the contributors of this book are under 25 at the time of publishing, having grown up with the internet as an integral part of their lives" (Roggenbuck et al. 2014, 5). Tao Lin is one such contributor, but more than any other work from alt lit, his novel *Taipei* has achieved the widest distribution and critical attention.

Tao Lin is also, according to compelling accounts, a sexual predator. His former girlfriend and fellow alt-lit writer E. R. Kennedy accused Lin of sexual abuse and plagiarism on Twitter in September of 2014, a year after *Taipei*'s publication (Ryan 2014, 1–3). The public disgrace of Lin, arguably the alt-lit movement's most visible figure, marked in many respects the end of the alt-lit movement (although many of its authors have enjoyed continued success, including Kennedy, as well as Lin, but no longer necessarily under the auspices of the "alt-lit" category). It is worth mentioning this for two reasons: first, that much of Tao Lin's work may in fact be at least partially attributable to Kennedy, and secondly, that Tao Lin can be considered a representative of a particularly (and "toxically") masculine articulation of techno-oriental affect. Like Yang, Tao Lin's explorations—unintentional or not—of techno-oriental affect are not only racialized but gendered within what is likely a misogynistic episteme.

As Tao Lin's third and most widely read full-length novel, *Taipei* describes an often-distracted, tech- and drug-addled meandering narrative focused on the relationship between Paul and a (presumably white) woman named Erin, also in her 20s, as the two partake of illicit drugs, acts of mischief, and various attempts at communication. Following in the footsteps of his previous novels *Eeeee Eee Eeee* and *Richard Yates*, *Taipei* is rife with Tao Lin's characteristic affectlessness, persistent in his writing as an emotional alienation and detachment from his surroundings, although *Taipei* is Lin's longest and most personal (if not, conventionally speaking, "intimate") work. In this sense, he has been frequently compared to Bret Easton Ellis, similarly infamous yet celebrated for his flatness, nihilism, and sensory detail more sociopathic than sensual.[9] But what is particular to Tao Lin's work, and to *Taipei* especially, is that this detachment is facilitated, in a very large way, by contemporary technology and social media (and, as I argue later, its almost unconscious attachment to racialization). Paul's life is largely narrated in a series of mundane details of moving through the world via technology, but he gradually gains a kind of "genuine" face-to-face connection with his lover Erin while visiting his family in Taipei. As Clancy Martin writes in his review of *Taipei* in the *New York Times*,

> Most of us take it for granted that we should focus on our conversations and the emotions they produce. But we take it for granted while sitting in a restaurant with a spouse, sending texts or checking Facebook or Googling the movie we're going to see. (2013, BR8)

A passage from midway through the novel is representative of Tao Lin's creative modus operandi:

> In a café in Ann Arbor around 10:30 p.m., two days later, Paul realized, when he remembered Erin's existence by seeing her name in Gmail, he'd forgotten about her that entire day (over the next three weeks, whenever more than two or three

days passed since they last communicated which they did by email, every five to ten days, in a thread Erin began the day she dropped him off at the airport, Paul would have a similar realization of having forgotten about her for an amount of time). Around midnight he drove his rental car to a row of fast-food restaurants near the airport and slept in a McDonald's parking lot. When he woke, around 2:45 a.m., he bought and ate a Filet-O-Fish from the McDonald's drive-thru. While trying to discern what, from which fast-food restaurant, to buy and eat next, he idly imagined himself for more than ten minutes as the botched clone of himself, parked outside the mansion of the scientist who the original Paul paid to clone himself and paid again to "destroy all information" regarding "[censored]. (Lin 2013, 109)

Like this passage, most of the novel's prose consists of dry details, fleeting observations, and non sequiturs, with a stubborn contemporaneity that feels less a prescriptive "commentary" on the "early millennial" generation (referring roughly to 20- and 30-somethings in the second decade of 21st century) and more of a descriptive immersion within the ontology of technologically mediated existence. Tao Lin is a member of this generation, being born in 1983 and 30 years old at the time of *Taipei*'s publication. In this passage, as in most of the novel, technological mediation has become naturalized as a means of accessing knowledge, and of existing in the social world; in the moment in this passage, Paul only remembers the existence of his partner "by seeing her name in Gmail," then proceeding to describe at length in the parenthetical about how the initial email thread had begun. Tao Lin then delves into the miscellany of Paul's consumption of fast food, bereft of sensory detail, but plunges the reader into Paul's imaginary musings of being a "clone of himself."

If we take this passage as stylistically representative of the novel, then it may seem confusing, at first glance, to consider *Taipei* as speaking to Asian American subjectification at all. After all, Tao Lin unambiguously eschews categorization as an "Asian American writer."[10] In a 2008 interview with Jessa Crispin of Bookslut, Tao Lin responds to a question about being Asian American with an aggressive postraciality:

> I think a person who has an identity-crisis about being both Asian and American, or a person who starts a magazine for Asian-Americans, or anything like that—if they aren't doing it in order to make money—is prejudiced, if prejudiced means treating people differently based on abstractions and not concrete, factual, and specific evidence from reality. If a person has "Asian pride" they are racist, I think, in most people's definition of racism, because it's the same as saying, "Asians are better than Germans, Canadians, and Africans."

Tao Lin's evaluation of "Asian pride" as "racist" is, of course, reflective of a reactionary colorblindness that has come to characterize the hegemony of the Obama-era "postraciality" that had loomed over U.S. racial discourse at the time of the novel's writing, uncritically equivocating the performative recuperation of a marginalized identity with the violence of white supremacy. Tao Lin's colorblindness reifies, in the words of Brandi Wilkins Catanese, "a fiction that divorces itself from the processes of history... since many institutions in our culture were created through concerted inattention to nonwhite culture in order to normalize whiteness" (2011, 36). Paul is, for all intents and purposes, a model minority protagonist, in terms of his internalization of white normalcy, his assimilation into American tech-hipster culture, and in fact his own endorsement of Asian orientalist stereotypes, all of which are consistent with Tao Lin's stated reactionary position on race. And yet, perhaps unwittingly, *Taipei* is something of an artifact of Asian American techno-orientalization and in fact demonstrates a complex relationship between this technological abandon and racialized, masculine masochism. For *Taipei*, race lurks as something of an inconvenient specter, always working to thwart the novel's own attempts to transcend it, and it often manifests itself through engagement with digital technologies.

For example, returning to the passage quoted earlier, it is telling that Paul imagines himself science-fictionally as "the botched clone of himself," which is certainly evocative of the (techno-)orientalist image of the mass-produced, non-individuated Asiatic horde. The "botched clone" is also suggestive of an affective relationship to the haze in which Paul finds himself, reminded of his lover's existence through checking email, sleeping in a parking lot, and consuming fast food with what seems to be a deadpan hipster self-amusement, reflecting an alienation from his own feelings, provoking him to wonder whether his thoughts and feelings are indeed "his own" or the "original's." Furthermore, the "botched clone" also, according to Paul's imagination, wishes to confront (or kill) the scientist who created him in the style of a Frankensteinian Oedipal drama. There is thus a silent, unexpressed violence implied in the cold, seemingly unfeeling state of being massified and de-individuated.

Indeed, this "botched clone" reference is one among many of similar massified, easily orientalizable metaphors. Throughout the novel, Paul makes a number of references to feeling "like a zombie,"[11] "cyborg-like,"[12] "robot-like,"[13] and so on, with each conjuring an image of an orientalized, de-individuated mass. *Taipei* never disavows or distances itself from such imagery; rather, it embraces its very ontology, the prose insistently remaining a detached, almost distracted, deadpan neutral. Although these figures are not *necessarily* orientalized—particularly given their presence in other works of a similar aesthetic (such as that of Ellis)—*Taipei* tends to describe Asian figures in similar terms, suggesting a homologous relationship between the Asian and the massified nonhuman. Indeed, Tao Lin seems at least partially aware of the orientalizing racialization of this imagery; when Paul reflects on the city of Taipei, early in the novel, he is fully aware of—and in fact does not challenge—the racialized notion of the orientalized mass:

> Because his Mandarin wasn't fluent enough for conversations with strangers—and he wasn't close to his relatives, with whom attempts at communication were brief and non-advancing and often koan-like, ending usually with one person looking away, ostensibly for assistance, then leaving—he'd be preemptively estranged, secretly unfriendable. The unindividualized, shifting mass of everyone else would

be a screen, distributed throughout the city, onto which he'd project the movie of his uninterrupted imagination. Because he'd appear to, and be able to pretend he was, but never actually be a part of the mass, maybe he'd gradually begin to feel a kind of needless intimacy, not unlike being in the same room as a significant other and feeling affection without touching or speaking. (Lin 2013, 17)

This early passage demonstrates a complex breadth of Paul's relationship to Taipei, and to Asianness, in general. Shy of lamenting his lack of Mandarin fluency, Paul's second-generation Asian American status renders Taipei inscrutable; Paul's relatives are described as "koan-like," and as a result of his alienation, he'd be both "preemptively estranged" and "secretly unfriendable." Tao Lin's choice of "unfriendable" is furthermore consistent with the novel's fidelity to interface-mediated existence, utilizing "friend" in the verb form as popularized by the dominant social media website Facebook. Then, the description becomes unapologetically (techno-)orientalist, describing Taipei's crowd as an "unindividualized, shifting mass," which is also evocative of Wesley Yang's "mass of faces that resemble it" quoted at the beginning of this chapter.

Perhaps unintentionally, this passage, alongside the others, suggests an intriguing connection between orientalist massification, affect, and digital technology, one that is congruous with Vincent Chin's becoming-car of the opening chapter. Here, however, Paul—unlike Wesley Yang—imagines a curious and uncanny dis/identification with the faceless (or, alternately, same-faced) Asiatic mass; his second-generation status prevents him from fully joining it, although he can racially "pretend" to, achieving a curiously alienated intimacy that Paul finds comforting or even pleasurable, if somehow "needless." Paul's liminal status as Asian American thus produces a desirable ennui, through which he can experience intimacy precisely by being a stranger, individuated by virtue of his Americanization, with the outward appearance of being a part of the mass, and with it, bearing flat affect and mass-reproducibility.

Moreover, I'd like to draw special attention to the *screen*, Paul's image of choice to describe his imagination of the Taiwanese horde. In Paul's fantasy, the mass of Asians *becomes* the screen itself—in this case, the movie screen. Part of Paul's desire, then, is to join the screen, which is simultaneously the undifferentiated mass and the cognitive prosthetic into technological mediation. This desire seems at least partly reflective of a Freudian death drive for the individual monad. This is also significant since the screen, either overtly or implicitly, is ubiquitous throughout the novel, seamlessly merging with Paul's sensory experience of the world. This intensifies as Paul interacts more with *computer* screens—that is, virtual interfaces. Such an interface, writes Alexander Galloway, is "less ... a surface" and more "a doorway or window," and "is not something that appears before you but rather is a gateway that opens up and allows passage to some place beyond" (2012, 30). The presence of the screen in *Taipei*—whether that is the screen of his smartphone, or his MacBook—is rarely mentioned as an actual, material object with which Paul interacts except, notably, when referring to the mass of undifferentiated Asians. Rather, as a doorway interface, the screen opens what Maurice Merleau-Ponty has called the "body schema" into the digital world. Merleau-Ponty describes the "body schema" as "a *compendium* of our bodily experience, capable of giving a commentary and meaning to the internal impressions and the impression of possessing a body at any moment" (2012, 113, emphasis in original), and "a total awareness of my posture in the intrasensory world" (2013, 114). Importantly, Merleau-Ponty's concept of the "body schema" dissociates the physical body itself from the felt experience of having a body, which also paradoxically opens the possibility of having a felt sense of the body extend beyond the body itself.

To Paul, the physical world and the digital world are phenomenologically indistinguishable. Just as Paul remembers Erin's existence through Gmail (which is analogous to Paul being aware of his posture when given the appropriate stimulus), Paul experiences his social world through the terms of digital mediation. Such experiences occur a multitude of times throughout *Taipei*, two examples of which are as follows:

> "Paul," said Erin, and grasped his forearm. They stopped walking. More aware of Erin's perspective, looking at his face (and not knowing what expression she saw or what he wanted to express), than of his own, Paul didn't know what to do, so went "afk," he felt, and remained there—away from the keyboard of the screen of his face—as Erin, looking at the inanimate object of his head, said "if I did I would tell you" and, emphatically, "I'm not lying to you right now." (Lin 2013, 106–107)

> "Jesus, look," said Paul pointing at an eerie building far in the distance, thin and black, like a cursor on the screen of a computer that had become unresponsive. He imagined building-size letters suddenly appearing, left to right, in a rush—*wpkjgijfhtetiukgcnlm*—across the desert. (Lin 2013, 151)

In the former passage, Paul goes "afk"—an early 2000s chat room acronym standing for "away from keyboard," signifying idleness from an actively live online social interaction—when he and Erin argue over a fairly inconsequential lie Erin had told.[14] In the latter passage, Paul notices a building as he and Erin walk to a rental car, which they subsequently drive to a Las Vegas wedding chapel to be rather spontaneously married. In both segments, interface with the computer screen serves as the first referent to describe Paul's sensory experience. In the first, "afk" becomes the metaphor to describe what is likely the evacuation of all affect altogether for Paul, a sudden absence and dissociation from the present moment. The metaphor also serves to performatively naturalize the referent, effectively expecting the reader to understand precisely what kind of affectual absence is being described. As Tao Lin spells it out— "away from the keyboard of the screen of his face"—the keyboard roughly stands in as Paul's sentient consciousness, while the screen becomes, again, the exterior access point for affect. When being "afk," Paul's head is even rendered an "inanimate object." Consequently, Paul's sudden technologized "idleness" makes him somehow thing-like, undergoing a kind of becoming-computer, or in Kriss Ravetto-Biagioli's terms, "digital uncanny," referring to "how nonhuman devices (surveillance technologies, algorithms, feedback, and data flows) anticipate human gestures, emotions, actions, and interactions, thus intimating that we are machines and that our behavior may be predictable precisely because we are machinic" (2019, 5).

Meanwhile, in the second passage, digital mediation infiltrates Paul's actual visual field. As Paul looks out to the distance, the prose relates a building to a computer image: the unresponsive cursor. The cursor—that is, the arrow that a computer user manipulates across the screen—is the phenomenological extension of the user's will in interacting with a visual computer interface, the omnipresent thing that allows the visual field of the screen to become variously graspable. In a sense, the cursor is a virtual prosthesis analogous to a fingertip but not quite (which, of course, is that which moves the cursor, via mouse or trackpad); as Maurice Merleau-Ponty reminds us, "It is never our objective body that we move, but our phenomenal body... since our body, as the potentiality of this or that part of the world, surges toward objects to be grasped and perceives them" (2012, 121). Of course, Paul doesn't perceive just a normal cursor, but an *unresponsive* one, implying that the building does not move despite his semiconscious willingness to move it in his mind. And then, reflexively, Paul imagines a string of letters the size of the building itself across the desert, suggesting that for Paul, the visual field of the material world and the visual field of the screen blur all together. For Paul, in other words, all the world—including his own face—is not a stage, but a screen.

Returning to the earlier passage, in which the orientalized mass of koan-like Asians becomes "the screen" of Paul's imagination, we can ascertain that for Paul, there is something Asian about the screen itself. That is, the screen, as the thing that renders objects flat for display or interaction, is homologous with the affective flatness with which Asiatic racial form has been associated. Despite Tao Lin's attempts to distance himself from race, and his own eschewing of the discourse of "Asian pride," *Taipei* finds itself thoroughly embedded in race by way of the screen, which serves simultaneously as Paul's self, other, and lens of perception. The more computerized or screenlike Paul becomes in a particular moment, the more he accesses the Asianness he paradoxically eludes. This demonstrates, as Sara Ahmed has brilliantly revealed, that orientalism possesses a phenomenological, vectored dimension, that orientalism is as much a sense of "orientating" in space as it is an epistemological-geopolitical formation.[15]

Intriguingly, the notion of Orient-as-distant-yet-reachable takes on a second valence when applied to Paul and his Asian American positionality. In his description of Taipei, Paul seems to assume the default "western" position of describing the oriental mass/horde, yet Paul disidentifies with it; the horde is at once desirable, uncanny, and familiar. That is to say, because of his lack of Mandarin fluency paired with his phenotypic likeness (which is, in sum, his Asian Americanness), Paul finds the Orient *culturally* both inscrutably distant and reachable. Yet, similar to the hypothetical Occidental position, it is the Orient's inscrutability that makes it appealing, except that for Asian American Paul, who looks like those he considers inscrutable, the appeal lies in the intimacy that comes from a cultural/racial failure. His face, like the "unindividualized mass" of Taipei itself, is a screen, the machine that renders objects flat for display.

In considering both Tao Lin/Paul's face-as-screen-as-Asian, and Wesley Yang's indistinguishable quasi-robot face, I turn to Deleuze and Guattari's discussion of "faciality" in relation to affect, as well as Giorgio Agamben's theorization of the face. Giorgio Agamben conceptualizes the face more generally as the embodiment of communication and human sociality. Agamben argues,

> My face is my *outside*: a point of indifference with respect to all of my properties, with respect to what is properly one's own and what is common, to what is internal and what is external. In the face I exist with all of my properties (my being brown, tall, pale, proud, emotional...); but this happens without any of these properties essentially identifying me or belonging to me. (Agamben 2000, 98, emphasis in original)

That is, for Agamben, the face is the point of access to the sociality of the external world—"only where do I find a face do I encounter an exteriority and does an *outside* happen to me" (2000, 99)—which enables the possessor of the face to be not only a subject, but also an object (the outside *happens* to them). Agamben implies that this facialized objecthood is integral to sociality more generally. Additionally, Agamben argues, "The face is not a *simulacrum*, in the sense that it is something dissimulating or hiding the truth: the face is the *simultas*, the being-together of the manifold visages constituting it, in which none of the visages is truer than any of the others" (98). In this regard, Agamben does not conceptualize the face as a kind of mask, an "inauthentic" obfuscation of interiority but, rather, an assemblage of the multiple affects that roughly coheres into the dynamic conceptualization of one's face.

In contrast, theorizing faciality in *A Thousand Plateaus*, Deleuze and Guattari note that the face not only possesses a hegemonic whiteness, but literally *is* whiteness:

> The face is not a universal. It is not even that of the white man; it is White Man himself, with his broad white cheeks and the black hole of his eyes. The face is Christ. The face is the typical European, what Ezra Pound called the average sensual man, in short, the ordinary everyday Erotomaniac. (1987, 176)

With whiteness, the face simultaneously signifies divinity (Christ) and sensuality and feeling ("average sensual man"); whiteness comes to embody both the holy and the virile ideals. "Faciality," then, is the apparatus by which faces are judged to pass or fail in relation to the ideal white face. As a consequence, Deleuze and Guattari continue, "Racism operates by the determination of degrees of deviance in relation to the White-Man face" (1987, 178). Yet, the face becomes something into which one effectively assimilates: "You don't have a face as slide into one" (1987, 177), write Deleuze and Guattari, formulating the face as not an a priori given, but a social construct.

Deleuze and Guattari are thus more pessimistic than Agamben, insisting on the face's already-racial normativity, while Agamben locates the properties of social categorization on the face while de-essentializing their signification. Also, roughly speaking, Agamben emphasizes the social objecthood that accompanies the face, while Deleuze and Guattari are focused on the assemblage's (approximately, the "subject's") becoming-face, of moving toward an affective normativity. Deleuze and Guattari's attention to faciality's technology of normalization runs contrary to Agamben's assertion that the face is not a "simulacrum." Although Agamben is correct to assert that the face is not inherently a dissembling mask, the face may be taken as a simulacrum in relationship to the racial normativity described by Deleuze and Guattari. That is, if the face "*is* the White Man," then the nonwhite face that strives toward recognition-as-face is, necessarily, a simulacrum of sorts, already inauthentic by way of its nonnormative racialization.

Neither Agamben's nor Deleuze and Guattari's discussion of faciality is rooted within a materialist or historicist analysis of how these "facialities" come to be, nor do they disclose their implicit colonial universalism, of which continental poststructuralism is often guilty. For example, the modern consolidation of faces around racial typologies cannot be dissociated from Francis Galton's composite portraits of different "racial" groups in the late 19th century, which explicitly sought to connect facial phenotypic markers to criminal tendencies, as David Green has aptly demonstrated. Nevertheless, and despite their overreach of the role of the face in producing racial capitalism,[16] Deleuze and Guattari successfully describe an affectively normative whiteness that establishes the parameters for not inscrutability, but scrutability, and with it the access to unconditional humanness that such legibility enables. Considering this notion of faciality alongside Alexander Galloway's observation that "there is no 'faciality' with the computer" (2012, 12), I would argue that this face-as-simulacrum forms the affective foundation of techno-orientalism itself. Wesley Yang's lamentation of the quasi-robot Asian face is, in effect, a lamentation that the Asian face cannot properly express the sensuality and affect to which the white face has unmediated, assumed access, simply because the parameters for such sensuality and affect have been set within white aesthetic terms from the beginning. The Asian face, as "barely distinguishable from a mass of faces that resemble it," is also a simulacrum, marked by a perceived uncanny reproducibility (which is, obviously, only perceived as uniform due to its deviance from white normativity). Tao Lin's Paul, meanwhile, would likely agree in this assessment, but unlike Wesley Yang, Paul finds intimacy in being among faces that are not strictly, by Deleuze and Guattari's formulation, "faces," even as Paul's cultural proximity to whiteness (via Americanization) renders him alienated from them. Paul, unlike Wesley Yang, seems to find comfort in sharing the same deviation from white faciality precisely while Taipei remains emotionally inscrutable (and thus, orientalized).

Intriguingly, Paul seems to anticipate this comforting alienation whenever he encounters other Asian bodies, even Asian American ones. Following the norm of white Anglophone literature, Tao Lin always racially marks Asians in *Taipei* (unlike white characters), and their presence often implies a foreignness that is not commented upon, even if that foreignness ends up being false. The most notable example occurs when Paul, drug addled and eating food and Adderall with (racially unmarked, presumably white) friends Fran and Daniel, notices a group of Asians while on the way to pick up a DVD in Daniel's apartment:

> On the walk to Daniel's apartment, to get *Drugstore Cowboy*, dozens of elderly, similarly dressed Asian men were standing in a loosely organized row, like a string of Christmas lights, seeming bored but alert, on a wide sidewalk, across from the Bar Matchless. Daniel asked one of them what movie they were in and the Asian man seemed confused, then said "Martin Scorsese" without an accent when Daniel asked again.
>
> Around forty minutes later Paul said "that looks like the same group of Asians ... we saw earlier," realizing with amazement as he saw Bar Matchless that they had unwittingly walked to the same place. (Lin 2013, 68)

Throughout this excerpt, the group of Asian men is described in conformist terms ("similarly dressed," "standing in a loosely organized row, like a string of Christmas lights") and Paul reductively racially marks them ("group of Asians"). Yet, the group of Asian men implicitly defies expectations; in response to Daniel's largely nonsensical (presumably, drug-influenced) question of "what movie they were in," the Asian man responds "without an accent." The Asian's accentlessness (or rather, to be linguistically precise, his possessing the same mainstream American accent) contradicts the expectation established by the orientalist foreign conformity implicit in the description, a racist expectation that Paul has internalized yet he himself disproves. Then, when "the same group of Asians" is encountered again, they signify a familiarity, that Paul and Daniel have "been there" before as the two young men, disoriented, try to navigate around the city. Not unlike racial form itself, the Asians in the line cannot be avoided. They persistently exist proximal to Paul despite his attempts to go elsewhere. They are, furthermore, not dissimilar to Paul in the sense that they are "without an accent," that is, presumably Asian American, despite the implication of Paul's assumption of their foreignness. They bear some semblance to what Sau-Ling Wong has termed "racial shadows," the figures upon whom undesirable Asianness is projected, thus "render[ing] alien what is, in fact, literally inalienable, thereby disowning and distancing it" (1993, 78), although unlike in Wong's formulation, Paul does not seem to viscerally abject the Asians so much as notice their abnormality within a barely disturbed indifference.

Later in the novel, when Paul first actually arrives in Taipei, he is riding the bus with Erin and his father, surrounded by highly technologized imagery, which makes him pause and reflect on technology more generally. Notably, his contemplation is inflected with a postmodern, cyberpunk dystopianism:

> It was around 10:30 p.m. Paul stared at the lighted signs, some of which were *animated and repeating like GIF files*... and sleepily thought of how technology was no longer the source of wonderment and possibility it had been when, for example, he learned as a child at Epcot Center, Disney's future-themed "amusement park," that families of three, with one or two robot dogs and one robot maid, would live in self-sustaining, underwater, glass spheres by something like 2004 or 2008. At some point, Paul vaguely realized, technology had begun for him to mostly only indicate the inevitability and vicinity of nothingness. Instead of postponing death by releasing nanobots into the bloodstream to fix things faster than they deteriorated, implanting little computers into people's brains, or other methods Paul had probably read about on Wikipedia, until it became the distant, shrinking nearly nonexistent somethingness that was currently life—and life, for immortal humans, became the predominant distraction that was currently death—*technology seemed more likely to permanently eliminate life by uncontrollably fulfilling its only function: to indiscriminately convert matter, animate or inanimate, into computerized matter, for the sole purpose, it seemed, of increased functioning, until the universe was one computer*. Technology, an abstraction, undetectable in concrete reality, was accomplishing its concrete task, Paul dimly intuited while idly petting Erin's hair, by way of an increasingly committed and multiplying workforce of humans, who receive, over hundreds of generations, a certain kind of advancement (from feet to bicycles to cars, faces to bulletin boards to the internet) in exchange for converting a sufficient amount of matter into computerized matter for computers to be able to build themselves. (Lin 2013, 166–167, emphasis mine)

Again, in this passage, we see Paul's visual field utilizing computerization as his primary referent ("lighted signs... animated and repeating like GIF files," which are short online soundless animated images that play on a loop). But this is also one of the rare moments of the novel that seems, at least ostensibly, critical of technology itself. Paul indulges a Heideggerean anxiety about the capacity for technology to become not just a human means to prosperity (represented by the science fictional underwater glass spheres and the life-sustaining nanobots) but a means for its own end. When Paul notes that technology is "more likely to permanently eliminate life," it is through the conversion of all other matter "into computerized matter." Considering Paul's consistent self-technologization throughout the entirety of the novel (appearing even in this passage as the streetlights as "GIF files"), it is abundantly clear that Paul himself undergoes this very process, becoming "computerized matter" itself. This conversion is, furthermore, heightened in Taipei and, presumably, East Asia more generally: "As the bus moved into denser parts of Taipei... Paul felt like he could almost sense the computerization that was happening in this area of the universe, on Earth" (Lin 2013, 167)—that is, that in Taipei, he draws closer to singularity. Thus, Taipei and Paul undergo parallel self-inflicted techno-orientalizations, conversion into "computerized matter."[17]

Yet, the fact that Paul feels an "intimacy" with such technologization implies a comfort with precisely that mode of affectless alienation with which he associates Asianness. Paul's relationship to techno-orientalized Taipei, and by extension to the fugue of computer-mediated abandon more generally, is coldly masochistic. But from where does this relationship emerge? Interestingly, in the second chapter of the novel, Paul reflects upon his adolescent relationship with his immigrant mother, wherein he exhibited some powerfully masochistic tendencies. In high school, Paul becomes extremely awkward and self-conscious, often paranoid that others are making fun of him. He begins to think of himself in rather mechanical terms:

> When he heard laughter, before he could think or feel anything, his heart would already be beating like he'd sprinted twenty yards. As the beating slowly normalized he'd think of how his heart, unlike him, was safely contained, away from the world, behind bone and inside skin … as if to artfully assert itself as source and creator … and later, after innovating the brain and limbs and face and limbs, to convert into productive behavior—its uncontrollable, indefensible, unexplainable, embarrassing squeezing of itself. (Lin 2013, 40)

Paul's adolescent self, in other words, conceptualizes his heart as unruly, involuntarily pulsing beside itself when anxious, but ruling his brain and body as if they comprised a machine ("innovating … to convert into productive behavior"). Not unlike Vincent Chin, he is techno-orientalized, but unlike Chin, Paul does so to himself, within the realm of his adolescent imagination. So, in response, he begins to ask his mother to punish him severely, in an attempt to psychologically remedy himself:

> In Paul's sophomore or junior year he began to believe the only solution to his anxiety, low self-esteem, *view of himself as unattractive, etc. would be for his mother to begin disciplining him on her own volition*, without his prompting, as an unpredictable—and, maybe, to counter the previous fourteen or fifteen years of "overprotectiveness," unfair—entity, convincingly not unconditionally supportive. *His mother would need to create rules and punishments exceeding Paul's expectations, to a degree that Paul would no longer feel in control*. To do this, Paul believed, his mother would need to anticipate and preempt anything he might have considered, factoring in that … he probably already expected, or had imagined, any rule or punishment she would be willing to instate or inflict, therefore she would need to consider rules and punishments that she would not think of herself as willing to instate or inflict. Paul tried to convey this in crying, shouting fights with his mother lasting up to four hours, sometimes five days a week. There was an inherent desperation to these fights in that each time Paul, in frustration, *told his mother how she could have punished him*, in whatever previous situation, *to make him feel not in control*—to, he believed, help solve his social and psychological problems—it became complicatedly more difficult, in Paul's view, for his mother to successfully preempt his expectations the next time. (Lin 2013, 41, emphasis mine)

In this early passage, Paul believes that his mother's punishments are capable of curing him of social anxiety, paradoxically by robbing him of social control. So extreme is his desire for punishment that he angrily chides his mother for *not* punishing him; hilariously, his mother ultimately fails to carry out his wishes, finding strictness and punishment utterly counter to her actual tendencies (which also, incidentally, counters the "Tiger Mother" discourse of Asian mothers mentioned at the start of this chapter).

Paul's insistence that his mother severely punish him reflects a masculine masochism, particularly as theorized by Deleuze. Deleuze argues that the mother-as-torturer—not the father—is the crucial figure in the symbolic order of masculine masochism, who operates to expel the father from the masochistic subject:

> Finally, he [the masochist] ensures that he will be beaten; we have seen that what is beaten, humiliated, and ridiculed in him is the image and the likeness of the father, and the possibility of the father's aggressive return. *It is not a child but a father that is being beaten*. The masochist thus liberates himself in preparation for a rebirth in which the father will have no part. (Deleuze 1989, 66, emphasis in original)

Deleuze's masculine masochism relies upon a powerful femininity that effectively exorcises the power and authority of the father rather than submitting to it. Paul, above all else, resents his mother for *not* taking away his sense of control, for not undermining his sense of agency and leaving his sense of individualism intact. Curiously, in this respect, Paul instead finds the satisfaction of the relinquishing of control in the various figurations of techno/oriental, from the fugue of the digital interface to the "screen" of orientalized masses, and later in the novel, from various hallucinogens.

In Paul's account of his childhood, his father is only briefly mentioned,[18] with much more of his early experience dominated by being placed in rudimentary English as a second language courses and, later, feeling social anxiety. This omission suggests the relative emotional absence of Paul's father, which, incidentally, mirrors the social anxiety that Paul feels in his adolescent years. This social anxiety, particularly given Paul's experience as a 1.5 generation Asian American growing up in a Mandarin-speaking household, can indeed be read as a racialized anxiety over the father, of inheriting a masculine Asianness that does not read properly in the white U.S. milieu of normative gender performance. Thus, Paul appeals masochistically (although unsuccessfully) to his mother in order to properly assimilate into the heterosexual economy, to be born anew with his psychology corrected.

Yet, as Deleuze describes, such masochism in fact idealizes coldness—that is to say, the flat affect that I have been discussing throughout this chapter. Deleuze describes coldness as "not the negation of feeling but rather the disavowal of sensuality" (1989, 52). Masochistic coldness, then, can be understood as deviation from normative faciality, a disavowal of the affects that signify a fully animate and expressive whiteness. Masochistic coldness entails the persistence of a rich inner life while converting the body into an inert, inanimate object, rendering the face into a screen, affectively "going afk." Technological mediation, then, becomes the means through which Paul actualizes the masochistic ideal he had sought throughout his childhood and adolescence. In doing so, he embraces the condition of becoming the racial-technological excess of postmodernity, ultimately taking pleasure from the flat affect of coldness, from becoming-screen, all the while ostensibly disavowing the relationship of race to narrative.

Of course, my analysis of *Taipei* is, after all, a counter-reading to what I am sure are Tao Lin's own intentions. Tao Lin would likely argue that *Taipei* would still be equally resonant if the central character were not Asian American, even as the presence of techno-orientalized Asiatic racial form persists throughout the novel's pages. Yet, much of what Tao Lin seems to inadvertently write and explore regarding Asian Americanness is explicitly and intentionally expounded upon by another Asian American writer whose name differs by only one letter: Tan Lin. Through Tan Lin's *Insomnia and the Aunt*, we find a second explicit example of the relationship between technological mediation, phenomenological embodiment, affect, and racial becoming.

She Becomes Furniture: Television, Race, and Memory in Tan Lin's *Insomnia and the Aunt*

Multidisciplinary artist and academic Tan Anthony Lin jokes that he is often confused with Tao Lin. On his Tumblr blog, Tan Lin writes,

> Tan Lin instead of Tao Lin
> McNuggets instead of Adderall
> Ambient Stylistics instead of Alt Lit
> Jogging instead of Internet Poetry
> Lulu instead of Scribd
> x instead of ' '
> BIZAARO WORLD WHAT WILL HAPPEN WHEN IT "COLLIDES"

Of course, the truth is that Tan Anthony Lin, born in 1957 in Seattle, Washington, is the senior of the two writers, although he must contend with the contemporary popularity of the similarly named Asian American author. Unlike Tao Lin, Tan Lin is not, demographically speaking, a member of the "post-1965" wave of Asian American authors, having closer generational commonality with Asian American writers prominent in the 1990s like Lois-Ann Yamanaka, Jessica Hagedorn, and Karen Tei Yamashita (although like Hagedorn, he seemed initially separate from preestablished Asian Americanist discourse). Yet despite the wholly justifiable need to distinguish the two men and their careers, a thematic resonance between the two authors nevertheless persists.

Loosely, his work has been characterized as "ambient literature," in which Tan Lin aims to pursue an aesthetic of "reading distractedly." In fact, throughout his oeuvre of poetry, Tan Lin frequently pursues questions of mediation and technology, utilizing Internet searches and other forms of online detritus to form pastiches of cyber-expression.[19] This philosophy is also strongly reflected in his 2010 book *Seven Controlled Vocabularies and Obituary 2004. The Joy of Cooking*, about which Tan Lin states that he "was interested in the book as dispersed ambient textuality, meta-data, or maybe just the allusiveness of the bibliographic that is referenced by a title, which I suppose the book itself and its ecosystems of reading" (Sanders 2010). In this sense, Tan Lin's literary work aims for particular moods and fugues related to being swarmed with data and information, trying to locate the "ambiance" of being surrounded by media at large.

For the purposes of this discussion, I turn to Tan Lin's short volume entitled *Insomnia and the Aunt* (2011). Whereas Tao Lin's *Taipei* is a semiautobiographical novel, Tan Lin's *Insomnia* is a fictive memoir and, out of all of Tan Lin's works, perhaps the most directly conversational about race and Asian Americanness. Curiously, Tan Lin's dreamlike, affectively insomniac text more consciously invokes and explores the themes of race, affect, and mediation that are only latently present in Tao Lin's *Taipei*. Furthermore, *Insomnia and the Aunt* is able to deploy the affect of technological mediation to the very practice of becoming Asian American, utilizing its ambient mood to capture the felt experience of television viewership, and by extension, becoming the television itself.

Insomnia and the Aunt is a slim 44 pages of prose intermittently interspersed by black-and-white images (visually similar to Tan Lin's preceding *Seven Controlled Vocabularies*)—the former a nonlinear reflection of Tan Lin on his fictive aunt, the latter a collection of iconic television images and presumed photographs from the author's past. In an interview with the Asian American Writers Workshop, Tan Lin states, "*Insomnia* is an ethnographic and sociological accounting, i.e. a fiction. This fiction concerns a group of people, Chinese people in America, and examines how Chinese people in America become Chinese people in America. And the answer is by watching TV" (Foote 2015, 2). *Insomnia* reflects upon a fictional childhood of Tan Lin, in which he spends time with his half-Chinese, half-English aunt who manages the Bear Park Motel in remote Concrete, Washington. In these summers, the narrator would spend entire nights with his aunt, literally watching television beside her for hours on end, reflecting on the nature of his aunt's presence in the shared space. In framing the prose to come, the narrator spends the first page contextualizing his aunt and uncle's trajectory, arriving from China to Washington state and opening a Chinese restaurant. Then, as the narrator describes,

> Their first restaurant went out of business, they moved to Seattle to open another one, I think it was called Ming's Garden, but they got tired of serving people American Chinese food, so in the early 80s they decided to close the restaurant down and travel east, *into* the wilderness. They settled in a place near North

> Cascades National Park, near an Indian reservation. My aunt has always told me, in an inconsequential sort of grammatical inversion, that this is "the story of your lives" only backwards, from America to the real America, from China to somewhere you've never been before. And like most Orientals in the mid-seventies (or "Asian people" as they have been called since the mid-nineties), there was never the slightest bit of emotion on her face when she told me this story. Someone said "The Oriental, we are good at killing emotions," and I think that person was right. (Lin 2011, 8, emphasis in original)

In this early paragraph, the narrator's aunt and uncle move away from the metropolitan center of Seattle (and, presumably, from the state's primary concentration of Chinese immigrants) and into "the wilderness," associated with "the real America." The "realness" of North Cascades National Park is implied by its proximity to an Indian reservation, implying a greater closeness with an essential "Americanness" by virtue of its proximity to indigeneity. We can thus initially understand the setting of *Insomnia and the Aunt* to be remote and closer to the bucolic "natural" than to the synthetic, evoking a sense of frontier Americana on the razor's edge of settler-colonial Manifest Destiny.[20] But it is notable that in this framed telling of his aunt's narrative, the narrator comments that "there was never the slightest bit of emotion on her face" and then proceeds to racialize it, finding truth in the notion that "the Oriental" is "good at killing emotions."

As an immigrant Chinese American, the narrator's aunt begins to serve as a quasi-allegorical figure of Asianness in America whom the narrator utilizes as a reference point to his own sense of self. Her affective flatness is also already resonant with the "going afk" of *Taipei*, but rather than interface with the Internet, the aunt is more fixated upon the television screen. Of course, there seems to be considerable difference between the relatively passive engagement with the television screen and the more active interactivity with the computer or phone screen—namely, the latter's "holding power," to borrow a phrase from Sherry Turkle. Yet, I would argue that the televisual and the informatic screens bear more similarity in terms of seizing their viewer/user in the liveness and presence contained in their temporality. Besides the fact that, as Philip Auslander has convincingly argued, television's ontology is ultimately rooted in live performance and the ideal of transporting the home audience into the theatrical liveness of the studio, television programming is organized around a concept of information overload and "flow." As Raymond Williams has written, television commercials are not so much "interruptions" of the programs as they are part of a larger experiential (and affective?) whole, a "flow, in which the true series is not the published sequence of programme items but this sequence transformed by the inclusion of another kind of sequence, so that these sequences compose the real flow, the real 'broadcasting'" (1990, 91). Phenomenologically speaking, the television screen produces a similar tidal wave of information as the Internet in *Taipei*, and correspondingly, an affective flatness that animates (or perhaps, de-animates) the central character's felt experience of being racialized.

The effect of such distraction and mental wandering is an impairment of focus, and an imprecision of memory. Throughout *Insomnia and the Aunt*, the narrator attempts to remember his aunt's visage but cannot do so adequately. He has only one photo of her that seems somehow unreal, and it is unreal partly due to the asymmetry of her Asianness with the narrative's setting:

> The only photograph of my aunt that I have managed to hold onto through the years has her wearing a white cowboy hat and dark sunglasses that seem out of place in the wilderness, and that signal the sort of disruption or lie that I associate with Asians in the movies or in Ohio where I grew up, or Asians in fast food restaurants like McDonalds, where I have never eaten and where I have never seen a Chinese person eating. I have watched hundreds of movies with Asians and fake Asians in them, and the one thing that makes them all the same (except the white Asians) is that the Asians never stare into your eyes through the glass of a TV screen and you are never allowed to look too deeply into theirs. I think it is for this reason that whenever I think about my aunt, and TV for that matter, I can never remember my aunt's eyes (they appear to belong to someone else), and think instead of Robert Redford, who said in an interview that it is necessary for the body to lie to the mind (not the other way around) when acting and that the various strata of lying are continually searching for each other in the wilderness that most people call the truth and my aunt calls television. For my aunt, TV can never really lie because it is on all the time, unlike the theatre, where there are all sorts of changes of scenery and which as a result goes on and off and is thus the perfect medium for telling lies one after another. But in my aunt's motel, the TV never goes off and all these changes are not changes at all; they're commercials. (Lin 2011, 10–11)

To both the narrator and the aunt, both truth and deception take on curious dimensions in relationship to the image. Beginning with the image of his aunt with the cowboy hat and sunglasses, the narrator notes that they "seem out of place in the wilderness" and immediately racializes that asymmetry. His aunt's apparel is a "disruption" or a "lie" somehow congruent with Asians in movies or in fast-food restaurants. The Asian in the fast-food restaurant is somehow a lie, and Lin is not entirely clear if this Asian is untrue because she doesn't exist ("I have never seen a Chinese person eating"), or if, ontologically, the Asian eating American fast food is somehow a contradiction. My reading inclines toward the latter; "Asians in the movies," for example, actually exist, and this parallels the structure of "Asians in fast food restaurants like McDonald's." This implies that the narrator is aware, at least in the abstract, that Asians are in fast-food restaurants—perhaps through televisual mediation—but that somehow their presence is equally asymmetrical and unsettling.

Then, the narrator considers the eyes of Asians in cinema, stating that "you are never allowed to look too deeply" into them. There is not a clear sense of who condones the looking, although it is likely some relationship between a U.S. cinematic norm of not focusing on Asians' faces to access their psychic interiority ("the Asians never stare into your eyes through the glass of a TV screen") and a disciplinary function that insists an aversion from the eyes altogether. The eyes, the primary visual locus of faciality and intersubjective interiority, are somehow inscrutable and illegible to memory, if they are read as Asian. This televisual racial logic extends so thoroughly to the narrator that he cannot, no matter how hard he tries, remember his own aunt's eyes, or perhaps, that he can remember what they look like but distrusts the authenticity of their appearance in his memory—"they appear to belong to someone else." His aunt's eyes, then, are not her own, perhaps because the narrator lacks the capacity to conceptualize her eyes-as-eyes, and by extension, her face-as-face, to reference back to Deleuze and Guattari's notion that the face "*is* the White Man." Tellingly, the narrator invokes one of the most emblematically handsome white men of all, Robert Redford, who comes to mind instead of his aunt's eyes. Redford's quote that acting consists of the "body lying to the mind" implies a precedence of bodily exteriority over psychic interiority when taking on the act of performance. As the narrator presents Redford's description of acting, "the various strata of lying are continually searching for each other in the wilderness that most people call the truth and my aunt calls television," he subtly invokes various traditions of theater and performance theory in conceptualizing the relationship between the performance and the "authentic"—Erving Goffman's well-known model of the "front stage" and "back stage," for example.[21] The body becomes a pastiche of various "strata of lying"—that is to say, performed personae, but for the aunt, this occurs not in the wilderness of truth, but in television. In other words, for the aunt (and also, arguably, the narrator), the raw material of embodied affectual expression primarily resides within the world of TV. Furthermore, the TV is somehow less "deceptive" than theater; the commercial obfuscates the theatricality otherwise witnessed in the staged scene change of drama (which is consistent with Raymond Williams' characterization of "flow," cited earlier in this chapter). For the aunt, the never-ending presence and liveness of the television[22] provides the very basis for its authenticity.

The narrator, furthermore, seems to be skeptical of when his aunt actually does demonstrate affective exuberance. Not too long after he arrives at the motel, his aunt is described as "crying in front of the lobby window, which is back lit like a movie set" (Lin 2011, 10) and then proceeds to dramatically take his bags to the same room in which he always stays. However, according to the narrator, her choreography is scripted; every time he comes to visit, she does exactly the same thing: "She will cry in exactly in the same manner, in front of the neon NO VACANCY sign in the window, with the same uncontrollable wailing and tears and half-Chinese words I do not understand" (Lin 2011, 10), "as if my aunt's life were endlessly re-passing a single point in time, like an actor in a sitcom or a car going past the same highway exit night after night on its way home" (Lin 2011, 10). It becomes clear, as the repeated late-night TV-watching binges illuminate, that there is something imitative, machine-like, and somehow "inauthentic" about her melodramatic display, that she is likely parroting the emotional abandon that she witnesses on television.

Within these passages and elsewhere, Asianness is already fake. This is not in the sense of Asian stereotypes being asymmetric with an essentialist Asian "reality"; rather, it is that Asianness signifies fakeness itself, in that Asian faciality does not project proper affective expression as normalized by the television. This sense of essential artificiality mirrors *Taipei* and its repeated references to clones and androids as analyzed earlier, except that in *Insomnia and the Aunt*, the racialization is overt. Moreover, just as the face "*is* the White Man," the aunt's television *is* America, while the Asian face is somehow less properly animate; as Mel Chen has described, animacy is "an often racialized and sexualized means of conceptual and affective mediation between human and inhuman, animate and inanimate, whether in language, rhetoric, or imagery" (2012, 10). Animacy and the distinctions it engenders functions as a technology of vertical ordering but also gestures to how the animate and the racial become mutually constitutive, whether through an excess of affect, its apparent absence, or a substantially qualitative aberrance. Conversely, a human's racialized thinglikeness can be understood on an affective basis.

Perhaps, as the narrator suggests in the opening page of *Insomnia and the Aunt*, "Orientals ... are good at killing emotions" because of a proximity to being racialized as thinglike, and by extension, somehow "fake" humans. Although in that opening passage, the narrator uses the word "emotions," but it is the narrator's read of his aunt's expressions that provokes this thought—that is to say, it is not so much emotion but affect, the exterior shimmering of feeling. Consequently, what the narrator interprets as the "killing" of the aunt's feelings is not necessarily the absence of feeling but, rather, the predetermined failure of the Asian face to be properly disciplined into the animacy of whiteness. The television then becomes the means by which that discipline is always aspired to but never actually achieved. As a consequence, the aunt is figured as perpetually in self-defeating transit, paradoxically attempting to escape the thinglikeness of Asianness by becoming the thing that is the television. Perhaps this could very well be the very essence of the Asian American condition: becoming thinglike in one respect (model minority) to escape being thinglike in another (inscrutably foreign).

Furthermore, in the process toward affective assimilation via the TV, the aunt undergoes a forgetting, allowing her own consciousness to become ahistorical and, conversely, the narrator encounters difficulty in remembering the aunt, except through a technologically mediated thingification:

> For an immigrant like my aunt, America is not the images on a TV, it basically is the TV, which is why she decorates it with paper doilies, vanilla incense sticks and stuffed Garfields. This is also why my aunt thinks all TV, even live TV, is canned, and why she thinks America is basically not a place or even an image, but furniture. For my aunt, the live broadcast of the Vietnam War of my youth and her early middle ages resembled a re-run. My aunt accordingly has very few memories of violence or even racism in America. TV has made her forget all these things. Likewise, it is very hard for me to remember her even though I miss her intensely. The more I miss

her the more she becomes furniture or a TV commercial for Tide detergent. (Lin 2011, 19–20)

To the aunt, America *is* the TV, and the TV in turn is understood as not just the series of images it displays, but as a material, physical object (hence her decoration of the device). Moreover, the narrator then implies that it is the physicality of the TV that makes the aunt believe that all TV is canned; it is the literal materiality of the television that confers its hyperreal uncanniness. Paradoxically, it is the artifice of its "cannedness" that makes the television somehow more authentically American, since "authentic" Americanness becomes defined by its thingness and objecthood. But importantly, from the narrator's standpoint, the aunt *herself* becomes thinglike in his memory; she becomes "furniture" or "a TV commercial for Tide detergent." Notably, the awareness of the television as furniture, and then the conversion of the aunt into furniture, is objectifying, but not necessarily for commodity consumption. Intriguingly, the narrator's longing for his aunt, and the cloudiness of his memory, while melancholic, falls short of a desire for the consumption of more goods. It is not the case, for example, that the narrator expresses a desire to acquire more Tide detergent to compensate for the loss of his aunt; rather, the presence of the detergent is the *effect* of a mediated cathexis. In any event, this thinglikeness operates to obfuscate, delete, or rewrite memory on some level, with the aunt detaching herself from racism, which is, interestingly, mentioned and even assumed but never overtly illustrated. Not unlike *Taipei*'s Paul, the aunt experiences race not through the overt confrontations of racism, but through the already-racialized frames of mediatization itself.

In his interview with Asian American Writers' Workshop, Tan Lin states regarding television watching in *Insomnia*,

> Mediation is surreal, but also utterly natural.... From a standpoint that is not necessarily mine, my aunt does not really exist. This makes perfect sense to me; she is an emanation of a TV set. But the same is true of the TV too. It has no life apart from my aunt. (Foote 2015, 2)

Although their stylistic strategies vary, *Insomnia* and *Taipei* share in common, to varying degrees, a naturalization of mediation—the ambiance of *Insomnia* allows thought and television images to blur into one another seamlessly for the first-person narrator to produce a non-narrative meditation, while Tao Lin's *Taipei* utilizes a cold close third person to demonstrate the phenomenological extension of Paul's sense of embodiment and of self into the digital landscape (and vice versa). However, *Insomnia* effectively completes what *Taipei* merely gestures toward, a psychic interiority of the self-consciously techno-mediated Asian American subject. The aunt and the television are enabled to only exist in relation to each other; the aunt, as the figure of becoming–Chinese American, is always liminally traversing from ontological fakeness to the object of furniture that promises normativity and belonging.

Part of *Insomnia*'s success in this regard is naturally due to Tan Lin's intentional conceit to engage with Chinese American subjectivity, but it is also worth considering that the screens in *Taipei* and the screens in *Insomnia* are every so slightly different. Although, as I have argued, *Taipei*'s Paul seeks out masochistic coldness through his engagement with digital technology, Alexander Galloway argues that "[t]o be 'informatically' present in the world, to experience the pleasure of the computer, one must be a sadist" (2012, 13). The fugue of the online interface is perhaps more sadistic than masochistic despite its coldness, inviting the user to inflict changes within the boundaries of its screen as a form of omnipotent telekinesis. Meanwhile, *Insomnia*'s television screen is more fundamentally an instrument of masochism in which the viewer's relationship is almost gloriously passive, more fully de-animating the subject than *Taipei*: whereas in *Taipei*, Paul would imagine himself as the botched clone or the screen of koan-like massified Asians, *Insomnia*'s aunt would become furniture itself.

Furthermore, *Insomnia* thwarts the sadism of interactivity through its usage of URLs in the footnotes. *Insomnia* metafictionally performs a form of Internet fugue through its footnoting of search engine results. There are 10 footnotes in the text, 9 of which include short, tangentially related quotes from online Internet articles, complete with Internet hyperlinks. For example, after the narrator explains that his aunt "has two or three American voices" (Lin 2011, 24) and that the "first voice is the English practiced by a Chinese person and it sounds like an answering machine" (Lin 2011, 24–26), the fifth footnote, indexed after "machine," written on the bottom page 26, states:

I can still hear his **voice**—Simpler Living—Naomi Seldin…

Feb 25, 2009 … There are 16 messages on my cordless phone/**answering machine**.… It **sounds like** you're honoring your father's memory in the right ways…

blog.timesunion.com/simplerliving/16-messages/6151/ - Cached

The appearance of this footnote is not precisely a clarification or a citation of an in-text reference, as a footnote in an academic text would be but, rather, more of a free association. The presence of the word "Cached" after the URL also directly indicates that this is meant to be read as a result from a Google search.[23] The URL, which is still live at the time of this writing, links to a blog post by Naomi Seldin describing her experience mourning her father by keeping his messages on her answering machine. This citation foreshadows the narrator's mourning of his aunt that, at this point of the text, has not yet actively begun. But it is worth noting that this link must be manually typed into a browser's URL bar, rather than merely "clicked," since, of course, the book is a physical book. In this way, *Insomnia and the Aunt* hoists the phenomenology of Internet browsing so characteristic of Paul in *Taipei* onto its Internet-savvy reader, who may momentarily rue the fact that this book is material rather than a clickable web page. This also paradoxically draws attention to the physical materiality of the book itself and its metatextual limitations as such. Whereas *Taipei* provides a portrait of a user primarily on his interface, *Insomnia and the Aunt* conjures an interface for the readers themselves. This technique ultimately serves Tan Lin's objective of creating an "ambient novel," producing a state of informatic distraction, teasing the reader to mentally wander in much the same way one would wander in an online interface, but ultimately resists the actualization of this wandering precisely through its materiality, its thinglikeness (contrasting here with the ethereal digital interface that it imitates). Thus, the digital sadomasochism portrayed in *Taipei* is both dismantled and refined in the televisual masochism of *Insomnia and the Aunt*. Nevertheless, both *Taipei* and *Insomnia* provide invaluable portraits of Asian American becomings within the regimes of cold, flat screens. But in the next, final chapter, we explore techno-orientalization within the screen itself, the digital realm of the video game.

6
White Skin, Yellow Flesh
Transhumanist Erotohistoriography in *Deus Ex: Human Revolution*

In Chapter 5, I explored the role of techno-orientalized racial form as a phenomenology of digitized media; here, I engage with the digital itself in the form of the video game *Deus Ex: Human Revolution (DX:HR)*, a game that, both representationally and structurally, remains attached to the techno-oriental form. Announced in 2007 and released in 2011 as the prequel to the 2000 cult classic *Deus Ex*, Eidos Montreal's video game *DX:HR* was roundly heralded as a monumental achievement of gameplay and digital aesthetics. With an average score of 90/100 among critics according to game review aggregator website metacritic.com, *DX:HR* is by nearly all measures a triumph in video game design, aesthetics, and narrative. As Arthur Gies of IGN writes, "It's a visionary, considered piece of work.... Human Revolution is a smart, rewarding piece of transhumanist noir that does justice not just to Deus Ex, but to the fiction that inspired it." However, like its 1980s filmic and literary cyberpunk predecessors, *DX:HR* is also guilty of obtuse techno-orientalist representations, positioning Asian-raced peoples as embodiments of the possibility of dystopian failure within the transhumanist future. This is particularly relevant due to not only the rise of societal gamification at large, but also the high rate of video game play among Asian Americans. According to the Nielsen Company's 2012 "State of the Asian American Consumer," Asian Americans "spend more time on video games than other groups" (Narasaki 2012, 10), particularly youth. The Northwestern University Center on Media and Human Development's June 2011 report "Children, Media, and Race" has demonstrated that Asian American youth aged 8–18 have the highest rate of video game and computer game play compared with youth in other racial demographics, spending 73% more time on video games and 83% more time on computer games per day on average compared with white children.[1] However, as Dean Chan writes, "Asian American gamers are, paradoxically, both hypervisible and out of sight" (2009). Moreover, as I have written elsewhere,

> North American video games have had a long contentious history with regard to Asian racialization. From the grotesquely racist *Shadow Warrior*, the techno-orientalist cyberpunk *Deus Ex* series, and the essentialist and stereotypical portrayals in Sid Meier's *Civilization* series and *Alpha Centauri*, to the comparatively benevolent but romanticizing *Jade Empire*, and the redemptive if masculinist *Sleeping Dogs*

(to name but a handful of easy examples), Asian racialization has had a persistent presence in the North American video game imagination, to varying degrees of epistemic violence or political potential. (Rivera 2017, 195)

The juxtaposition of high rates video gaming among Asian Americans with Asian Americans' purported ubiquity and invisibility in the world of gaming is a grotesque if familiar representational challenge. In this regard, *DX:HR* is contiguous with rather than exceptional from North American video game conventions, a game heavily played by the very demographic that it representationally caricatures, but I would argue that its retrofuturistic techno-orientalism, combined with the phenomenological immersion inherent to the medium, offers a peculiar route to practice Asian American masochism. In other words, for the Asian American gamer to not just play, but take pleasure, in assuming the roles and scripts of *DX:HR* requires closer examination. In examining *DX:HR*, I take on what Christopher B. Patterson has recently called an "'erotics of play,' wherein social meanings are constructed through pleasure, passion, and intimacy" (2020, 13). As a game, a medium governed predominantly by active and direct interactivity,[2] *DX:HR* provides an opportunity for the Asian American gamer to experience not only their own body-as-stereotype, but their own body-as-other. This is precisely how *DX:HR* presents potentially generative possibilities for the Asian subject who plays it and engages its deeply problematic gameworld. A first-person action/role-playing game, the cyberpunk science fiction game places the player in the perspective of its protagonist, Adam Jensen, explicitly described as a thirty-four-year old Caucasian male who has fully augmented cybernetic limbs and organs. As security chief of the human augmentation firm Sarif Industries, Jensen unravels a massive conspiracy pertaining to the controversy of human (or, more specifically, transhumanist) augmentation itself, all unfolding in the *Blade Runner–*inflected imagery of an imagined 2027 AD. In a sense, the video game allows its player to explore the architecture of a structure of feeling,[3] in this case, one that houses the techno-oriental becoming-machine itself. Not unlike Ariane Cruz's description of pornographic fucking machines as "not merely extensions of their white inventors and the white male imaginary but as embodiments of white masculinity" (2016, 196), *DX:HR* is an immersion into both the phenomenology of neoliberal whiteness and the techno-orientalism that is its queer excess. Yet it is also a terrain for the masculine (but not exclusively masculine) Asian American subject to masochistically exercise a mode of what Elizabeth Freeman terms "erotohistoriography," a deployment of violent erotics to contend with one's own subject formation.

Through a reading of *DX:HR*, this chapter concludes the previous four threads of model minority masochism, an Asian American cultural politics that locates itself in slippages, role reversals, and unintuitive affects. I operate from an understanding of the game as a realm of open signification, analyzing not just the content and form of the object in question—the game itself—but the practice of playing from the perspective of an Asian American male-identified subject (that is, myself). The male Asian American player of *DX:HR* becomes the transhumanist white man in order to play within the structure of fantasy, opening discomforting corridors of racial possibility. As I illustrate in this final chapter, *DX:HR* is a private theater for the racially depressed, presenting a virtual world of self-annihilation for the Asian American gamer that pries open wounds of racialization for investigation and reflection.

Racial Phenomenology and Transhumanist Neoliberalism

To return to David Palumbo-Liu's quote,

> [t]he nature of Asian American social subjectivity now vacillates between whiteness and color. Its visibility is of a particular texture and density; its function is always to trace a racial minority's possibilities for assimilation.... Asia/America resides *in transit*, as a point of reference on the horizon that is part of *both* a "minority" identity and a "majority" identity. (1999, 5)

However, the formal and aesthetic structures of the video game *DX:HR* enable such an "in-transit" social subjectivity to be felt through the artifice of the gameworld, by inviting the Asian American player into flesh, and particularly in white flesh, which is central to theorizing Asian American engagement with the video game. Through the invocation and invitation of flesh, *DX:HR* thus suggests that racial form has a phenomenological dimension as well as a textual one, a "texture and density" to racialization.

To put it bluntly, *DX:HR* is a game about flesh, that performs flesh, that is an extension of flesh. This may seem counterintuitive, due to the common-sense understanding that gaming and digital media enable a liberatory *dis*embodiment, a meditative fugue that I explored at length in Chapter 5 in Tao Lin's *Taipei*. Indeed, this very sentiment is the crux of John Perry Barlow's famous 1996 assertion in his "A Declaration of the Independence of Cyberspace": "Ours is a world that is both everywhere and nowhere, but it is not where bodies live" (1996). In contrast, I would argue that virtual space—which includes video gaming as much as it includes cyberspace—contains rather than eschews the body. I follow in the tradition of feminist technocultural scholarship such as that of Allucquère Rosanne Stone, N. Katherine Hayles, Lisa Nakamura, Amanda Phillips, Bo Ruberg, among others, all of whom note the continued (if somewhat different, often heightened) relationship of the body to the technological apparatus, particularly in regard to the continuity of gender, race, and other markers of bodily difference within the virtual realm.[4] But rather than the body per se, I turn to flesh as the key concept of game embodiment.

When I state that *DX:HR* is a game of flesh, I draw from both Black feminism and phenomenology. In her monumental essay "Mama's Baby, Papa's Maybe," Hortense Spillers makes a distinction between flesh and body: flesh is the matter of embodiment associated with the captive subject position, while the body represents a wholeness that belongs to the liberated, free subject. Unlike flesh, the body is abstraction, a prerequisite for personhood. For Spillers, flesh denotes "its seared, divided, ripped-apartness, riveted to the ship's hole, fallen, or 'escaped' overboard" (1987, 67), with the enslaved Black person as the central example. As Anne Cheng summarizes in *Second Skin*,

> if the captive black female body has provided a rich source of irresistible and destructive sensuality, turning that body into a 'thing' ('being for the captor'), then 'flesh' with all its material fissures, tears, scars, and ruptures serves as a crucial and ethical reminder of the injuries inflicted on that body. (2010, 119)

In her reading of Spillers, Amber Jamilla Musser writes, "Flesh connects bodies to the external world by emphasizing the various conditions that make bodies visible in particular ways; it is about power and difference" (2014, 19). Michelle Ann Stephens adds, "It is this scratched up, fleshy body, the body made subject to racially and sexually sadomasochistic acts, a body that shows the very edges and seams of its cuts and splits, which is then covered over by the skin of race" (2014, 4). Thus, in the Spillersian mode, flesh is the haptic location of racialized embodiment, the physical matter that slavery rendered fungible, the material site of scarification and mutilation, with "cultural seeing by skin color" hiding the "hieroglyphics of the flesh" (1987, 67).

Meanwhile, Gayle Salamon draws from Maurice Merleau-Ponty, who deploys the concept of phenomenological flesh to provide a conception of transgender subject formation. Salamon's deployment is useful here: she writes that flesh is not synonymous with bodily matter, as "neither matter nor mind, but partakes of both these things and yet cannot be described as a mixture of them" (2010, 65). Rather, writes Salamon, "flesh" is a felt phenomenological extension that actually anticipates the body itself; "*Flesh is that which, by virtue of psychic investment and worldly engagement, we form our bodies into*, rather than the stuff that forms them" (2010, 64). In both Salamon's transgender account and Spillers' account of Black captivity, flesh *precedes* the body ("before the 'body,' there is 'flesh,'" writes Spillers, 67), and perhaps both grasp at a kind of prelinguistic intelligibility, although their descriptions are in reverse. Spillers' flesh is material, the "stuff" of bodies, while Salamon's is the indentations of the bodily schema *into* which the body itself forms.

I do not consider Spillers and Salamon to be arguing over a definition of flesh so much as productively disaggregating flesh from the body for different critical projects. Yet, both of their articulations are crucial to understanding the racial-sexual nexus of *DX:HR*.

Phenomenologically, I consider flesh here as an extension of feeling a body, of mapping out the potential spatial motility in which a body can "exist." Importantly, Salamon's phenomenological articulation of flesh offers a theoretical foundation to analyze the felt embodiment of the Asian American gamer in the white digital hegemony of *DX:HR*, naming the liminal interstices between subject and cultural object and opening this "flesh" to inquiry. But the violence of the video game, within its world, converts bodies into flesh in the Spillersian sense; as I will explain later, the game's conclusion is premised upon the lacerated, charred conversion of body back to flesh in order to consolidate racial otherness.

Moreover, racial subjectification exists in phenomenological flesh as well; this is, after all, an extension of the argument of the previous chapter, that race exists in the shaping of perception and interface itself. Racial embodiment entails Frantz Fanon's oft-cited "epidermal racial schema," which encapsulates "A slow construction of my self as a body in a spatial and temporal world" (2008, 91). For Fanon, to be racialized is to have a body, to be overdetermined by it over a gradual temporality, and the fleshy practice of *DX:HR* heightens this awareness altogether. Although Fanon's description of the epidermal racial schema—a crucial racial intervention into phenomenological thought more generally—is grounded in the context of postcolonial Francophone Blackness, his formulation still retains import for the Asian American body. To be racialized as Asian in the United States—and correspondingly, to undergo Asian American subjectification in dialogue with that racialization—is at least partly to be cognizant of one's own body, at least discursively and visually, as "Asian," relative of course to "others." In this regard, *DX:HR* follows the 1980s cyberpunk convention of establishing Asianness as the paradigmatic Other of cybernetic technofuture; *DX:HR* offers an expanse of Asian bodies to slay. For the Asian American subject extending their flesh into the gameworld, this produces a paradoxical state, one that I argue bears masochistic potential.

Although I would argue that the medium of the first-person video game is "fleshy" on the whole (and indeed, in a game such as this, there is also the haptic sensation of the controller vibrating when receiving damage, etc.), *DX:HR* diegetically emphasizes this fleshiness through its particular articulation of transhumanism, which in this game is coded as an ideal white liberalism, of the bounded and perfectly autonomous individual, against techno-orientalized deviance. Put another way, flesh is the terrain upon which *DX:HR* carves its transhumanist explorations. In the online publicity leading up to the release of *DX:HR* in August 2011,[5] Eidos Montreal emphasized three interrelated elements: its choice-driven agentic gameplay, its "cyberrenaissance" aesthetics (including, notably, extensive interactions with racialized Asian peoples), and its explicit engagement with transhumanist philosophy, all of which ultimately inform each other in *DX:HR*. The game immerses its player into a phenomenological experience of white liberal transhumanism, both diegetically and non-diegetically,[6] placing the player into the (un)comfortable role of an augmented whiteness.

In fact, it is perhaps more accurate to say that transhumanist augmentation becomes whiteness itself. In an interview with GameSpot,[7] *DX:HR* Art Director Jonathan Jacques-Belletete (who also served as the face and body model for Jensen's appearance) boasts the game's direct engagement with transhumanist thought, including the work of Joel Garreau, who in turn describes transhumanism as an intellectual and social movement dedicated to "the enhancement of human intellectual, physical and emotional capabilities, the elimination of disease and unnecessary suffering, and the dramatic extension of life span" (2005, xiii). Put simply, transhumanism can be understood fundamentally as the ideology of the "technologically-positive," utilizing new technologies to "enhance" the "human." In this sense, as Nick Bostrom states, transhumanism is at the center of human intellectual curiosity since its inception, though Bostrom traces contemporary transhumanist thought to the works of the Enlightenment, with an "emphasis on individual liberties, and ... its humanistic concern for the welfare of all humans" (2005, 4).

Accordingly, transhumanist thought trends toward individualist advancement over ideological intervention in its utopian conceptualizations. Garreau, writing in the early 2000s, points to a series of contemporary U.S. cultural tendencies necessitating the rise of transhumanist thought:

> The inflection point at which we have arrived is one in which we are increasingly seizing the keys to all creation.... It's about what parents will do when offered ways to increase their child's SAT score by 200 points.... What fat people will do when offered a gadget that will monitor and alter their metabolisms. What the aging will do when offered memory enhancers. (2005, 11)

Here, Garreau concerns himself not with educational equity, nor with societal perceptions of fatness; transhumanist human augmentation provides individuals with the capacity to succeed within a system taken as a given. Furthermore, Garreau implies that these augmentations, these prostheses, are external products, purchasable externalities to allow those with the means to succeed and leapfrog over those who presumably do not. Indeed, Cary Wolfe aptly argues that since transhumanism is essentially a conservative extension of white Enlightenment humanism, its discourses consequently deify the atomized Kantian individual, the white masculine rational ideal of the social contractarian imaginary. Despite transhumanists' attempts to distance themselves from the "specter of eugenics,"[8] transhumanism nevertheless shares a discursive resonance with eugenic notions of "human" "perfection—"human" insofar as the modern concept of the "human" has been racialized at least since the Enlightenment as both Sylvia Wynter and Charles Mills have astutely reminded us,[9] and "perfection" dependent upon full able-bodiedness and able-mindedness.

Bodily ideality and whiteness consequently haunt the transhumanist thought upon which *DX:HR* draws. Moreover, Adam Jensen is not just a transhumanist messiah (the biblical resonance of "Adam" certainly isn't subtle), but a white supercrip.[10] Jensen gains his augmentations in the introductory tutorial segment of the game that ends with his suffering mortal wounds at the hands of a black-ops augmented mercenary group called the Tyrants; Sarif engineers then proceed to augment his body to save his life. He gains cybernetic augmentations without consent to "correct" a disability imposed upon him against his will. Jensen thus simultaneously embodies the restoration of that which had been castrated, at once absence and ideality, prosthesis as virtuosity.

In its fleshiness, *DX:HR* is both representative and exceptional of the first-person action game. It is representative in that its general gameplay mechanics of movement, camera control, and leveling up are emblematic of this gamic form. However, it is arguably exceptional in its explicit diegetic mapping of cybernetic augmentations onto the main character's body that directly correspond to not just to statistical improvements in performance, but in "felt" phenomenological differences in gameplay altogether. In *DX:HR*, flesh manifests not just through the lived experience of being Adam Jensen, but also through the systematic form through which Jensen is augmented, allowing the player to form Jensen's body into the flesh of the player. In the game, as the player controls Adam Jensen and progresses, they gradually acquire "Praxis Points," which in turn can be spent in further augmenting parts of Jensen's body. As shown in Figure 6.1, the player can exercise agency in choosing which body parts to augment, such as head, torso, arm, skin, legs, eyes, etc.—each augmentation having a different effect in the gameplay experience. Upgrades are thus literally mapped onto the digital anatomy of the avatar and then experienced in the digital flesh. To enhance stealth, the player can choose to augment Jensen's skin so that he can turn invisible for a few seconds at a time, or perhaps his legs so that he emits less sound.

As Jensen incrementally gains transhumanist augmentations to his body throughout the game—which can alternatively make Jensen faster, more perceptive, stronger, et cetera—the alterations to the sense of being Jensen are not just seen or heard, but proprioceptively felt, affecting the player's very capacities to act within the gameworld, especially from the immersive first-person viewpoint of the game. The leveling up of Adam Jensen procedurally literalizes the ideological Enlightenment (and correspondingly, transhumanist) ideal of atomized self-improvement by mapping it onto his body, and invisibilizing it through its first-person interface. Jensen is, in fact, a cybernetic transhumanist Homo economicus, described by Foucault as "an entrepreneur of himself, being for himself his own capital, being for himself his own producer, being for himself the source of [his] earnings" (2008, 226). After all, Jensen develops principally in economic terms. As a role-playing game, in which the player does not simply play for a few minutes competitively for a round or two but,

Figure 6.1 The Augmentation Menu. From *Deus Ex: Human Revolution*, courtesy of Square Enix.

rather, progresses for a total of over 20 hours in one continuous storyline, *DX:HR* is a game in which the player invests a significant amount of what Edward Castronova terms "avatarial capital," a compelling virtual accumulation of "experience points and attributes" (qtd. in Nakamura 2009, 140) that is the product of the player's narrative labor. This is particularly the case in a high-agency game like *DX:HR*, in which the player feels that they crafted the narrative and the character build according to personal gameplay preferences. To accumulate avatarial capital, the player constructs a selfhood through flesh, located on the assemblage that is Adam Jensen's white cyborg pastiche of a body. *DX:HR* is emblematic of Turkle's declaration that "games hold out a ... promise," that is, "the promise of perfection" (2005, 86). Such is the procedural rhetoric[11] that undergirds the leveling up of Jensen as a character: mediated through the supercrip body, *DX:HR* phenomenologically produces an immersive ideal of not only liberal, but *neo*liberal, individualism that brings affective shape to the unboundedness of masculine whiteness. It produces whiteness as experience through action, and the Asian American player, as potential model minority, is welcome (if not explicitly) to step inside, to blur the boundary between self and other as they control white transhuman Adam Jensen through techno-orientalist transhuman Hengsha.

In this first-person view, Jensen's race is unmarked like whiteness itself, exhibiting its emblematic "invisibility ... as a racial position" (Dyer 1997, 3) yet contrasting with the many racial others present in the game, since whiteness is "precisely the absence of culture ... the empty and therefore terrifying attempt to build an identity based on what one isn't and on whom one can hold back" (Roediger 1994, 13). After all, as Lisa Nakamura aptly argues in *Digitizing Race*, the default "subject of interactivity" of digital media is hegemonically understood as white and male (2008, 15). *DX:HR* thus procedurally literalizes the ideological white Enlightenment transhumanist ideal of atomized self-improvement by mapping it onto the body, and invisibilizing it through its first-person interface. Except in some dialogue and cinematic sequences, and when Jensen ducks for cover, the game primarily transpires in first-person view, effectively immersing the player into Jensen's subjectivity as they make these various gameplay choices throughout the game (see Figure 6.2). In this first-person presentation, in which the screen is almost always displaying what the character/avatar sees (even the Heads-up Display (HUD)—a first-person gamic convention usually understood to be nondiegetic—is understood to be a diegetic reflection of Jensen's augmented vision, since the HUD does not appear pre-augmentation), the player does not only empathize with Jensen, but *becomes* Jensen in the gameworld. As Alexander Galloway asserts, the first-person subjective view in video games establishes "an intuitive sense of affective motion" to "facilitate an active subject position that enables and facilitates the gamic apparatus" (2006, 69). If the player has adequate competence over the controls, looking, movement, and firing weapons become seamless, a virtual extension of embodiment in a three-dimensional landscape.

However, *DX:HR*'s various gameplay modalities offer more than combat: one can choose to confront mission objectives with gun combat, stealth, conversational persuasiveness (such as in "social boss" interactions[12]), computational competence, or

Figure 6.2 A gameplay screenshot of an augmented "social boss" negotiation with Tong, the owner of "The Hive" bar & nightclub in Hengsha. Personality traits and rhetorical success measurement are represented in the top corners, while the bottom displays the player's dialogue options for Jensen. From *Deus Ex: Human Revolution*, courtesy of Square Enix.

some combination of these abilities. Choices—both the strategic "reactive" choices of in-time combat and the tactical choices of character augmentation—provide a particular agentic pleasure in the video game. Even the narrative conclusion of *DX:HR* depends on the player's actions; the player can choose one of four outcomes for the transhumanist future depending on the opinion they have formed regarding human augmentation through playing the game. It is largely through this agency that *DX:HR* retains its holding power,[13] deeply entrenching the consciousness of the player into the presence of the gameworld. The *becoming-avatar* in the first-person video game grants something like (but not quite) embodiment, echoing Nigel Thrift's theorization of contemporary automobiles as "extensions of [their drivers'] bodies" (2004, 47), especially through technologies of transubstantiation such as ergonomics and driving software that extend the bodily schema over the device itself.

The agency and immersion of the game all heighten the sense of flesh and of investment, in which the player plays a part in the authorship of the game's narrative; through actions in a rule-bounded gameworld, the player is neither spectator nor author but a participant somewhere in between. The gamer of color is thus placed in a circumstance in which the distinction between subject and object is blurred, especially while assuming the role of the white transhumanist cyborg. But above all, through the becoming-avatar and the extension of phenomenological flesh, the medium itself presents a kind of masochistic becoming-machine; granted, in a different sense than we have seen in the first few chapters of this text. Nevertheless, we see a union of form and content in *DX:HR*; becoming-machine and techno-orientalism are hand in hand.

Echoes of Ebens: Detroit, Erotohistoriography, and Techno-Orientalism

DX:HR shamelessly deploys techno-orientalism to render its aesthetic legible as cyberpunk, projecting anxieties that have haunted the genre since its inception in the Japanophobic 1980s. *DX:HR* art director Jonathan Jacques-Belletete refers to the aesthetic of the game as "cyberrenaissance," drawing from the visual vocabulary of both the Italian Renaissance[14] and the cyberpunk imagery in films such as *Blade Runner* and novels such as William Gibson's *Neuromancer*, both of which are undisputedly the most influential paragons of the cyberpunk genre that were birthed in 1980s science fiction. However, as Lisa Nakamura writes: "[Cyberpunk]'s emphasis on machine-enabled forms of consciousness seems to glorify, at times, the notion of the posthuman, which is also coded at times as the postracial. Despite this coding, however, race is all over cyberpunk's future terrains" (2002, 61). In addition to the abundance of neon, grit, and corporate domination over all aspects of social life, *DX:HR* is replete with an abundance of techno-orientalist imagery (specifically, sinophobic techno-orientalism), which was quite intentional; after all, as described in promotional videos, Jonathan Jacques-Belletete indicates that the inclusion of Asian settings is almost a requirement for (the nostalgic, retrofuturistic) cyberpunk. Such displays become particularly prevalent once Adam Jensen arrives in Hengsha. The Shanghai island in 2027 (which, as of this writing, is far from a speculative cyberpunk dystopia and is instead a small farming community) has been converted into a literally two-layered mega-metropolis dominated by the Chinese augmentation firm Tai Yong Medical, which operates the upper layer of habitation and monopolizes the city's sunlight. The lower level consists of Hengsha's criminal elements, red-light districts, and freakishly augmented Triad agents called "Harvesters," who scavenge for prosthetic body parts to attach to their own bodies. In Hengsha, Jensen explores the Hung Hua brothel, a cybernetic bordello with sexualized Asian women with straight bob haircuts, a throbbing techno beat interspersed with feminine gasps playing as a persistent soundtrack in the background. There, the player-as-Jensen can choose to play the White Savior role and assassinate (or frame for an arrest) a Chinese man who coerces the sex workers into augmenting themselves, in exchange for a reward in the form of money and potentially a Praxis point. Interestingly, even within a game replete with choice-driven gameplay, the game does not offer the choice to solicit services from the Hung Hua sex workers—Jensen remains loyal to his kidnapped white girlfriend (and chief Sarif scientist) Megan Reed—and thus retains his position of white male liberal-democratic moral superiority in contrast to the amoral, patriarchal, and sexually deviant Orient. Of course this cliché sinophobia morally justifies a particularly telling dialogue option of Jensen's when he speaks to a bouncer in the neighboring nightclub The Hive (also obviously evocative of stereotypical Asian conformity and "swarmlike" character), in which he remarks that "all of you look alike."

Thus, *DX:HR* presents a juxtaposition of two neoliberal transhumanisms: Adam Jensen, biblically named in *DX:HR* as a figure of once-pure origin, literalizes and embodies not the techno-orientalist dystopia of transhumanist civilization's Asian discontents, but the transhumanist ideal that takes white male individualism to its most glorious conclusion, a beacon of where transhumanism *could* lead, in contrast to the dirty techno-oriental nightmare presented in Hengsha, marked by vice, poverty, and exploitation. Techno-oriental filth is the dystopian excess of the transhumanist vision, a cautionary horror of augmentation—and the neoliberal subjectivity it euphemizes—gone wrong. Consequently, acting through the first-person identification with Jensen presents a dissonant (if perhaps mundane and not wholly unexpected) experience for the gamer of color, who is placed in a circumstance in which the distinction between subject and object is blurred altogether, especially while assuming—and mastering—the role of the white cyborg.[15]

But within the action of the gameworld, interactivity lends such mastery both a performatic dimension and an erotic one. Concerns of theater apply directly to video game studies—perhaps even doubly so—given that video games represent a form of intensified, privatized performance for its users.[16] However, the video game is a cultural production whose mode of identification exceeds the Aristotelian empathy with the protagonist of drama; it is a mode in which the player *becomes* the avatar or gaze onscreen itself. Insofar as they act upon the gameworld, the gamer is neither strictly a performer, character, or audience member. In performance terms, the gamer blurs the boundaries between performance and mise-en-scène, for, in Clara Fernández-Vara's words,

> the player parallels both the audience of the theatre play, and the interactor of software. The player is an active performer because she is also an interactor; but she is also the audience of the performance, since she is the one who makes sense of the system and interacts accordingly. (2009, 6)

Indeed, as Sherry Turkle argues, the video game provides a relationship of fusion, that whereas in "pinball you act on the ball ... [i]n *Pac-Man* you are the mouth" (2005, 70). In gaining such a sensation of existing in the gameworld, the gamer develops a relationship with the game not unlike that of an erotic encounter, rife with tactility, fantasy, pleasure, and perhaps emotional attachment. After all, as Sherry Turkle demonstrates, the video game's holding power possesses "roots [that] are aggressive, passionate, and eroticized" (2005, 66), invoking altered states that "combine a feeling of ominipotence and possession—they are a place for manipulation and surrender" (2005, 83).

Through the immersion of the gameworld, the player's fusion with the avatar or first-person gaze blurs the distinction between identification and desire; in Thomas Foster's words, "desire *for* machines often becomes difficult to distinguish from the desire to *be* a machine, and vice versa" (2005, 82).¹⁷ Thus, as a space that one inhabits and acts upon, techno-orientalized Hengsha literalizes Sara Ahmed's description of the status of the Orient as a reachable object:

> Orientalism ... would involve not just making imaginary distinctions between the West and the Orient, but would also shape how bodies cohere, by facing the same direction. Objects become objects only as an effect of the repetition of this tending 'toward' them, which produces the subject as that which the world is 'around.' The orient is then 'orientated'; *it is reachable as an object given how the world takes shape 'around' certain bodies.*" (Ahmed 2006, 120, emphasis mine)

DX:HR's interactive techno-orientalism makes the Orient an object reachable by the player-as-transhumanist-Jensen while simultaneously establishing the Orient's irreconcilable otherness by exhibiting Hengsha's improper "orientation," especially given its transgression of sexual propriety. *DX:HR*'s techno-orientalism imbues Hengsha with a sleazy, dirty affect against which Jensen's transcendent whiteness is counterposed. Thus, for the player with a body racialized as Asian, the game silently necessitates an asymmetric identification not only with Jensen, or even the white male gaze, but also with the imperial white male sense of engaging with the world in a process of epistemological marginalization and its consequent colonial mastery. It is a fantasy of conquest of a *reachable* techno-orient, a sensory space whose bodies are not unlike that of the player themself.

As the Asian American player engages with the epistemologically violent, stereotypically techno-orientalist setting of Hengsha, *DX:HR* illuminates the possible slippage of roles between the Asian stereotyped and the white master enabled by the structure of fantasy for the Asian player themself, which is, in this case, techno-orientalist. We can find a similar relation within Asian American theater critique: both Josephine Lee and Anne Anlin Cheng, in analyzing David Henry Hwang's *M Butterfly*,¹⁸ variously suggest that stereotypes and the fantasies that deploy them may in fact be uncomfortably necessary catalysts for pleasure itself. Strikingly, in examining the character Song Liling—the male-identified Chinese spy who performs idealized Orientalized femininity to seduce and manipulate male French diplomat René Gallimard—Cheng links stereotype, pleasure, and the fluidity of roles of power within the erotic encounter:

> One might say Song has ... not only learned how to be with a white man, but also how to *be* the white man. This suggests that, within stereotype's necessary and repeat performance, the *other* identificatory position available for the one stereotyped is not another stereotype ... but the role of the master. The difficult lesson of *M. Butterfly* is therefore not that fantasy exists, as the playwright himself asserts in his afterword, but the more politically distressing idea that fantasy may be the very way in which we come to know and love someone—to come to know and love ourselves. (2000, 127, emphasis in original)

The player has "not only learned how to be with a white man, but also how to *be* the white man" within the ludic magic circle of the techno-orientalist fantasy gameworld. To become Jensen is to master Jensen; to master Jensen is to master techno-orientalist Hengsha, which in turn is to master, in Josephine Lee's words, "the body-as-stereotype." However, such mastery is simultaneously a submission, as the player is, despite the significant agency afforded by *DX:HR*'s game mechanics, still bounded by a racist techno-orientalist narrative if one wishes to succeed. The player is as much "bottom" as "top" to the game itself, and pleasure can arise from this ambiguous doubling of position. Moreover, as I have argued earlier, despite the problematics of techno-orientalism, it is a racial form that is not altogether eschewed by Asian America; to recall again Rachel C. Lee and Sau-Ling Wong, "the Asian (American) cyborg is not solely the construct of the West, but also a self-invention that can take on model minority dimensions" (2003, xiv). The Asian American relationship to techno-orientalism, like Song's relationship to white masculinity, is complex and masochistic, heightened even more so in the video game medium as a consequence of its flesh.

Thus, I again turn to the work of Elizabeth Freeman and her concept "eroto-historiography: a politics of unpredictable, deeply embodied pleasures that counters the logic of development" (2005, 59). Erotohistoriography also "posits the value of surprise, of pleasurable interruptions and momentary fulfillments from elsewhere, other times" (2005, 59), deriving pleasure from the inappropriate. Freeman examines particular instances of "politically incorrect" queer sexual pleasure as performing a form of subjective excavation, locating rich potential in a "'bottom' historiography" that would usually be intuitively dismissed as internalized oppression (2005, 65). In discussing S/M, for example, Freeman states that "S/M relentlessly physicalizes the encounter with history and thereby contributes to a reparative criticism that takes up materials of a traumatic past and remixes them in the interests of new possibilities for being and knowing" (2010, 144). Freeman's formulation of S/M is instrumental in conceptualizing how both graphically and epistemologically violent video games such as *DX:HR* can potentially reorganize "the relationships among emotion, sensation, and historical understanding" through the usage of "icons and equipment from traumatic pasts" (2010, 168), excavating knowledges through the epidermal-racial schema of the flesh. I would assert that *DX:HR* offers the same potential for the Asian American subject, a sadomasochistic encounter in which Asian racialization materializes into an object of media.

That said, if we consider the Asian American playing of *DX:HR* to be an erotohistoriographic gaming practice, then what historiography is it performing? It is a historiography of the very species of techno-orientalism I have elaborated in the first two chapters, a racialization of mechanization ultimately rooted in the Detroit auto industry, the setting of Vincent Chin's murder. Although much of the second half of *DX:HR*'s narrative transpires in techno-orientalized Hengsha, the majority of the first half of the game occurs in Detroit, Michigan. As it happens, Jacques-Belletete mentions that Detroit was chosen as the opening setting precisely due to its history with the automotive industry:

> For Detroit, the idea was to show the reinvention of the city through Sarif Industry's heavy investment in the field of biotech research and manufacturing. If the city's glorious past was about the automotive industry, it would now be revived through the cybernetic industry. We even decided to reinforce this concept by having old car factories turned into biomechanical assembly lines, which in turn creates a strong visual message for the location. (Agnello 2012)

There is thus an intentional through line from the Detroit auto industry to that of human augmentation within the mythos of *DX:HR*. The machinic appearance of human augmentation of *DX:HR* furthermore lends human augmentation an industrial aesthetic compatible with a twentieth-century conception of Detroit, and, similarly, Fordist mechanization. However, in contrast with the multi-tiered vertical Hengsha, which speaks to a kind of dystopian extravagance in spite of its perverse underclass, Detroit's landscape more uniformly reflects the depressive bleakness of urban decay. With the exception of the Sarif Industries headquarters, the cityscape of *DX:HR*'s Detroit is dominated by deteriorating alleyways, gangs, and poverty, complete with a tragically predictable antiblack caricature. Within mainstream gaming journalism, *DX:HR* received negative publicity about its extremely stereotypical and antiblack portrayal of a homeless Black woman named Letitia (who serves as an informant for Jensen), a minstrelesque representation whom Evan Narcisse calls "a really bad part of a really good game" that "look[s] and sound[s] like a homage to Amos 'n' Andy" (2011).[19] In any event, it is through the stereotypical caricature of Letitia that Jensen and the player receive an assessment of the socioeconomic conditions of city; if the player has Jensen ask her about the city's mood, Letitia responds:

> Oh, things ain't looking good, Cap'n. People losing their jobs, their homes, locking everything they's own inta those, uh, garage-door storage units 'round town, hoping nobody breaks in an' steals stuff. Mr. Sarif gonna save us, he better do it, soon.... Just feels like this whole city's waiting to explode.

Through the absurdity of a 2027 Black person speaking a caricatured pre-1980s (African-American vernacular English) AAVE, *Deus Ex* displays a continuation of the contemporary Detroit that conforms to its blighted postindustrial stereotype. As Letitia implies, Sarif Industries is purported to be the corporate savior of the community through its investment, although its effectiveness in doing so is predictably disappointing. Still, *DX:HR*'s Detroit, possessing a largely unemployed and ultimately postindustrial workforce, resonates deeply with Vincent Chin and Ronald Ebens' Detroit of 1982. The parallels are rife, down to the presence of roboticism to the preoccupation with outside Asian competition. As a consequence, despite the game's transhumanist futurism, *DX:HR* ultimately draws upon a historical nostalgia, accessing a structure of feeling indexing the aesthetic and logic of U.S. 1980s cyberpunk, from the local urban decay to the existential threat of techno-orientalism, including the very setting of the Vincent Chin murder. But Adam Jensen is provided an opportunity that

Ronald Ebens was never afforded: a chance to travel to Asia and slay the very Asian competition that has conspired to disenfranchise him.

Enter the Dragon Lady: Masochism and the Annihilation of Self and/as Other

No character embodies the techno-orientalist yellow peril quite as obtusely as Zhao Yun Ru, the CEO of Chinese cybernetics company Tai Yong Medical, rival of the Jensen's American company Sarif Industries. Of the multiple antagonists of *DX:HR*, Zhao is the ultimate villain behind the conspiracy to control the world through augmentation implants. Mysterious, empowered, duplicitous, and cunning, Zhao is, quite blatantly, a Dragon Lady—she is even literally referred to as "the Dragon Lady" in text-based diegetic documents found throughout the Tai Yong facility. And yet, I argue that the final confrontation with Zhao is the moment that most illuminates *DX:HR*'s game-specific, masochistic, erotohistoriographic potential for the Asian American subject.

Jensen first personally encounters Zhao when he breaks into Tai Yong Medical in search for clues to find his (white) girlfriend Megan; Zhao plays the China Doll role, pleading to Jensen that she is a smaller pawn in a larger game, extending a hand to touch his face to distract him with her exotic-erotic Oriental feminine wiles, before she turns around and locks him in her office as she calls up her guards, whom Jensen must either defeat or sneak past (see Figure 6.3).

Figure 6.3 Adam Jensen (foreground) confronts Zhao Yun Ru, CEO of Tai Yong Medical Corporation. From *Deus Ex: Human Revolution*, courtesy of Square Enix.

Zhao's treachery escalates throughout the game's narrative. Approximately two-thirds of the way through the game, a brief, violent seizure hits the entire augmented population on Earth, Jensen included, which causes both the game's controller and the display to shake. News reports identify the mass seizure as an augmentation software bug, but, fortunately, Tai Yong Medical advertises having created a software repair patch. As Jensen, the player can choose to visit a clinic and have the patch applied, which ceases any future seizures, or the player can choose to distrust the patch, and the duplicitous, unclean Chinese science that it implies, and proceed through the game without it. The former choice results in Zhao's ability to literally neutralize Jensen's augmented upgrades during his battle with a powerful commando. To augmented civilians less powerful than Jensen, the Tai Yong patch even enables Zhao to remotely control their actions like a puppeteer. Thus, Zhao's Tai Yong upgrade is an infection of Oriental software that not only poisons but also completely threatens the player's sense of individual bodily autonomy. The Tai Yong patch is racialized and orientalized, possessive of a queer potential to render subjects—and most threateningly, white subjects—non-normative. As Chen has written, "the queerest bioterrorist is one who is remote, racialized "otherwise," and hybrid: both human painting agents and microcosmic pollutants that, almost of their own accord, invade the body through plenitudes of microcosmic sites ... sites the state cannot afford to acknowledge, for the queer vulnerabilities they portend" (2011, 271). In this case, the toxic Oriental infection renders some mediocre (as in Jensen), and others mindless conformist automotons, barbarous hordes made Chinese sycophants of the Dragon Lady queen. The game thus rewards the misogynist orientalist paranoia that validates this digital toxicity. While human augmentation serves as a biopolitical "corrective" to disabled bodies (which are then, subsequently, othered once more through augmentation's hypervisibility), augmentation then becomes additionally racialized: some upgrades are "trustworthy" while others are "foreign" tools that lie in wait, like the Manchurian candidate, to execute their collectivist Oriental agenda. Jensen's augmentations represent the normative, safe routes for evolution, while the optional Tai Yong upgrades present the peril of a techno-oriental dystopia. The player will feel the oncoming weakness should they choose to take the East into their body.

But it is in the final encounter with Zhao that the game is at its most sadomasochistic for the Asian American player. As the final boss (villain) to slay in *DX:HR*, Zhao connects herself to a massive network of quantum computers called the Hyron Project, invented by her co-conspirator-turned-traitor Hugh Darrow (who, as the "father of augmentation," was the inventor of most of the technologies—Zhao, the Oriental, replicates, appropriates, and steals from this white man's genius), that would enable her to regain complete control of the augmented human population. She connects the Hyron's fiber optics to her own nervous system, which suspends her from the ground, giving her an almost arachnid appearance as her Oriental body is fused with the massive technological apparatus, though she is protected, safely secure behind bulletproof glass (see Figure 6.4).

Figure 6.4 Zhao linked to the Hyron Project in the final battle of DX:HR. She is shielded by a wall of invisible bulletproof glass. From *Deus Ex: Human Revolution*, courtesy of Square Enix.

The conventional strategy to defeat Zhao in this confrontation is to attack the Hyron machine, which in turn has four other "drone" women linked in as slaves to the central processing unit. In a frenetic battle, the player-as-Jensen can dodge the Hyron's weaponry and slay the hapless, blinded drone women who have given their souls to the machine, which will result in Zhao's protective glass screen collapsing, leaving her open to attack. However, there is an alternate method: if Jensen was fortunate enough to pick up the experimental laser rifle earlier in the game, he can literally shoot through the glass to annihilate Zhao. This particular method is striking on several levels; there is an unsettling sense of violent masculine penetration, for one. Furthermore, glass is an invisible protection, an uncanny fetish-element of the digital age that transforms the three dimensional into the two dimensional, that transmutes tactile objects into objects of visual display. But for the Asian American player in particular, I moreover suggest that the glass is not entirely transparent; the glass that shields Zhao is a Lacanian mirror in which the Asian American player confronts the image of both self and other, or perhaps, self as other. Zhao is suspended in the machine, not unlike how the Asian American player is also suspended in the playing of the game, submitting to the machine's techno-orientalist aesthetic. Through the glass, the Asian American player faces the image of themselves and must annihilate themself in order to progress. For the male-identified Asian American player, it is a forced choice, an affiliation with gender over race, of completing the virtual access to model minority whiteness through racialized misogyny.

In any event, no matter how Zhao is slain, her body is literally incinerated in a brief cinematic sequence that plays when her health falls to zero; as she wails an otherworldly shriek of anguish, her human body is charred to a crisp and collapses to the floor. Jensen renders her overcooked meat, confronted with the sad reality of her organicity. Zhao, techno-oriental techno-fetishist, paradoxically cannot transcend her humanity because she is, as nonwhite, as Oriental, not human enough. The player, in turn, whose flesh has extended into the combat of the game, experiences a kind of orgasmic relief at the defeat of Zhao; her burning, contorted, but almost postcoital corpse is the climactic reward after hours of developing augmentations and maximizing Jensen's strength (see Figure 6.5).

For the male Asian American gamer, the player whose racial-epidermal schema aligns with Zhao's, it is a moment of simulated self-annihilation. In "being" the white man, the male Asian American player is positioned as simultaneously "top" and "bottom" of the erotic gaming encounter, a strange mixture of excitement and shame as the player is paradoxically coerced into a position of dominance in which one simultaneously incinerates self and other, both embodied by Zhao. In other words, the male player's self has expanded beyond the body of Jensen, embodying the white male subject and the Asian female object at once. Provocatively, the naked exercise of power coupled with pleasure in this game, as in S/M, displays the means by which domination and submission as positional categories themselves blur altogether. To dominate Jensen is to submit to his transhumanist whiteness. To dominate *as* Jensen is to submit to techno-orientalism. But perhaps, to submit to techno-orientalism is to deploy, in Freeman's words, "the uses of physical sensation to break apart the present into fragments of times that may not be one's 'own,' or to feel one's present world as both conditioned and contingent" (2010, 141). Thus, such an erotohistoriographic engagement in the game implies a productive inappropriateness, a means by which flesh reveals itself as imbricated within the ubiquity of power, to feel the "present world as both conditioned and contingent," allowing for slippage between the white male master and the dominated techno-orientalized.

To take pleasure in the slaying of Zhao is not necessarily to take pleasure in killing an Asian woman, nor even in occupying the space of heteropatriarchal whiteness; such pleasure is perhaps instead a masochistic invitation into the wound of racialization, whose traumatic nature becomes reconfigured in the moment of pleasure. I suggest that *DX:HR* offers for the masculine Asian American player (who again, to stress the specificity of *action* in games, is not merely a *reader*) a potential articulated by Darieck Scott regarding Samuel Delany's racially masochistic erotica:

> the traumatic past is exacerbated as it is also soothed, the wounds both bandaged and bled; and it is in that body-psyche nexus wherein what we call the sexual operates that this contradiction is held and that both psychic pain and the effects, if not the content, of language undergoes a transformation. (2010, 236)

But unlike both Scott's description here and Freeman's theorization of the erotohistoriographic, the interactive techno-orientalism of *DX:HR* explicitly highlights not

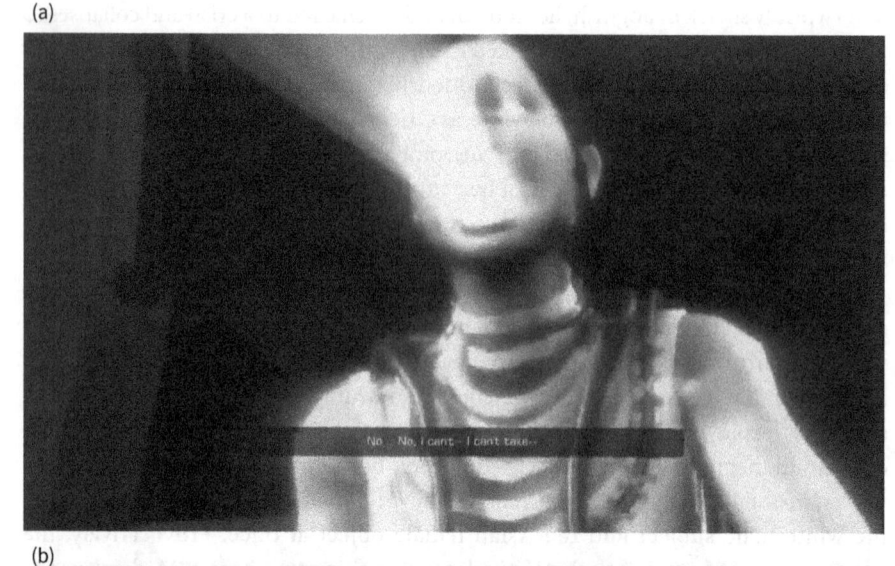

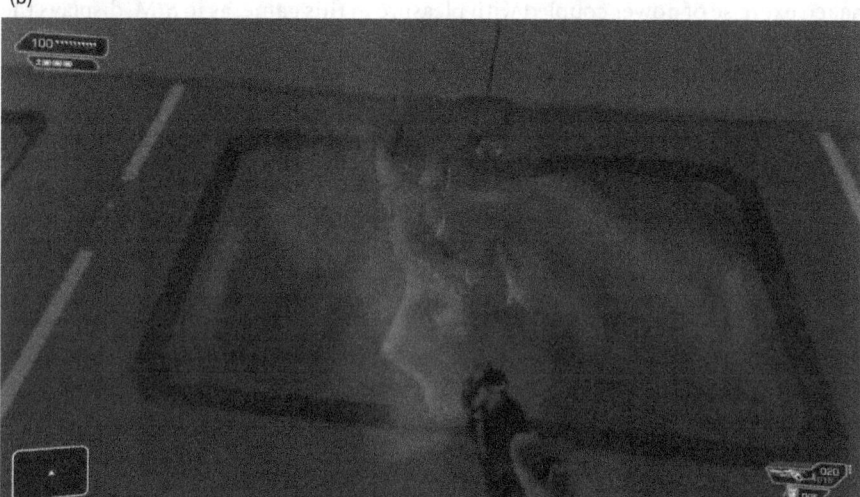

Figure 6.5 Top: Zhao dies screaming in battle victory cutscene. Bottom: Zhao's charred corpse, gameplay still. From Deus Ex: Human Revolution, courtesy of Square Enix.

only past racializations but also a transhumanist future, locating racial futurity in a complexly masochistic configuration upon racialized flesh.

The Asian American immolation of Zhao, the annihilation of the techno-orientalized self and/as other, may be more than mere internalized misogynist racism or abjection of the orientalized self; it might also be a creative mode of reflection. But this erotohistoriographic masochism of the flesh enables a claim to both a collective memory and a negotiation of a contentious future. As Rey Chow explains,

> [T]his extra dimension of the historicity of having-been-rendered-object needs to be recognized as a dimension of intellectual and artistic creativity, one that bears a sticky, messy historical imprint—namely, a claim to a (collective) memory of being aggressed against and the masochistic pleasures and pains that typically accompany such a claim. (2012, 181)

Phenomenologically, this is achieved in *DX:HR* through the extension of flesh from self to other, the player at once doubled in the position of subject and object of violence. This gamic erotohistoriography inverts the secondary masochism of the early Freud; rather than inwardly directed sadism, this is outwardly directed masochism, a re-performance of the abjection of racialized excess. That is, by assuming the role of Adam Jensen and slaying Zhao, the masculine Asian American player experiences, virtually, the simultaneous pleasure and nausea of assimilation and model minoritarianism.

Thus, we see a self-punishment, an annihilation of techno-orientalized yellow peril in favor of a cybernetic, unmarked masculine whiteness. The player here becomes-machine to kill a racial cyborg, having undergone a process not unlike Zhao's. Not only does *DX:HR* present an erotohistoriography of exclusion; it also incorporates (assimilates?) its player into the gameworld in order to slay the Asian who has been an irreconcilably foreign threat yet has also tried to play the white man's game but was driven mad from hubris. There is, at once, shame and pleasure, in both the player and Zhao, of both complicity with becoming-machine and the annihilation of its results. This could very well be the affective condition of model-minoritized Asian Americanness itself, the expulsion of one's own racial shadow[20] for the promise of full liberal personhood.

Somewhere within panethnic Asian American subjectivity, between the re-performed eulogies for Vincent Chin and the demolished walls of the Monkawa boarding house, remain the charred ephemera of Zhao Yun-Ru. As the player moves past the remains to the conclusion of *DX:HR*'s narrative, they leave behind a part of their flesh, graspable only when subjected to its familiar historical traumas. In this regard, model minority masochism upholds a Faustian promise, of a pleasure of self-completion twinned with the ash left from orgiastic immolation. But it is also a way of knowing, or perhaps a means of feeling, the kinesthetic weight of history, offering a cognitive map of racialization through the black and gold corridors of cyberpunk Hengsha and Detroit. Beneath the game's regime of intelligibility lies the possibility of the erotic, the cybernetic, within which Asian American subjectivity may find something like self-recognition.

Coda

Sankyoufocoming

It is 2005. I am a nineteen-year-old college freshman, stepping into the white stage light of the black box theater in Roble Gym. I let the silence onstage linger for a few moments, take a deep breath, slap on an eerily superficial smile, and begin:

> I went to the crafts shop the other day in search of
> glue to mend some broken promises
> I browsed through acres and mules
> growing grass and running rivers
> exchanging furtive glances with the shopkeeper
> who led me to the storage room labeled "Golden Mountain"
> and it was there I saw the store's most popular item
> listed for little more than half a soul
> the Model Minority
> Funny, 'cause I was going to assemble one myself
> but my lazy unemployed ass was stuck to the sofa
> so I never got around to it
> But I made a New Year's resolution
> to be a better citizen so I
> decided to do it

I take a beat. I am cruel now.

> so I started with a
> shifty serpentine spine I'd find
> in the dumpster behind a minstrel show
> and laced it with wooden chopsticks
> still stained with chow mein and chop suey
> that dribbled from the billion chins in the phone book
> It didn't need a heart but a fortune cookie
> that snapped satisfactorily,
> Sankyoufocoming Sankyoufocoming Sankyoufocoming Sankyoufocoming
> with a bow and a chow sieu bao in hand

then some electronic bones I could activate by remote control
but I got some interference from the couch potato next door

who guffawed as my man walked into
a wall of Rambo's bullets

(I mime getting shot by a machine gun, collapse, and rise again.)

It was okay though, since I could
make another one that looked
exactly the same

So I suited him with thick skin
and slanty eyes that white guys think
are hard to see out of
then the mouth of a mouse
and the wang of a Wang
I stir-fried him to crispy perfection and
he was alive!

And now, I escalate, commanding the model minority I have assembled, bowing with each "sankyoufocoming":

Go, model minority
Display yourself in a glass case with a glass ceiling
and be satisfied with your being
a middle manager
Sankyoufocoming Sankyoufocoming Sankyoufocoming Sankyoufocoming
Be that rat in the rat race
'Cause labyrinthine ghettos will constrain your pace
And as you stand, pose
for National Geographic pornos
side by side with Whitey
as you're spared from the clutches of Affirmative Action
so you can complain about being too excellent too
Go to the brothel, model minority
and find a steamy piece of that American Wet Dream
Blonde and pale and bathing in cash
Try to woo her with your Elvis impersonation
as your shadow pantomimes white pantomiming black
and she'll laugh and think you're cute like a dog
(which, by the way, you *don't* eat)

she won't let you touch but she'll let you jerk of in front of her
Sankyou.
Sankyou
Sankyou
Sankyou
> while Martin and the liberals sweep racism away
> to make the world safe for the Melting Pot
> The smelting pot of the Golden Mountain and golden skin
> Go, model minority and bark beside Ashcroft
> peel off immigrants like a banana
> and write books for the Hoover Institute
> about how you are living proof that the system works
> and that two Wongs
>> make a White
>> after all
>
> SANKYOUFOCOMING!
> I drop here. A long quiet. Slowly, as I rise:

Go, model minority
and find solitude in the white void

While I keep shopping for glue
to mend broken promises

In many respects, this piece that I had written as a teenager never fully let me go. As I grew older, more thoroughly trained in queer and feminist thought by mentors such as Cherríe Moraga, I would come to wince at some of the lines, as I do now, that reproduce the logics of white heterosexism. Yet for all of the political and aesthetic imperfections of this spoken word poem, I cannot help but realize, rather belatedly, that I had been pursuing the questions of this book all along. This poem, simply and literally titled "Model Minority," contains much of the argument I put forward in the preceding pages: the model minority is an artificial assemblage with mechanical attributes, chooses to aspire to white ideals (including the appropriation of Blackness), and, in the context of George W. Bush–era neoconservatism, supports state surveillance and the erosion of civil liberties ("bark besides Ashcroft" was, at the time, a rather unsubtle reference to torture apologist John Yoo). But above all, I was punishing this model minority. Flogging him. This model minority that my narrator had assembled, but, as I performed, conjoined with me. The poem begins as farce, transitions to sadistic cruelty as I describe the model's grotesque construction, and finally concludes with a deeply masochistic self-loathing, as it becomes clear that my commands to the model minority are, in fact, commands to myself.

Three years later in 2008, this piece would serve as one monologue in *R&L*, a full-length choreopoem I wrote to speak to 21st-century Asian Americans of my generation. It, too, was a fairly didactic performance, but one that advanced the ideas that found their way into this book. In the opening monologue, the character Helen, modeled blatantly after elder Japanese American radical Yuri Kochiyama, excoriates the Asian American audience:

> God, sometimes, I look at you young
> Orientals and I think
> you all got more in common with
> *hakujin* [white devils]
> than yourselves.
> The next time I see a Chinese guy who rallies
> against affirmative action I swear
> I'm gonna get him skin lightening cream
> and Jackie Chan eye surgery.
> They called us model minorities
> and we're eating it up.
> We're snorting the shit they've fed us
> and what are we doing? We're getting good grades
> and moving to neighborhoods
> where there ain't no black folks
> pretending that we—we've always belonged.
> (beat)
> What happened to us?
> What ever happened to the days
> when "Asian American" meant something, eh?
> When we linked arms in the struggle,
> with blacks and Hispanics and poor whites,
> we were all brothers and sisters united
> for a better world
> rather than a better paycheck?
> (beat)
> I still remember,
> because brother Malcolm died in my arms.
> He was shot so many times
> and I just kept whispering to him
> not to die, please, we need you,
> brother Malcolm.
> Brother Malcolm was shot by a fellow black man.
> I tell you all,
> that's what we're doing to ourselves.
> Still.
> We are killing
> the heroes
> in ourselves.

The figure of Helen, herself an embodiment of the Afro-Asian superego I described in Chapter 3, personifies the mother figure of masochism, lambasting fellow Asian Americans for their full embrace of American liberal capitalism and the ideology that sustains it. Her warning that "we are killing the heroes in ourselves" is meant to suggest not only a kind of racial cowardice—echoing, rather problematically, a Frank Chin–style valorization of masculine pride—but also that the notion of "Asian American" is far from the nostalgic construction of solidarity that it had been in the Asian American movement.

I wrote these words in the context of early-21st-century Stanford University, which one of my dissertation committee members (and fellow Stanford alumnus) humorously coined "the capital of neoliberalism." For nearly my entire time as an undergraduate involved in various forms of activism, I was constantly exhausted by Asian American peers who chose to not get involved with the many racial justice, labor, and anti-imperialist movements on campus. Anecdotally, I felt that the vast majority of Asian American students conformed precisely to model minority stereotypes of pursuing relatively apolitical STEM careers in medicine, engineering, and of course Silicon Valley tech, all while the small Asian American activist vanguard of which I was a part regularly worked to "dispel" the model minority as "myth." And yet, I had doubts; I wondered whether it was *we* who were quixotic, unrealistic, enthralled by what Arjun Appadurai has termed a "nostalgia without memory," yearning for an Asian American subjectivity that purposefully ignored the material conditions of a largely embourgeoised Asian American community to instead perform an affect of radicality. And as was the case in the first "Model Minority" poem, I could not fully externalize the model minority from myself, an Asian Stanford student protective of his GPA. Helen's admonition was not only for the Stanford audience, but for me, as well.

Years later, I would read about the case of another Asian American freshman: Chun Hsien Michael Deng, whose story opened this book. I was not entirely sure what to feel. I found myself both in Deng and in the fraternity brothers who tortured him, those brothers who assumed the role of white male tormentor in order to reveal the "truth" of Asian men's suffering. If a tree falls in the forest, and no one is around to hear it, does it make a sound? If an Asian man is subjugated but does not feel that he is suffering, is he a proper subject of ressentiment?

It is now 2020. The Taiwanese American entrepreneur Andrew Yang, founder of Venture for America and author of *Smart People Should Build Things*, recently ran for the nomination for the Democratic candidate for president of the United States. Although he was not the only high-profile Asian American who sought the nomination for the 2020 election—now–Vice President Kamala Harris is of course Indian American—Yang has worn his (East) Asianness on his sleeve. Although he was always a long shot for the nomination, Yang's campaign garnered a surprising amount of momentum, even polling ahead of several more established politicians, campaigning on a platform of a universal basic income of $1000 a month for every U.S. citizen, and focusing much of his discourse on the perils of automation.

But curiously, Andrew Yang's campaign for the presidency was, in many respects, the culmination of the many threads of model minority masochism I have described throughout this book, often embracing model minority and techno-orientalist tropes, combining them in spectacular fashion. He and his supporters wore hats and pins that read "MATH" (an acronym for "Make America Think Harder," a satirical remix of "Make America Great Again"). He bolstered a campaign fundraising video in which he appears as a Star Wars hologram appealing to his supporters to contribute funds. During one nationally televised debate on September 12, 2019, he quipped, "I'm Asian, so I know a lot of doctors." He publicly called for forgiveness of Shane Gillis, a comedian whose racial epithets included calling Yang himself a "Jew chink" (Feuerherd 2019, 1). Yang has, moreover, been accused of masculinist, sexist management practices, such as firing a female employee who questioned him on gender-based pay disparities and firing another woman for getting married and thus less "committed" to the company. Model minoritarianism, masculinism, techno-orientalism, and embrace of racialization are all curiously wedded together in a single logic of model minority masochism. And Yang has followers, with considerable numbers of young people uniting in what has been called the "Yang Gang" to support his candidacy, many of whom (but far from exclusively so) are Asian American men.

With the COVID-19 coronavirus pandemic raging in 2020, generating a widespread spike in Sinophobia and anti-Asian violence more generally (emblematic in Donald Trump's quip of "kung flu"), Andrew Yang penned an op-ed in the *Washington Post* in April 2020 entitled "We Asian Americans Are Not the Virus, but We Can Be Part of the Cure." He opens with an anecdote of grocery shopping, with several other (presumably non-Asian) people in the space eyeing him suspiciously. "And then, for the first time in years," he writes, "I felt it. I felt self-conscious—even a bit ashamed—of being Asian." But then, after lamenting anti-Asian bigotry, Yang pitches a textbook model minority answer to the problem: "The truth is that people are wired to make attributions based on appearance, including race. The best thing that could happen for Asians would be to get this virus under control so it isn't a problem anymore. Then any racism would likely fade." He draws parallels to the Japanese American 442nd infantry battalion, arguing for exceptional assimilationism, moreover, uncritically assuming Asian Americans to be a techno-oriental population of health and tech wizards whose technical expertise is uniquely qualified to combat the virus. He urges his fellow Asian Americans to "wear red white and blue" and concludes his article to demand: "Demonstrate that we are part of the solution. We are not the virus, but we can be part of the cure."

Yang's position is, politically speaking, diametrically opposed to the admonition from Helen in *R&L*, and, yet, what the two positions hold in common is a disappointment with the Asian America of their respective contemporary moments. For Helen (and, by extension, me in 2008), Asian Americans have selfishly attached themselves to the temptations of whiteness and American capitalism and must turn outward to build coalitions of color; for Yang, Asian Americans are selfishly dwelling too much on their sense of victimization and must turn outward to prove their worth to an American mainstream. Opposite politics, but common sadomasochistic flagellation.

Unsurprisingly, Yang drew sectors of the Asian American left to publicly criticize him. Jenn Fang, feminist public intellectual and author of the popular Asian American blog *Reappropriate*, writes,

> Andrew Yang says he is reclaiming negative stereotypes to empower nerdy Asians. But, efforts to reclaim negative slurs and stereotypes can only go hand-in-hand with sophisticated conversation about how those stereotypes are damaging and unrepresentative of the community when taken at face value. Yang does not do this. There is nothing subversive towards the Model Minority Myth in selling an "I *heart* Math" t-shirt.

But, Fang also belabors extensively the mythology of the model minority, and the familiar ways in which the model minority has been instrumentalized to obfuscate Asian American economic diversity and legitimate suffering. In this regard, not only does Yang represent the reactionary aspects of model minority masochism; he also draws out its more progressive, Asian Americanist, moral masochistic form, the punishment of the figure who embraces model minoritarianism, he who is also embarrassingly representative of (and thus part of) ourselves. This dialectic should be quite familiar to us by now.

In the echoes of the becoming-machine in 1980s Detroit, in the touchscreens and televisions of the contemporary Asian American literary imagination, in the muscled ressentiment of the Green Goliath, in the mournful yet impossible jazz notes of Chet Monkawa, in the digitized dystopia of the video game interface, racial masochism's life persists in what it means to perform, and to approximate "being," this uncanny thing called "Asian American." What I hope to have offered here is not a definitive or static model of an identity but, rather, an impressionist portrait of a social relation, wherein the convergence of historical, aesthetic, and ethical forms have coagulated into something that exceeds the sum of the parts of panethnicity. To rephrase the immortal title of Carlos Bulosan's magnum opus, Asian America is in the affect; it is in the liminal zones of human and machine, interior and exterior, model minority and perpetual foreigner, pain and pleasure.

In closing, I hope to gesture to a futurity within a painful encounter with trauma, and I wonder if it is through a masochistic critique that there may be a futurity beyond what ressentiment and melancholia have allowed. Of course, it is possible that this may not be the case; in the end, masochism remains more descriptive than prescriptive, and even as it contains its various telic ideals, the various masochisms may, in fact, thwart each other. The model minority masochism of becoming-machine and the moral masochism against it may coexist only in a deathly embrace. Yet, this antinomy may be precisely what is needed in order to achieve an Asian American cultural politics that is more reflective of those interpellated under its sign, yet also transformative in its relationship to power and self-formation.

Despite my critique of the moral-masochistic "ideal critical subject" throughout this text, I nevertheless believe that an Asian Americanist radicality is needed more urgently than ever. The political heart of those early poems still beats beneath my anxious ambivalence. In the era of global far-right authoritarianism, the waves of nativism, exclusion, and overt white supremacy have re-entrenched themselves in the national mainstream. At first glance, my critique of ressentiment and melancholia may seem critical of resistance movements, but in reality, it was *white* ressentiment, not unlike that which killed Vincent Chin (and, in fact, concentrated in similar geographic areas), that propelled Donald Trump into office in 2016. Recalling the Lordeian truism that "the master's tools will never dismantle the master's house," moral economies of woundedness have grave limitations in their transformative potential simply by relying on the individuation and essentialism that animates racial capitalism.

The Asian American model minority itself can be conceived as one such "master's tool," an embodiment of respectability politics itself, and operationalized as a technology via techno-orientalism. Racial masochism contends with its underlying logics even as it sometimes embraces it, or sometimes *precisely* by doing so. Not unlike Donna Haraway's cyborg in the 1980s, the monstrosity formed by militarism and capitalism that can in turn lead to its undoing, the self-objectifying, self-punishing, masochistic Asian American may offer a modest first glimpse into an Asian American subjectivity not only of resistance, but of corrosion. The robot may leak battery acid, after all. And the masochist may be the most capable among us to feel something like freedom.

Notes

Introduction

1. Drawing from Jodi Melamed's critique of neoliberal multiculturalism (2006).
2. The model minority is fundamentally assimilationist, although it can easily draw from the orientalist perpetual foreigner imagination—take, for example, *New York Times* columnist Nicholas Kristof's comment in his 2015 op-ed "The Asian Advantage" that "I'm pretty sure that one factor is East Asia's long Confucian emphasis on education."
3. Lee's terminology is particularly precise, although it is nearly the same concept as the "bad subject," first applied to Asian American literary studies by Việt Thanh Nguyễn in *Race and Resistance*, who in turn is indebted to its first articulation by Michel Pêcheux, whose "bad subject" is the one who resists the Althusserian hail of interpellation.
4. For example, Daryl Maeda's history of the rise of Asian American identity can, in fact, validate this position given the historical roots of the very term "Asian American" as an intentionally revolutionary identity, not unlike the rise of "Chicano/a" for Mexicans in the United States.
5. Ellen Wu, *The Color of Success: Asian Americans and the Origins of the Model Minority* (2014), and Madeline Hsu, *The Good Immigrants: How the Yellow Peril Became the Model Minority* (2015). As Ellen Wu writes, the development of "Asian Americans as the model minority—a racial group distinct from the white majority, but lauded as well assimilated, upwardly mobile, politically nonthreatening, and *definitively not-black*" (2014, 2, emphasis in original)—is partly the result of Chinese and Japanese American responses to shifting national and transnational circumstances in the prewar, internment, and postwar periods.
6. Louis Althusser and Michel Foucault agree on this basic point, even if their conceptual frameworks architecturally differ. Judith Butler writes, "Whether by interpellation, in Althusser's sense, or by discursive productivity, in Foucault's, the subject is initiated through a primary submission of power" (1997b, 2). While Althusser describes the hail of interpellation, that responding to the call of "hey you" (his metaphor for ideology) converts one into a subject because the person hailed "has recognized the hail was 'really' addressed to him, and that 'it was *really him who was hailed*'" (2001, 174, emphasis in original), Foucault meanwhile models power as a circuitous force that constitutes society and subjects themselves, insisting "We should not ... be asking subjects how, why, and by what right they can agree to being subjugated, but showing how actual relations of subjugation manufacture subjects" (2003, 45).
7. After all, to cite a Foucauldian truism, "Where there is power, there is resistance, and yet, or rather consequently, this resistance is never in a position of exteriority in relation to power" (1978, 95).
8. In a similar maneuver, Shimakawa's *National Abjection* explores the performance of an Asian American body that has been historically abjected through legal means—exclusion acts, internment, and so on—and attempts to forge a form of subjecthood despite having been consigned the status as abject refuse. With legal exclusion established as a definitive

paradigm for Asian American racialization, Shimakawa turns to Kristeva's articulation of abjection to characterize the psychic condition of Asians in the United States.

9. These more recent historical studies revise Robert G. Lee's influential historical framework, in which the racialization of Asians in the United States follows six stages according to the economic conditions of the United States: "the pollutant, the coolie, the deviant, the yellow peril, the model minority, and the gook" (1999, 8). Although Lee's typology remains quite valuable as an analytic, Hsu's and Wu's accounts problematize, for example, the notion that the model minority's origins arose cleanly in the Cold War—and that, in fact, its origins can be traced to the beginning of the century.

10. As Lisa Lowe and David Lloyd write in their introduction to *The Politics of Culture in the Shadow of Capital*, "'culture' obtains a 'political' force when a cultural formation comes into contradiction with economic or political logics that try to refunction it for exploitation or domination" (1997, 1). Similarly, I conceptualize cultural politics as a domain of racial and ethnic strategy in order to confront, subvert, or submit to modes of exploitation and violence. It is within the domain of cultural politics that cultural production gains political force, cohering or exploding various formulations of identities and collectivities.

11. Sigmund Freud's highly influential descriptions of masochism ultimately form the foundation for much of masochism theory for the twentieth century. The early Freud of "Three Essays on the Theory of Sexuality" (1905) considered masochism to be a secondary psychic function, one that stemmed from an inwardly turned sadism: "masochism is nothing more than an extension of sadism turned round upon the subject's own self, which thus, to begin with, takes the place of the sexual object" (1989, 252). However, as Freud began to pursue study of *thanatos*, the death drive, in *Beyond the Pleasure Principle* (1920), Freud revised his model of masochism to be "possibly" primary rather than secondary, arguing that masochism reflects the instinctual drive of the subject to return to a state of inactive death.

Jacques Lacan takes this latter Freudian notion of masochism and situates masochism as being the primary function, with sadism as its secondary. In fact, Lacan states, "sadism is merely disavowal of masochism" (1998, 186), in which the sadist exists primarily for the masochist's fantasy. Crucially, both sadism and masochism, argues Lacan, are founded upon self-objectification: "the subject assuming this role of object is precisely what sustains the reality of the situation of what is called the sado-masochistic drive, and which is only a single point, in the masochistic situation itself. It is in so far as the subject makes himself the object of another will that the sado-masochistic drive not only closes up, but constitutes itself" (1998, 185). Under the Lacanian paradigm, masochism is principally a perversion of becoming the object of the drive, and the other's *jouissance* beyond the pleasure principle, that is, toward death.

12. Within relational psychoanalysis, masochism is something of a different order altogether, being not primarily invested in sexual pleasure at all but, rather, a narcissistic moral economy of suffering and recompense. According to Victorian literary scholar John Kucich, who draws from the tradition of relational psychoanalysis, masochism should be understood primarily as a fantasy structure, rather than limited to (though not excluding) the scene of chains and whips of the popular imagination. In fact, notes Kucich, the contemporary consensus among psychoanalytic clinicians is that "masochism should be understood within a narcissistic technology, not a sexual one" (2007, 22), with the extension of the self as the primary preoccupation of masochism. Kucich's pre-Oedipal relational

model of masochism furthermore argues that various fantasies of omnipotence are the "primary narcissistic compensation that masochism provides" (2007, 22), including the omnipotence of others: "By exaggerating his or her suffering, the masochist can provoke fantasies, too, that an unknown, infinitely sympathetic rescuer will someday appear. The projection of omnipotence onto others serves the masochist in a more general way by producing a morally simplified and thereby controllable world in which judgments about others are always absolute and always the masochist's narcissistic needs" (2007, 24–25). The pre-Oedipal masochism of relational psychoanalysis that Kucich describes is not tethered to sexual pleasure but, rather, to fantasy, the pleasure of imagining, itself.

13. Moreover, Deleuze disagrees with Freud and Lacan on masochism's relationship to sadism, arguing that masochism is completely separate from sadism, since sadism relies upon a process of "negation," opposed to the "suspense" of masochism. Furthermore, argues Deleuze, masochism is temporal, requiring long durations of suspense between painful strikes.

14. In his June 1982 interview with the *Advocate*, "Sex, Power, and the Politics of Identity," Foucault gleefully celebrates S/M as "inventing new possibilities of pleasure with creative parts of their bodies," declaring it "a creative enterprise, which has as one of its main features what I call the desexualization of pleasure" (1994b, 165). Foucault dissociates pleasures from sex, noting the fascinating dimension of how S/M derives pleasure from parts of the body that are not the sex organs.

15. Leo Bersani builds upon Foucault to explore how the masochist does not technically enjoy pain itself, but "rather a passion for pleasure so intense that extreme pain is momentarily tolerated (rather than loved for its own sake) as necessary to bring the masochist to that biochemical threshold where painful stimuli begin to produce pleasurable internal substances" (1995, 94). The thrill of masochism then becomes a thrill of "self-shattering" in which "the ego renounces its power over the world.... Through pain, S/M dramatizes (melodramatizes) the potential ecstasy in both a hyperbolic sense of the self and the self's renunciation of its claims on the world" (Bersani 1995, 95).

16. This is echoed in Judith Butler's *Psychic Life of Power*: "To desire the conditions of one's own subordination is thus required to persist as oneself." Butler continues, "What does it mean to embrace the very form of power—regulation, prohibition, suppression—that threatens one with dissolution in an effort, precisely, to persist in one's own existence? It is not simply that one requires the recognition of the other and that a form of recognition is conferred through subordination, but rather that *one is dependent on power for one's very formation,* that that formation is impossible without dependency, and that the posture of the adult subject consists precisely in *the denial and reenactment of this dependency*" (1997b, 9, emphasis mine). This "denial and reenactment" of the dependence on power sets the conditions for a masochistic encounter with racialization, for the racialized subject depends on racialization in order to achieve legibility. Here, Butler uses the word "desire," but masochism gestures not just to desire; masochistic critique asks whether not just desire but *pleasure* exists in that nexus of power and subjectification, asking if subjugation lays the groundwork of what Celine Parreñas Shimizu has titled "productive perversity" (2007, 6). In his first volume of *The History of Sexuality*, Foucault pronounced that "Pleasure and power do not cancel or turn back against one another; they seek out, overlap, and reinforce one another. They are linked together by complex mechanisms and devices of excitation and incitement" (1978, 48).

17. This text aspires to be the first full-length study deploying masochism to map model minority subjectivity and Asian American cultural politics, but this is far from the first to discuss masochism within Asian American cultural production. Josephine Lee, for example, locates masochistic pleasure in Song's occupying of a stereotype in *M Butterfly*: "It is easy to argue that what gives pleasure is the subversion of the stereotype.... But this position is complicated by Song's pleasure in his own performance: he is thrilled not only by his duping of Gallimard but also, the play suggests, by the fantasy of being loved as a butterfly" (1997, 118–119). Additionally, masochism itself is of particular prominence within Asian American scholarship already: Daniel Y. Kim describes Asian American masculinity as characterized by "self-loathing, masochism, and melancholy" (2005, 143), while erin Khuê Ninh suggests that the debt-bound daughter of Asian American literature is disciplined into a self-immolating masochism as a consequence of the micropolitics of capitalism manifest in the Asian immigrant family. This text builds upon these works by bringing masochism to the fore, with attachment to model minoritarianism.
18. It is curious to contrast this imaginary of mass reproducibility to that described by Christopher Bush in his 2007 essay "The Ethnicity of Things in America's Lacquered Age." Bush, in describing Gilded Age *japonisme* in the United States, describes a fetishism of Japanese objects that conceptualizes them as *not* mass-produced; rather, the Japanese people *themselves* all universally possessed an inclination toward aesthetic craftsmanship. This imagination of Japan would shift as Japan rose to become an industrial power, and East Asia on the whole became conceptualized as being fundamentally imitative. This could be one of the primary distinctions between more "generic" East Asian orientalism and more contemporary techno-orientalism.
19. As Andreas Huyssen writes in "The Vamp and the Machine," his reading of Fritz Lang's *Metropolis*, "The fears and perpetual anxieties emanating from ever more powerful machines are recast and reconstructed in terms of the male fear of female sexuality, reflecting, in the Freudian account, the male's castration anxiety.... Woman, nature, machine had become a mesh of significations which all had one thing in common: otherness; by their very existence they raised fears and threatened male authority and control" (1986, 70).
20. Similarly, in her examination of gendered cyborg imagery from the 18th to 20th centuries, Jennifer González argues that the advent of modern technology produced "a situation in which the relation—and the distinction—between the machine and the human became a question of gender and class. Those who had access to certain machines were privileged, and those who were expected to behave like certain machines were subjugated. The same is true today" (1999, 60).

Chapter 1

1. This is partially, though not entirely, true, for according to most accounts, Chin threw the first punch. However, this does discount the escalation that happened prior to the first act of physical violence.
2. Many of which are covered in this chapter, but the Chin case is prominent in such legal scholars' texts as Frank Wu's *Yellow* and Robert S. Chang's *Disoriented*, and Helen Zia's *Asian American Dreams*.

3. I refer to "Asianness" and "Asian Americanness," but I wholeheartedly reject any essentialist notions of either of these descriptors. I analyze these abstractions precisely as abstract constructions.
4. Moreover, the material conditions of 1980s Detroit were in dialogue with its aesthetics. As Ben Williams recounts, Detroit's Black community is not only the birthplace of "Motown" soul music, but also American techno music: "techno is a specifically African American variation on the themes of inner-city collapse explored by [cyberpunk artists Alvin] Toffler, [Ridley] Scott, and [William] Gibson, a variation that teleports African diasporic traditions into the disembodied world of computer networks" that "soundtracks the decaying industry of Detroit" and "leaves the city behind for the new global space of postindustrial capitalism" (2001, 155). Galster also remarks that "it's not surprising, with its alien-like work environments stressing machine-like precision, that Detroit later would become the acknowledged birthplace of Techno music" (2012, 4). Furthermore, Galster's remark about "robocops" extends to the Detroiters' 2011 campaign to erect a massive statue to the cyborg hero of the same name from the iconic film by Paul Verhoeven.
5. According to Kurashige, Detroit has been a harbor for Asians to seek refuge from various forms of "persecution and exploitation"—early Chinese immigrants moving away from the West Coast, Filipinos working in the Ford factories, Southeast Asian refugees uprooted by the Vietnam War. This has also been accompanied by relatively cautious cultural politics—Japanese Americans, for example, encouraged to not cluster together and instead assimilate into the white mainstream (2002, 53).
6. Thus far, I have referred to Asian American "subjecthood" when, strictly speaking, the term "subject" is ultimately an inadequate descriptor in relationship to Deleuze and Guattari's description of "becoming." Deleuze and Guattari prefer "assemblage," implying a model that "lean[s] more to collection, combination, assembling" (Puar 2007, 4). Jasbir Puar favors the assemblage over the (intersectional) subject, arguing that the assemblage "de-previlege[s] the human body as a discrete organic thing" (2007, 5) and does "not privilege bodies as human, nor as residing within a human/animal body" (2007, 5). That said, my usage of the term "subject" is not mutually exclusive of the Deleuzian model of assemblage as described by Puar, and neither, I would argue, are many strands of critical theory; for example, the Foucauldian model of subjectivation as described in Volumes 2 and 3 of *The History of Sexuality* entailing "technologies of the self" are quite compatible with the assemblage. What I reject, as cultural theory at large seems to have soundly rejected for decades, is the notion of the soundly unified, universal subject. Thus, I will deploy the terms "assemblage" and "subject" more or less interchangeably, except to highlight particular aspects at various points.
7. Invoking, as Julia Kristeva writes, "one of those violent, dark revolts of being, directed against a threat that seems to emanate from an exorbitant outside or inside, ejected beyond the scope of the possible, the tolerable, the thinkable. It lies there, quite close, but it cannot be assimilated" (1982, 1). As David Leiwei Li and Karen Shimakawa have separately demonstrated in *Imagining the Nation* (2000) and *National Abjection* (2003), respectively, Asians in America had been legally abject since at least the mid-20th century (in Li's account), or since the 19th century (in Shimakawa's), victims to a politic of exclusion beginning with the 1882 Chinese Exclusion Act and continuing all the way through 1965 immigration reform and beyond. In Shimakawa's narrative, the psychic life of abjection manifested legally, performatively codified to enact a persistent racial exclusion.

8. As I will detail at greater length in Chapter 4, ressentiment is related to but different from masochism, in that ressentiment seeks revenge for injustice while masochism seeks self-punishment, although both operate from injury as its affective or libidinal fuel.
9. The masochist's violence may consequently demonstrate the inverse of the relationship of masochism and sadism articulated in Freud's early work—that is, that masochism is simply inwardly directed sadism rather than its own independent function, although Freud would change his position in *Beyond the Pleasure Principle*—in that what appears to be sadistic catharsis is secondary to a dominant narcissistic masochism.
10. I refer here to Mikhail Bakhtin's classic *Rabelais and His World*, in which he describes the medieval carnivalesque as a finite period in which the "fools" are "elected kings" (1984, 385), demonstrating the capacity for the festive to possibly overturn society and its social norms.
11. Zia has had a tendency toward the magnification of normative respectability in other works, as well. For example, as Colleen Lye argues in "The Literary Case of Wen Ho Lee" (2011), Zia (as coauthor of *My Country Versus Me*, Wen Ho Lee's memoir) goes to great lengths to establish Lee's apparent naiveté and subsequent political education, establishing Lee as a dutiful adherent of the American Dream, in order to underscore the injustice that is inflicted upon him.
12. As many have noted the narrative similarities between the Vincent Chin case and the murder of Emmett Till in 1955, so exist similarities between the figuration of Lily Chin and Mamie Till. Both women were tireless activists whose grief was publicly demonstrated to reveal the wrongness of their sons' deaths in order to demand some form of justice denied to them by the juridical court system. But while Lily Chin is most iconically figured with the dignified photo of her son resting on her lap, Mamie Till is best known for her powerful and controversial demand that her horrifyingly mutilated son be displayed in an open casket. The image of Lily Chin is homologous with the whole and respectable Vincent, while Mamie Till is figured with the material annihilated Black body.
13. The sanitization of Chin effectively worked to turn Chin into a martyr for a budding Asian American cause. One can certainly analyze the Chin affair, and the ACJ's work in particular, through martyrdom as a primary optic. In *Martyrdom and Memory: Early Christian Culture Making*, Elizabeth Castelli writes that "American martyrdom has historically had far more to do with political conflicts and especially with race" (2004, 192), and that "[t]he language of martyrdom serves in these different examples as a way of assigning a broader symbolic meaning to an event that might otherwise be interpreted as senseless and capricious violence" (2004, 193). Hate crimes in particular, according to Castelli, bear the discursive legacy of early Christian martyrdom that "floats in the background uncannily, as a distant analogy, a narrative resource, and an object of ambivalent nostalgia" (2004, 193). But martyrdom, too, is entwined with masochism. Using the discourse of British imperialists as an example, John Kucich writes, "What is particularly striking about British imperial culture is how often it mythologized victimization and death as foundational events in the teleology of empire.... The foundational myth [of Captain Cook] ... revolved around the sanctification implicit in the imperial martyr's suffering—a sanctification that allied imperial pain with redemption and with the beginning, rather than the end, of history. In short, sanctification transformed the pain and finality of death or defeat into pleasurable fantasies of ecstatic rebirth or resurrection" (2007, 5).

Chapter 2

1. See Karen Shimakawa's *National Abjection* (2001) and Joshua Chambers-Letson's *A Race So Different* (2013).
2. Well in line with the history of racialized people in the United States—the Buffalo Soldiers, the Tuskegee Airmen, the 442nd Infantry Battalion, the American Indian code talkers, and so on—utilizing military service to demonstrate loyalty and perform equality.
3. As Stephen Best and Saidiya Hartman have written regarding the question of slavery reparations in the writings of Ottobah Gugoano, "justice is beyond the scope of the law, and redress necessarily inadequate. If what has been done cannot be undone, then the forms of legal and social compensation available are less a matter of wiping the slate clean than of embracing the limited scope of the possible in the face of the irreparable, and calling attention to the incommensurability between pain and compensation" (2005, 1–2). *Chinoiserie* gestures toward this form of reparation, although, as I argue, it remains limited by its attachments to normative grievability.
4. Documentary theater is a medium well rehearsed within performance studies, and like all such works, the UC Hastings re-enactment provokes the question posed by Carol Martin: "not everything in the archive is part of the documentary.... What is the basis for the selection, order, and manner of presentation of materials from the archive?" (2006, 9). Consequently, continues Martin, "The process of selection, editing, organization is where the creative work of documentary theatre gets done" (2006, 9). In other words, documentary theater is a curatorial medium, defined as much by its selections from the archive as much as that from its omissions, all the while creating "its own aesthetic imaginaries while claiming a special factual legitimacy" (2006, 10), and "[a]s staged politics, specific instances of documentary theatre construct the past in service of the future the authors would like to create" (2006, 10).

Chapter 3

1. Third-generation American; grandparents immigrated to the United States.
2. Here, I note 1992 as a key historical inflection point due to the Los Angeles riots / LA rebellion, which occurred from April 29 to May 4, 1992, waged principally by Black and Latinx communities outraged over the acquittal of the police officers who brutally beat African American motorist Rodney King. As David Palumbo-Liu, Helen Jun, Claire Jean Kim, and others have discussed, the mainstream media also rhetorically positioned Korean American business owners as victims of the uprising, wherein Koreans were very blatantly demonstrated as entrepreneurial model minorities in contrast to criminalized Blackness. It should be noted that the LA riots also occurred in the wake of the murder of Latasha Harlans, an African American teenager, by a Korean grocer who accused her of theft and did not serve jail time in the resulting trial, which occurred one week before the riots. The spectacle of the LA riots also signaled to many within Asian American activist communities the collapse of the Asian/Black coalition.
3. Within Black/African American studies, the most notable confrontation of Afro-pessimism has been an ongoing critique from Fred Moten, who forcefully argues that Black life, rather than Black social death, should be the locus of critical attention; Moten also argues that it is not *social* death that constitutes Blackness, but *political* death (2013). Within ethnic

studies more broadly, one of the most compelling critiques of Afro-pessimism comes from Iyko Day, who writes: "According to Sexton, no other oppression is reducible to antiblackness, but the relative totality of antiblackness is the privileged perspective from which to understand racial formation more broadly. But unlike the way feminist and queer critical theory interrogate heteropatriarchy from a subjectless standpoint, Sexton's entire point seems to rest on the very specificity and singularity—rather than subjectlessness—of black critical theory's capacity to understand race. The privilege of this embodied viewpoint similarly relies on rigidly binaristic conceptions of land and bodily integrity" (2015, 112). That is, Sexton requires an ossification of the subject, and an essentialist equivalence between the body and the subject, in order to make claims to Black exceptionalism. Moreover, Day makes reference to the "subjectlessness" of feminist and queer critical theory, a valuation most assertively pushed by Grace Hong and Roderick Ferguson in *Strange Affinities*, that difference in women of color feminism and queer of color critique is "not a multiculturalist celebration, not an excuse for presuming a commonality among all racialized peoples, but a clear-eyed appraisal of the dividing line between valued and devalued, which can cut within, as well as across, racial groupings" (Hong and Ferguson 2011, 11). This heterotopian woman of color feminist model, according to Hong and Ferguson, furthermore counters the epistemology of "ideal types" that undergirds the logics of cultural nationalisms that we see equally in Afro-pessimist and Afro-Asian coalitional thought (namely, the resistant Black subject), seeking instead a cultural politics that acts "as a rejection of the ways in which bourgeois and minority nationalisms create idealized identities" (Hong and Ferguson 2011, 11) altogether.
4. As Kim rightfully notes, Chin's literary specialty is "the self-loathing, masochism, and the melancholy that define Asian American masculinity" (2005, 143).
5. A profound irony, given Hortense Spillers' indispensable 1987 essay "Mama's Baby, Papa's Maybe: An American Grammar Book," which psychoanalytically dwells on the supposed and pathologized absence of the Black father with respect to the notorious 1965 Moynihan Report.
6. The "first wave" consisting of Frank Chin, Momoko Iko, and other playwrights who worked in the 1960s and '70s with East West Players, Asian American Theater Workshop, and others. See Lee's indispensable *A History of Asian American Theater* for a thorough historical overview.
7. From the article: "'I wanted to include everything,' Gotanda says by phone from his Berkeley home. 'I did all kinds of research and was deeply invested in the whole political and cultural backdrop from their birth to Chinese parents in Siam in 1811 to their arrival in Boston nearly 20 years later. But then I just let go and decided to write whatever I write and not worry about history.'"

. . .

"This is a reimagining of their lives," the playwright says.
(Jones 2011).
8. For the purposes of this discussion, my analysis will be focusing on the 2007 script of the play produced at ACT. Interestingly, some of the scenes discussed in this chapter were cut in the 2014 version of the script in the interest of streamlining character interactions, but I have decided to focus on the 2007 version primarily because of its more overt treatment of Afro-Asian thematics and, secondarily, its greater tendency toward stylistic homage to August Wilson in the form of monologic poetic flourishes.

9. E.g., Japanese American 442nd Regiment / 100th Battalion and the African American 332nd Fighter Group and 477th Bombardment Group in the Second World War, and the African American 92nd and 93rd Infantry Divisions in the First World War, to name but a handful examples. Much of this military participation can be attributed to strategic movements within their respective communities in an effort to win U.S. mainstream acceptance.
10. On November 20, 2014, Chinese American NYPD officer Peter Liang shot and killed unarmed African American Akai Gurley in Brooklyn, New York. Unlike a number of white police officers who similarly killed unarmed Black people in the same period, Liang faced indictment. In response, Chinese Americans rallied in massive numbers to protest what they perceived as "unfair treatment" of a Chinese American police officer, demanding charges be dropped. Some pro-Liang protesters even shockingly compared Liang to Vincent Chin, a comparison that Chin's niece Annie Tan vehemently rejected. On April 19, 2016, Liang was sentenced to five years of probation and 800 hours of community service and never served a day in jail.

Chapter 4

1. Perhaps most emblematic of this strategy is the work of Frank Chin. For example, *Chickencoop Chinaman* (1972) problematically dwells on the recuperation of the Asian father while remaining skeptical of the representational possibilities of Asianness itself, which has been "corrupted" by the feminizing force of orientalism. This leads to Chin's valorization of other modes of non-Asian masculinities that he inhabits yet decidedly avoids "mimicking," such as the cowboy masculinity of John Wayne.
2. For a particularly rigorous treatment of the Wen Ho Lee affair, see Colleen Lye (2011). In Lee, Lye articulates the cultural figure of the Asian American scientist, one who becomes enmeshed in an ambivalence between model minority complacency and Asian American "consciousness-raising."
3. The *Planet Hulk/World War Hulk* narrative follows a fairly traditional Aristotelian tragedy structure in which the hero is doomed by his tragic flaw (*hamartia*), and catharsis emerges from the hero's downfall as a result of this flaw.
4. Examples abound, although some of the most iconic and canonized would be Carlos Bulosan's *America is in the Heart* (1946), John Okada's *No No Boy* (1957), and many of the writings of the *Aiiieeeee!* anthology co-edited by Frank Chin, Lawson Fusao Inada, Shawn Wong, and Jeffery Paul Chan (1974). See the Introduction to this volume for a fuller explanation.
5. Furthermore, Nietzschean ressentiment is congruent with the racial melancholia described by Anne Cheng, which unconsciously feeds upon racial injury. One difference between ressentiment and melancholia is affective; ressentiment pivots primarily upon revenge and anger, while melancholia is a perpetual elongation of grief (additionally, this distinction can easily be problematically gendered). While ressentiment gestures toward a futurity, in reality it is as tethered to the repetition of trauma; meanwhile, melancholia refuses resolution altogether. The agent of ressentiment glorifies their position of structural weakness in order to seek revenge, while melancholia grips hold of the oppressed subject's "moment of truth" and seeks to rehearse it.

6. See David Kim's *Racial Castration*, Daniel Kim's *Writing Manhood in Black and Yellow*, Nguyen Tan Hoang's *A View from the Bottom*, and Celine Parreñas Shimizu's *Straitjacket Masculinities*.
7. This and similar phrases appear throughout Miek's speech in the *Hulk* comics as onomatopoeias for science fictional insectoid noises, or perhaps xenobilingualism. They do not appear to have concrete linguistic content for the Anglophone reader, however.
8. In the latter years of his career, Foucault theorizes "conduct" as an apparatus of governmentality, considering the multivalent resonances of "conducting others," "conducting oneself," "lets one be conducted," et cetera, as a means by which governmental power is not just collective and external, but individualized and internal. In Foucault's *Security, Territory, Population* lectures, counter-conduct is a mode of intervening within power relations, playful and subversive in its operations (while never being completely "outside" of conduct itself), often assuming an ethics of deliberate failure. Notably, Foucault's first example of counter-conduct is Middle Ages asceticism, a counterintuitive choice due to the fact that asceticism seems to be directly associated with the essence of Christianity (2007, 204–205). Yet, Foucault argues that asceticism in fact subverted the logic of pastoral power, as "ascesis is an exercise of self on self; it is a sort of close combat of the individual with himself in which the authority, presence, and gaze of someone else is, if not impossible, at least unnecessary," (2007, 205). In this sense, ascesis is perhaps desubjectifying, a form of subjective self-destruction that weakens the hold of the subjectifying gaze (or, alternatively, the interpellating hail). "Second," continues Foucault, "ascetism is a progression according to a scale of increasing difficulty.... And what is the criterion of this difficulty? It is the ascetic's own suffering" (2007, 205). The metric of asceticism's "progress," then, is suffering itself, the capacity for the ascetic to inflict pain on oneself, and establishes a telos in which suffering only magnifies over time. The resonances of moral masochism, as summarized Silverman, with Foucault's asceticism are clear, sharing "an exercise of self on self" and an intentional temporal vector toward increasing suffering. But whereas ressentiment also seeks suffering, doing so to feed the revenging subject, moral masochism instead seeks out suffering as an ethical self-punishment. If moral masochism is, additionally, a counter-conduct, then it is one that disrupts "the processes implemented for conducting others" (2007, 201); in this case, the field of power relations that determines the subject's normative relations to pleasure and pain.
9. It is exceptionally amusing in this regard, particularly through the presence of Amadeus' supergenius sister Marie Curie Cho, who operates a flying mobile command center masquerading as a gourmet Korean barbecue food truck.

Chapter 5

1. The 1974 anthology *Aiiieeeee!: An Anthology of Asian-American Writers*, co-edited with Jeffery Paul Chan, Lawson Fusao Inada, and Shawn Wong, is emblematic in this respect, although Chin's tendency toward declaring the Asian American mainstream a group of "racial Uncle Toms" is consistent throughout his writings on race. See Daniel Y. Kim's *Writing Manhood in Black and Yellow: Ralph Ellison, Frank Chin, and the Literary Politics of Identity* for a comprehensive account of Chin's expressions of masochistic masculinity.

2. One of several traditions of affect theory, another of which being that of Sylvan Tomkins, adapted later by Eve Sedgwick. For the purposes of this discussion, I open with Deleuze and Guattari's formulation.
3. Jameson would later revise his discussion of postmodernism in *Antinomies of Realism* (2013), although it is worth noting that he not only retains but centralizes affect and its corresponding phenomenology as one of the key pillars of realism.
4. For example, Chela Sandoval has pointedly written that women of color within the United States have never had the privilege of access to the whole bourgeois ego in the first place. "'[F]ragmentation' is neither an experience nor a theoretical construct peculiar to the poststructuralist or postmodern moments. Indeed, the fragmentation or split subjectivity of subjection is the very condition against which a modernist, well-placed citizen-subject could coalesce its own sense of wholeness.... Indeed, the condition recently claimed as the 'postmodern splitting off the subject' is one of the conditions that conquered and colonized Westerners were invited to survive under modernist and previous eras, if survival were a choice" (2000, 32, 3). However, as Jodi Melamed's critique of contemporary neoliberal multiculturalism would indicate, part of the rationalization of racial capitalism has been in the incorporation of minoritized, racialized subjects into the auspices of bourgeois individualism in order the legitimize the continued violence and exploitation of surplus labor of communities of color as a whole.
5. For example, in "Feeling Brown, Feeling Down," José Muñoz clearly elucidates that racial normativity is performed and reiterated via affect: "normativity is accessed in the majoritarian public sphere through the affective performance of ethnic and racial normativity. This performance of whiteness primarily transpires on an affective register. Acting white has everything to do with the performance of a particular affect, the specific performance of which grounds the subject performing white affect in a normative life world" (2000, 68). Muñoz thus importantly demonstrates how race and its accompanying technologies of normativity are produced through affect, and that certain racialized affects can be conceptualized quantitatively relative to one another. Consequently, not only is affect racialized, but racialization itself is, at least in part, affective. In particular, emphasizes Muñoz, Latina/os are characterized by a kind of affective excess relative to whiteness, which presents the Latina/o subject as being affectively unruly under the white normative regime.
6. Although I have chosen to focus on a postmodern techno-orientalism, it is true that these aspects of mechanized Asiatic racial form in the western hemisphere go considerably further back to the late 19th century and early 20th century, and not exclusively to the United States. In Cuba in the early 20th century, for example, Alfonso Hernandez Catá described Chinese coolies as "mechanized meat."
7. In my discussion of Asian American affect, I am in dialogue with Jeffrey Santa Ana's monograph *Racial Feelings: Asian America in a Capitalist Culture of Emotions*, which aims to explore how "the racial feelings" under U.S. liberal capitalism "affect the perception of Asians both as economic exemplars and as threats," and how "Asian Americans in their own cultural works characterize, accommodate, and resist their discursive portrayal as economic subjects in a capitalist culture of emotion" (2015, 5). Noting, following Arlie Hochschild, Michael Hardt, and the later Fredric Jameson, that contemporary racial capitalism has moved toward an "affect economy" in which economic relations become emotionally charged, Santa Ana argues that Asians become emotionally valued as both model minorities and threats under this new paradigm, and that their own emotional responses

can potentially upend their roles under neoliberal capitalist schema. The examples of white resentment and Japanophobia in Detroit in Chapters 1 and 6 illustrate much of Santa Ana's point, many of his observations in such emotional-economic associations are quite apt, and I concur with Santa Ana that under contemporary capitalism, emotion and affect have exploded as primary terrains of valuation and exchange. However, Santa Ana does not substantially distinguish between *emotion* and *affect*, as affect scholars such as Brian Massumi, Rei Terada, and Jameson have done. As Terada has written, emotion is conscious and psychological, whereas affect is located centrally in the body (2001, 4), which supports Massumi's assertion that emotion is individuated while affect is "a prepersonal intensity corresponding to the passage from one experiential state of the body to another and implying an augmentation or diminution in that body's capacity to act" (1987, xvi). Santa Ana's discussions center primarily around politicized anger or "feeling normal," which are more properly qualitative emotions held by subjects—that is, named emotions—rather than affects, as he often characterizes them. More akin to Muñoz's take on Latinidad than Santa Ana's case of racialized emotion, this chapter asks how Asianness—not as an essentialized identity but as a constructed structural position—can be understood *as an affective state itself*. That is, Asianness not precisely as crude biology nor a summation of anthropologically shared cultural attributes but, rather, an affective coagulation that intensifies the grid of intelligibility that forms the epistemic latticework of postmodernity itself.
8. Tao Lin has publicly acknowledged the semiautobiographical nature of *Taipei*. In an interview with *Entertainment Weekly*, he describes the process of writing *Taipei* as editing "25,000 pages" of his memory "into a 250-page novel." As a consequence, he considers it his magnum opus, stating: "I used, as source material, everything I know or have felt or experienced, or could imagine knowing or feeling or experiencing, up to this point in my life." As a consequence, it may be fair, in a limited sense, to equate Paul with Tao Lin himself in this analysis.
9. In an interview with Kelley Hoffman of *Interview Magazine*, after the publication of his second novel *Richard Yates*, Lin addresses this comparison to Ellis with a degree of befuddlement, conceding that possibly he shares Ellis' sense of humor, as well as a similar degree of empathy for his characters. However, Lin asserts that while Ellis considers his own characters "immoral," Lin does not consider the morality of his characters at all; Lin states that he is unabashedly amoral in his valuations at large. Amusingly, Lin does not comment on the stylistic similarity of prose with Ellis.
10. This eschewal is not necessarily unique, since a number of writers of Asian American descent have made similar disavowals. For example, Ping Chong, discussed in Chapter 2, has focused the majority of his work on non-Asian American subjects and often resists being clustered in the same category as David Henry Hwang and Philip Kan Gotanda. Similarly, Chang-Rae Lee turned many heads in the literary world with *Aloft*, which centers on an Italian American family with barely any mention of Asian Americanness whatsoever. However, neither Chong nor Lee has expressed the kind of open hostility to the Asian American label as Tao Lin, who has decried it as outright "racist."
11. "he [Paul] observed neutrally that, though he was drooling a little and probably the only non-dancing person in the room, no one was looking at him, then moved toward the room's iPod with the goal-oriented, zombie-like calmness of a person who has woken at night thirsty and is walking to his refrigerator and changed the music to 'Today' by the

Smashing Pumpkins" (Lin 2013, 74); "Erin asked how Paul felt and he murmured 'zombie-like' without moving his head" (Lin 2013, 160).

12. "In his state of medium euphoria, with intensely dull eyes and an overall cyborg-like demeanor, Paul stared briefly at the cofounder of *Vice* before turning and moving away with an earnest, uncertain feeling of disappointment" (Lin 2013, 112).

13. "due to 2mg of Klonopin remained poised, with a peaceful sensation of faultlessness, physiologically calm but mentally stimulated, throughout the night, as if beta testing the event by acting like an exaggerated version of himself, for others to practice against, before the real Paul, the only person without practice, was inserted for the actual event" (Lin 2013, 65); " 'I don't think I've ever told anyone. I don't think I cared if anyone knew. I was just like, "I saw a UFO." I think I was extremely bored. I was like a bored robot' " (Lin 2013, 104); "… reacted to Paul's robot-like extroversion with what seemed like barely suppressed confusion" (Lin 2013, 112).

14. Erin had initially claimed Paul was the only one Erin had told about her experience wearing purple and glitter in 4th grade, in order to attract UFOs. In this scene, Erin realizes she had told one of her other friends, as well; Paul then accuses Erin of lying.

15. "Orientalism," writes Ahmed, "involves a form of 'world facing'; that is, a way of gathering things around so they 'face' a certain direction" (2006, 118). In effect, Ahmed asserts that the Occident forms phenomenologically through the organization of collective bodies facing toward an imagined, constructed Orient far beyond the (Eastern) horizon that is always, to varying degrees, objectified and desired. As a consequence, "[t]he orient is then 'orientated;' it is reachable as an object given how the world takes shape 'around' certain bodies" (2006, 120). Through Ahmed's formulation, we can consider how orientalism has both vectored and spatialized aspects, that the imagined Orient is simultaneously distant ("over the horizon") and graspable ("*just* over the horizon").

16. Specifically, I take issue with Deleuze and Guattari's notion that "Racism operates by the determination of degrees of deviance in relation to the White-Man face"; this presupposes a narrow definition of racism in terms of individual bigotry as opposed to broader systemic, material structures that render entire populations exploitable, precarious, or vulnerable to premature death, to paraphrase Ruth Wilson Gilmore.

17. Such conversion invokes what Martin Heidegger has termed "Enframing" in his oft-cited text "The Question Concerning Technology." According to Heidegger, Enframing is both the essence of modern technology and "the way in which the real reveals itself as standing-reserve" (1977, 23). That is to say, Enframing is material and perceptual conversion of the real—consisting of largely inert objects—into "standing-reserve," which is, loosely, resources and objects that are utilizable. The danger of modern technology, warns Heidegger, is the conversion of human beings themselves into standing-reserve. Although on a historical level, such conversion has already literally happened on a wide and apocalyptic scale via the trans-Atlantic slave trade (an unsurprising oversight for the active Nazi Party member that Heidegger was), Heidegger's Enframing is nevertheless instructive in elucidating the relationship between Paul and his technologically mediated existence. By becoming increasingly technologically mediated, Paul effectively Enframes his own consciousness and his own body; the fact that Paul sees a distant building as "a cursor" suggests this very shift. Furthermore, the previous descriptions suggest that Taipei's Enframing exceeds even that of Paul's, and with it, the techno-orientalist associations with robots, clones, and zombies.

18. "Paul's father was 28 and Paul's mother was 24 when they alone (out of a combined fifteen to twenty-five siblings) left Taiwan for America" (Lin 2013, 36). This is the only mention of Paul's father during the childhood reflection in Chapter 2 of his book.
19. One of Tan Lin's most celebrated works to this effect is his book 2007 *HEATH*, which consists of a wide variety of media including blog posts, Really Simple Syndication (RSS) feeds, and handwritten notes. *HEATH* and a number of other texts utilize a series of footnotes consisting of Google searches to emphasize their status as "meta-text." This also applies to the central Tan Lin text of his chapter, *Insomnia and the Aunt*.
20. With its setting, *Insomnia and the Aunt* resonates with that of Tseng Kwong Chi's *Expeditionary Series* of photographs, in which Tseng inserts himself into vast, frontier landscapes of North America. As Iyko Day argues in *Alien Capital*, Tseng's exaggeratedly Chinese, self-orientalized presence in the photos subverts the universalism and settler-colonial romanticism of these photos, deploying a disidentificatory "Chinese drag" that highlights "the managed interplay of life, degeneration, and death as a central feature of settler colonialism and projected onto nature" (2016, 82). In *Insomnia*, the setting plays a similar role, gesturing to a kind of campy frontier Americanness, although its role is secondary to the exploration of the television set and the flattening of affect.
21. As described in Goffman's well-worn text *The Presentation of Self in Everyday Life*, the "front stage" is a collection of personas and behaviors that cater to particular public settings, while the "back stage" is the ostensibly authentic, although what becomes clear from this foundational work of performance theory is that the "authentic" is itself also actually performative.
22. I turn again to Philip Auslander, who writes: "Although the question of authentic television form remained unresolved, early writers on television generally agreed that television's essential properties as a medium are *immediacy* and *intimacy*" (2008, 15) and that "Unlike film, but like theatre, a television broadcast is characterized as a performance in the present. This was literally the case in the early days of television when most material was broadcast live. Even now that most television programming is prerecorded, the television image remains a performance in the present in an important sense" (2008, 15). Thus, according to Auslander, television has a medium ontology of liveness, and by extension, ambiance. But unlike theater, in which the actors must break or change scenes, television could feasibly be left on indefinitely without an interruption of "flow."
23. Before 2011, "Cached" and "Similar pages" were standard links alongside search results on the Google search engine, the former of which allowed users to access cached, previously saved versions of websites that were no longer strictly live. Since 2011, the links were removed from the individual search results.

Chapter 6

1. Calculations in essay based on data on Tables 22 and 27 on pages 17 and 19, respectively.
2. As argued in Galloway (2006).
3. A nod here to, of course: Williams (1977), 132–133.
4. Stone, for example, asserts that "the physical/virtual distinction is *not* a mind/body distinction. The concept of mind is not part of virtual systems theory, and the virtual component of the socially apprehensible citizen is not a disembodied thinking thing, but rather a different way of conceptualizing a *relationship* to the human body" (2001, 40).

5. Online viral publicity was quite ambitious, including a Flash website for Sarif Industries (sarifindustries.com), a pro-augmentation Sarif advertisement (http://www.youtube.com/watch?v=UWmeBeRb1RY), and an anti-augmentation agitprop video by the fictional activist group "Purity First," which evokes imagery of the 1999 Seattle World Trade Organization (WTO) protests (https://www.youtube.com/watch?v=akaos1U8Rto).
6. The diegetic/non-diegetic distinction has appeared in literary and film studies, but in video game theory it has been most explicitly articulated by Alexander Galloway in *Gaming: Essays on Algorithmic Culture*, in which he defines the diegetic as elements that exist as part of the gamic narrative (e.g., nonplayer characters to interact with, items to acquire, the room through which one is walking, ambient noise that is part of the environment), and the non-diegetic as those elements that are tacitly understood to not be a representation of what is "actually happening" in the game (e.g., the Main Menu or Game Over screens, soundtrack music that is not explicitly played from a source in game's setting).
7. GameSpot's Deus Ex Human Revolution Art Interview: http://www.youtube.com/watch?v=_8o1izAq7ig.
8. See Nick Bostrom's "History of Transhumanist Thought" (2005) and Allen Buchanan et al.'s *From Chance to Choice* (2000).
9. Charles Mills, in *The Racial Contract*, argues that race is the central political system that has defined and organized "Western" civilization and notions of the "human" since the Enlightenment, dividing humanity between the white and the nonwhite, with "black" representing the epitome of the bestial, the barely human. Mills points to Emmanuel Kant, considered widely to be "the most important moral theorist of the modern period" who "is *also* the father of the modern concept of race" (1997, 70), and that this "famous theorist of personhood is also the theorist of subpersonhood" (1997, 70), who derived much of his evidence from early eugenic studies that placed whites at the top of the racial hierarchy.
10. As Richard Harris writes, the supercrip "is seen in characters like the superhuman and selfless paraplegic who wheels hundreds of miles to raise money for cancer research or the blind girl who solves the baffling crime by remembering a crucial sound or smell that sighted people had missed. Sometimes the two even coexist in the same person, as in *The Miracle Worker's* Helen Keller, at first bitter and inept, almost animalistic, until she is 'tamed' by the saintly teacher Annie Sullivan, after which she goes on to be almost superhuman. A covert message of both of these portrayals is that *individual* adjustment is the key to disabled people's lives; if they only have the right attitude, they will be fine" (2004, 85).
11. In reference to Ian Bogost's *Persuasive Games* (2010).
12. The "social boss" is another innovative selling point for the *DX:HR* gameplay. Unlike in many role-playing games with dialogue choices, it is both possible to fail and to not succeed by using the same dialogue choices in every playthrough. To succeed, a player must choose dialogue options according to the character's body language and vocal intonations, which are randomized per playthrough. Failure does not mean a "Game Over" like in other games (which would normally prompt the player to "try again")—rather, the game continues, and the player must proceed with the consequences of that failure, which may include, for example, a character shooting himself in the head and thus cutting off any potential aid he may give Jensen in the future.
13. Reference here to Sherry Turkle's description of the video game's ability to monopolize the player's attentive focus and to immerse oneself in the world of the game.

14. In the same GameSpot interview referenced earlier in this essay, Jacques-Belletete points to Renaissance studies of human anatomy (such as da Vinci's) as an origin point for transhumanist thought. The imagined 2027 of *DX:HR*, according to Jacques-Belletete, is also a kind of "renaissance" period for human augmentation technology before the impending social collapse that occurs in the game's climax—the dystopian "cyberpunk" era thus looms on the horizon. Consequently, Jacques-Bellette decided to employ a consistent and dominating black-and-gold color scheme throughout the game—gold representing a Renaissance "golden age," and black representing dystopian cyberpunk.
15. Such slippage recalls Kobena Mercer's essay "Just Looking for Trouble," in which he describes his uncomfortable pleasure with Robert Mapplethorpe's objectifying photographs of Black men: "Once I acknowledge my own location in the image reservoir as a gay subject—a desiring subject not only in terms of sharing a desire to look, but in terms of an identical object-choice already there in my own fantasies and wishes—then the articulation of meanings about eroticism.... I am forced to confront the rather unwelcome fact that as a spectator I actually occupy the very position in the fantasy of mastery previously ascribed to the centered position of the white male subject!" (1993, 104) Mercer suspects that he, too, as a queer Black man, desires mastery of the nude Black bodies in Mapplethorpe's infamous photographs, identifying himself both with the desiring subject and the desired object at once, not unlike the Asian American gamer playing *DX:HR*. Yet, in both Mapplethorpe's photos and in *DX:HR*, the racialized object of representation (in Mapplethorpe's case, the gay Black man; in *DX:HR*'s, the techno-orientalized Asian) is not the likely audience for the work. Consequently, Mercer finds his engagement with Mapplethorpe's work simultaneously offensive and generative, discomfortingly finding himself sharing the same "fantasy of mastery" as the white male subject.
16. I am thus indebted to Clara Fernández-Vara's framework of analyzing video games as a genre of performance, especially given how video games, like other modes of performance, demonstrate "a special ordering of *time*, a special value attached to *objects*, *nonproductivity* in terms of goods, *rules*, and performance spaces" (2009, 2). Consequently, Josephine Lee's assertion on Asian American theater remains germane to Asian American video game studies: "That Asian Americans enact Orientalized stereotypes is often interpreted as a form of misguided internalization of cultural oppression, as ideological brainwashing rather than a conscious decision or choice. But this only partially accounts for the complexity of responses when Asian Americans articulate an *ambivalence about the desire felt for the body-as-stereotype*" (1997, 91).
17. It is worth noting that Foster's articulation here does not refer to video games, but technofetishism, and the representational figure of the desiring machine. Nevertheless, I argue that his description here still applies, particularly given the video game machine's necessity for a human operator in order for its narrative to actualize.
18. Hwang's 1988 play, the first play written by an Asian American to win a Tony Award, subverts Puccini's *Madame Butterfly* narrative, describing the tale of how Chinese spy Song Liling, an anatomically male person, performs ideal orientalized femininity as a woman for male French diplomat Rene Gallimard to seduce him and procure state secrets.
19. Interestingly, in this same article, Eidos Montreal released a statement in response: "Deus Ex: Human Revolution is a fictional story which reflects the diversity of the world's future population by featuring characters of various cultural and socioeconomic backgrounds.

While these characters are meant to portray people living in the year 2027, it has never been our intention to represent any particular ethnic group in a negative light."
20. Reference to Sau-Ling Wong's concept of the same name, descriptive of the racialized companion who conforms to the same stereotype as the protagonist's and thus undermines their own assimilation.

Bibliography

2Pac. "Dear Mama." Track 9 on *Me Against the World*. Interscope, 1995, CD.
Agamben, Giorgio. *Means without Ends: Notes on Politics*. Translated by Vincenzo Binetti and Cesare Casarino. Minneapolis: University of Minnesota Press, 2000.
Agnello, Anthony John. "Jonathan Jacques-Belletete, *Deus Ex: Human Revolution* Art Director." The Gameological Society. April 26, 2012. http://gameological.com/2012/04/jonathan-jacques-bellette-deus-ex-human-revolution-art-director/.
Ahmed, Sara. *Queer Phenomenology*. Durham: Duke University Press, 2006.
Althusser, Louis. *Lenin and Philosophy and Other Essays*. New York: Monthly Review Press, 2001.
Alvarado, Leticia. *Abject Performances: Aesthetic Strategies in Latino Cultural Production*. Durham: Duke University Press, 2018.
Amin, Kadji. *Disturbing Attachments: Genet, Modern Pederasty, and Queer History*. Durham: Duke University Press, 2017.
Auslander, Philip. *Liveness: Performance in a Mediatized Culture*. London: Routledge, 2008.
Bakhtin, Mikhail. *Rabelais and His World*. Translated by Hélène Iswolsky. Bloomington: Indiana University Press, 1984.
Barlow, John Perry. "A Declaration of the Independence of Cyberspace." *Electronic Frontier Foundation*. February 8, 1996. https://www.eff.org/cyberspace-independence.
Barthes, Roland. *Mythologies*. Translated by Annette Lavers. New York: Hill and Wang, 1972.
Baudrillard, Jean. *America*. London: Verso, 2020.
Beer, Matt. "Does 'Buy American' Buy Trouble? Detroit Killing Shows that Boosterism Can Breed Racism." *The Detroit Times*, June 2, 1983, 7.
Benjamin, Walter. *Illuminations: Essays and Reflections*. New York: Schocken Books, 1968.
Bersani, Leo. *Homos*. Cambridge, MA: Harvard University Press, 1995.
Best, Stephen, and Saidiya Hartman. "Fugitive Justice." *Representations* 92 (Fall 2005): 1–15.
Bhabha, Homi. *The Location of Culture*. New York: Routledge, 1994.
Bogost, Ian. *Persuasive Games: The Expressive Power of Videogames*. Cambridge, MA: MIT Press, 2010.
Bostrom, Nick. "A History of Transhumanist Thought." *Journal of Evolution and Technology* 14, no. 1 (April 2005): 1–25.
Bridges, Kim Chang-Mi, et al. Constitution for American Citizens for Justice. 1984. Materials Relating to the Vincent Chin Case, 1981–1990 (bulk 1983–1985), Asian American Studies Collection. Ethnic Studies Library, University of California, Berkeley.
Brown, Wendy. *States of Injury: Power and Freedom in Late Modernity*. Princeton: Princeton University Press, 1995.
Buchanan, Allen, Dan Brock, Norman Daniels, and Daniel Wikler, eds. *From Chance to Choice: Genetics & Justice*. Cambridge, Cambridge University Press, 2000.
Bush, Christopher. "The Ethnicity of Things in America's Lacquered Age." *Representations* 99, no.1 (Summer 2007): 74–98.
Butler, Judith. *Excitable Speech: A Politics of the Performative*. New York: Routledge, 1997a.
Butler, Judith. *The Psychic Life of Power: Theories in Subjection*. Stanford, CA: Stanford University Press, 1997b.
Butler, Judith. *Undoing Gender*. New York: Routledge, 2004.

Castelli, Elizabeth. *Martyrdom and Memory: Early Christian Culture Making.* New York: Columbia University Press, 2004.
Catanese, Brandi Wilkins. *The Problem of the Color[blind]: Racial Transgression and the Politics of Black Performance.* Ann Arbor: University of Michigan Press, 2011.
Chambers-Letson, Joshua Takano. *A Race So Different.* New York: New York University Press, 2013.
Chan, Dean. "Being Played: Games Culture and Asian American Dis/Identifications." *Refractory: A Journal of Entertainment Media* 16 (November 2009). https://webarchive.nla.gov.au/awa/20110216114918/http://blogs.arts.unimelb.edu.au/refractory/2009/11/16/being-played-games-culture-and-asian-american-disidentifications-dean-chan/.
Chan, Sucheng. *Asian Americans: An Interpretive History.* Boston: Twayne Publishers, 1991.
Chang, Juliana. *Inhuman Citizenship: Traumatic Enjoyment and Asian American Literature.* Minneapolis: Minnesota University Press, 2012.
Chang, Robert. *Disoriented: Asian Americans, Law, and the Nation-State.* New York: New York University Press, 1999.
Chen, Mel. "Toxic Animacies, Inanimate Affections." *GLQ: A Journal of Lesbian and Gay Studies* 17, nos. 2–3 (2011): 265–286.
Chen, Mel. *Animacies: Biopolitics, Racial Mattering, and Queer Affect.* Durham: Duke University Press, 2012.
Chen, Tina. *Double Agency: Acts of Impersonation in Asian American Literature and Culture.* Stanford: Stanford University Press, 2005.
Cheng, Anne Anlin. *The Melancholy of Race.* Oxford: Oxford University Press, 2000.
Cheng, Anne Anlin. *Second Skin: Josephine Baker & the Modern Surface.* Oxford: Oxford University Press, 2010.
Cheng, Anne Anlin. *Ornamentalism.* Oxford: Oxford University Press, 2018.
Chiang, Mark. *The Cultural Capital of Asian American Studies.* New York: New York University Press, 2009.
Chin, Frank. "Riding the Rails with Chickencoop Slim." *The Greenfield Review* 6, Nos. 1 & 2 (Spring 1977): 80–89.
Chin, Frank. *The Chickencoop Chinaman/The Year of the Dragon: Two Plays.* Seattle: University of Washington Press, 1981.
Chin, Frank, Jeffery Paul Chan, Lawson Fusao Inada, and Shawn Wong, eds. *Aiiieeeee! An Anthology of Asian-American Writers.* Washington, DC: Howard University Press, 1974.
"Chinese On Leong Association, for Immediate Release." Memo. March 23, 1983. Asian American Studies Collection. Ethnic Studies Library, University of California, Berkeley.
Chong, Ping. *Chinoiserie.* In *The East/West Quartet.* New York: Theatre Communications Group, 2004.
Chow, Rey. *The Protestant Ethnic and the Spirit of Capitalism.* New York: Columbia University Press, 2002.
Chow, Rey. *Entanglements, or Transmedial Thinking about Capture.* Durham: Duke University Press, 2012.
Choy, Christine, and Renee Tajima-Pena, dirs. *Who Killed Vincent Chin?* New York: Filmmakers Library, Inc. 1987.
Chu, Patricia. *Assimilating Asians: Gendered Strategies of Authorship in Asian America.* Durham: Duke University Press, 2000.
Chuang, Marisa. "The HOW, WHO, and WHAT's of the American Citizens for Justice Committee." Pamphlet, n.d. Box 4. American Citizens for Justice Archives. Bentley Historical Library, University of Michigan, Ann Arbor.
Chuang, Marisa. "Statement at Public Hearing, Detroit City Council (prepared by Dr. Marisa Chuang and delivered by Mr. Bonlap Chan)." Unpublished speech. July 7, 1983. Box 4.

American Citizens for Justice Archives, Bentley Historical Library, University of Michigan, Ann Arbor.

Chude-Sokei, Louis. *The Sound of Culture: Diaspora and Black Technopoetics*. Middletown: Wesleyan University Press, 2016.

Chuh, Kandice. *Imagine Otherwise: On Asian Americanist Critique*. Durham: Duke University Press, 2003.

Chun, Wendy Hui Kyong. *Control and Freedom: Power and Paranoia in the Age of Fiber Optics*. Cambridge, MA: The MIT Press, 2006.

Comay, Rebecca. "The Sickness of Tradition: Between Melancholia and Fetishism." Chapter 5 in *Walter Benjamin and History*. Edited by Andrew Benjamin. London: Continuum, 2006. pp. 88–101.

Crispin, Jessa. "May 29, 2008: A Short Interview with Tao Lin." *Bookslut*. May 29, 2008. http://www.bookslut.com/blog/archives/2008_05.php. Accessed 16 April 2016.

Cruz, Ariane. *The Color of Kink: Black Women, BDSM, and Pornography*. New York: New York University Press, 2016.

Darden, Joe T., and Richard W. Thomas. *Detroit: Race Riots, Racial Conflicts, and Efforts to Bridge the Racial Divide*. East Lansing: Michigan State University Press, 2013.

Day, Iyko. "Being or Nothingness: Indigeneity, Antiblackness, and Settler Colonial Critique." *Critical Ethnic Studies* 1, no. 2 (Fall 2015): 102–121.

Day, Iyko. *Alien Capital: Asian Racialization and the Logic of Settler Colonial Capitalism*. Durham: Duke University Press, 2016.

Deleuze, Gilles. "Coldness and Cruelty." In *Masochism*. New York: Zone Books, 1989. pp. 9–142.

Deleuze, Gilles, and Féliz Guattari. *A Thousand Plateaus: Capitalism and Schizophrenia*. Translated with a foreword by Brian Massumi. Minneapolis: University of Minnesota Press, 1987.

"Deus Ex: Human Revolution." *Metacritic*. http://www.metacritic.com/game/pc/deus-ex-human-revolution.

DuBois, W. E. B. *The Souls of Black Folk*. New York: Barnes & Noble Classics, 2005.

Dyer, Richard, *White*. London: Routledge, 1997.

Dyer-Witheford, Nick, and Greig de Peuter. *Games of Empire: Global Capitalism and Video Games*. Minneapolis: University of Minnesota Press, 2009.

Eidos Montreal. *Deus Ex: Human Revolution, Augmented Edition*. Video Game for Xbox 360. Eidos Montreal, 2011.

Eng, David. *Racial Castration: Managing Masculinity in Asian America*. Durham: Duke University Press, 2001.

Eng, David. *The Feeling of Kinship: Queer Liberalism and the Racialization of Intimacy*. Durham: Duke University Press, 2010.

Espiritu, Yến Lê. *Asian American Panethnicity: Bridging Institutions and Identities*. Philadelphia: Temple University Press, 1992.

Fang, Jenn. "Andrew Yang's Problematic Reinforcement of the Model Minority Myth." *Reappropriate*. 13 September 2019. http://reappropriate.co/2019/09/andrew-yangs-problematic-reinforcement-of-the-model-minority-myth/

Fanon, Frantz. *Black Skin, White Masks*. New York: Grove Press, 2008.

Fawaz, Ramzi. *The New Mutants: Superheroes and the Radical Imagination of American Comics*. New York: New York University Press, 2016.

Fernández-Vara, Clara. "Play's the Thing: A Framework to Study Videogames as Performance." *DiGRA 2009: Proceedings of the 2009 DiGRA International Conference: Breaking New Ground: Innovation in Games, Play, Practice and Theory* (2009). http://www.digra.org/digital-library/publications/plays-the-thing-a-framework-to-study-videogames-as-performance/.

Feuerherd, Ben. "New 'SNL' Cast Member Shane Gillis Referred to Andrew Yang as a 'Jew ch-nk.'" *Page Six*. September 14, 2019. https://pagesix.com/2019/09/14/new-snl-cast-member-shane-gillis-referred-to-andrew-yang-as-a-jew-ch-k/.

Fickle, Tara. *The Race Card: From Gaming Technologies to Model Minorities*. New York: New York University Press, 2019.

Foote, David. "Your Closest Relative Is a TV Set." *Asian American Writers' Workshop*. July 8, 2015. http://aaww.org/your-closest-relative/.

Foster, Thomas. *The Souls of Cyberfolk: Posthumanism as Vernacular Theory*. Minneapolis: University of Minnesota Press, 2005.

Foucault, Michel. *The History of Sexuality. Volume 1: An Introduction*. New York: Random House, 1978. Print.

Foucault, Michel. *Technologies of the Self: A Seminar with Michel Foucault*. Edited by Luther Martin, Huck Gutman, and Patrick Hutton. Boston: University of Massachusetts Press, 1988.

Foucault, Michel. "Questions of Method." Chapter 9 in *Power*. Edited by James D. Faubion, 223-239. New York: The New Press, 1994a.

Foucault, Michel. "Sex, Power, and the Politics of Identity." *Ethics: Subjectivity and Truth*. Edited by Paul Rabinow, 163-174. New York: The New Press, 1994b.

Foucault, Michel. *Society Must Be Defended: Lectures at the Collège de France, 1975-1976*. New York: Picador, 2003.

Foucault, Michel. *Security, Territory, Population: Lectures at the Collège de France, 1977-1978*. Translated by Graham Burchell. New York: Picador, 2007.

Foucault, Michel. *The Birth of Biopolitics: Lectures at the Collège de France, 1978-1979*. New York: Picador, 2008.

Frank, Dana. *Buy American: The Untold Story of Economic Nationalism*. Boston: Beacon Press Books, 1999.

Freeman, Elizabeth. "Time Binds, or, Erotohistoriography." *Social Text* 23, nos. 3-4 (Fall-Winter 2005): 57-68.

Freeman, Elizabeth. *Time Binds: Queer Temporalities, Queer Histories*. Durham, Duke University Press, 2010.

Freud, Sigmund. *The Freud Reader*. Edited by Peter Gay. Translated by James Strachey. New York: W. W. Norton & Company, 1989.

Fujino, Diane. *Samurai among Panthers: Richard Aoki on Race, Resistance, and a Paradoxical Life*. Minneapolis: University of Minnesota Press, 2012.

Fukuzawa, David. "Public Relations Problem/Case Study." Essay for JRN 670, Central Michigan University, December 1988. Box 4, American Citizens for Justice Archives, Bentley Historical Library, University of Michigan, Ann Arbor.

Galloway, Alexander. *Gaming: Essays on Algorithmic Culture*. Minneapolis: University of Minnesota Press, 2006.

Galloway, Alexander. *The Interface Effect*. Cambridge: Polity Press, 2012.

Galster, George. *Driving Detroit: The Quest for Respect in the Motor City*. Philadelphia: University of Pennsylvania Press, 2012.

Garreau, Joel. *Radical Evolution: The Promise and Peril of Enhancing Our Minds, Our Bodies—and What It Means to Be Human*. New York: Doubleday, 2005.

Gies, Arthur. "Deus Ex: Human Revolution Review." *IGN*. August 23, 2011. http://www.ign.com/articles/2011/08/24/deus-ex-human-revolution-review-2?page=2.

Goffman, Erving. *The Presentation of Self in Everyday Life*. New York: Anchor Books, 1959.

Gonzáles, Jennifer. "Envisioning Cyborg Bodies: Notes from Current Research." In *Cybersexualities: A Reader in Feminist Theory, Cyborgs, and Cyberspace*. Edited by Jenny Wolmark. Edinburgh: Edinburgh University Press, 1999. pp. 264-279.

Gotanda, Philip Kan. *After the War*. Unpublished manuscript, 2007. Microsoft Word file.

Gotanda, Philip Kan. *I Dream of Chang and Eng*. Unpublished manuscript, 2013. Microsoft Word file.
Haraway, Donna J. *Simians Cyborgs and Women*. New York: Routledge, 1996.
Hardt, Michael. "Affective Labor." *boundary 2* 26, no. 2 (1999): 89–100.
Harris, Cheryl. "Whiteness as Property." *Harvard Law Review* 106, No. 8 (June 1993). pp. 1707–1791.
Harris, Richard Jackson. *A Cognitive Psychology of Mass Communication*. Mahwah: Lawrence Erlbaum Associates, 2004.
Heidegger, Martin. *The Question Concerning Technology and Other Essays*. Translated by William Lovitt. New York: Garland Publishing, Inc. 1977.
Higginbotham, Evelyn Brooks. *Righteous Discontent: The Women's Movement in the Black Baptist Church, 1880–1920*. Cambridge, MA: Harvard University Press, 1993.
Hoffman, Kelley. "Tao Lin on Bret Easton Ellis, Indulgence." *Interview Magazine*. August 20, 2010, http://www.interviewmagazine.com/culture/tao-lin.
Hong, Grace, and Roderick Ferguson, eds. "Introduction." *Strange Affinities: The Gender and Sexual Politics of Comparative Racialization*. Durham: Duke University Press, 2011. pp. 1–23.
Hsu, Madeline Y. *The Good Immigrants: How the Yellow Peril Became the Model Minority*. Princeton: Princeton University Press, 2015.
Huang, Vivian L. "Inscrutably, Actually: Hospitality, Parasitism, and the Silent Work of Yoko Ono and Laurel Nakadate." *Women & Performance: A Journal of Feminist Theory* 28, no. 3 (2018): 187–203.
Hughey, Matthew. "Cinethetic Racism: White Redemption and Black Stereotypes in 'Magical Negro' Films." *Social Problems* 56, no. 3 (August 2009): 543–577.
Huyssen, Andreas. *After the Great Divide: Modernism, Mass Culture, Postmodernism*. Bloomington: Indiana University Press, 1986.
Iijima, Chris K. "The Era of We-Construction: Reclaiming the Politics of Asian Pacific American Identity and Reflections on the Critique of the Black/White Paradigm." *Columbia Human Rights Law Review* 29, no. 1 (Fall 1997): 47–90.
Iijima, Chris K. "Pontifications on the Distinction between Grains of Sand and Yellow Pearls." Chapter 1 in *Asian Americans: The Movement and the Moment*. Edited by Steve Louie and Glenn K. Omatsu. Los Angeles: UCLA Asian American Studies Center Press, 2001. pp. 2–15.
Jacques-Belletete, Jonathan, interviewee. "GDC 2010: Deus Ex: Human Revolution Art Interview." YouTube video, 11:43. March 15, 2010. https://www.youtube.com/watch?v=_8o1izAq7ig.
Jameson, Fredric. *The Political Unconscious: Narrative as a Socially Symbolic Act*. Ithaca: Cornell University Press, 1981.
Jameson, Fredric. "History and Class Consciousness as an 'Unfinished Project.'" *Rethinking Marxism* 1, no. 1 (1988): 49–72.
Jameson, Fredric. *Postmodernism, or, the Cultural Logic of Late Capitalism*. Durham: Duke University Press, 1991.
Jameson, Fredric. *The Antinomies of Realism*. London: Verso, 2015.
Jeon, Joseph Jonghyun. *Racial Things, Racial Forms: Objecthood in Avant-Garde Asian American Poetry*. Iowa City: University of Iowa Press, 2012.
Johns, Adrian. *Piracy: The Intellectual Property Wars from Gutenberg to Gates*. Chicago: University of Chicago Press, 2010.
Jones, Chad. "Philip Kan Gotanda's 'I Dream of Chang and Eng.'" *San Francisco Chronicle*. March 3, 2011. http://www.sfgate.com/thingstodo/article/Philip-Kan-Gotanda-s-I-Dream-of-Chang-and-Eng-3161857.php.
Jun, Helen Heran. *Race for Citizenship: Black Orientalism and Asian Uplift from Pre-Emancipation to Neoliberal America*. New York: New York University Press, 2011.

Juul, Jesper. *The Art of Failure: An Essay on the Pain of Playing Video Games.* Cambridge, MA: MIT Press, 2013.

Kang, Jay Caspian. "What a Fraternity Hazing Death Revealed about the Painful Search for an Asian-American Identity." *New York Times.* August 9, 2017. https://www.nytimes.com/2017/08/09/magazine/what-a-fraternity-hazing-death-revealed-about-the-painful-search-for-an-asian-american-identity.html.

Katz, Jack. *How Emotions Work.* Chicago: University of Chicago Press, 2000.

Kim, Claire Jean. *Bitter Fruit: The Politics of Black-Korean Conflict in New York City.* New Haven: Yale University Press, 2000.

Kim, Daniel Y. *Writing Manhood in Black and Yellow: Ralph Ellison, Frank Chin, and the Literary Politics of Identity.* Stanford: Stanford University Press, 2005.

Kim, Elaine. *Asian American Literature: An Introduction to the Writings and Their Social Context.* Philadelphia: Temple University Press, 1982.

Koshy, Susan. "The Fiction of Asian American Literature." *The Yale Journal of Criticism* 9, no. 2 (1996): 315–346.

Koshy, Susan. "Morphing Race into Ethnicity: Asian Americans and Critical Transformations of Whiteness." *boundary 2* 28, no. 1 (Spring 2001): 153–194.

Kresnak, Jack. "22 Facing Indecency Charges in Raid on Club." *Detroit Free Press.* December 15, 1983, 6A.

Kristeva, Julia. *Powers of Horror: An Essay on Abjection.* Translated by Leon S. Roudiez. New York: Columbia University Press, 1982.

Kucich, John. *Imperial Masochism: British Fiction, Fantasy, and Social Class.* Princeton: Princeton University Press, 2007.

Kurashige, Scott. "Detroit and the Legacy of Vincent Chin." *Amerasia Journal* 28, no. 3 (2002): 51–55.

Kurashige, Scott. *The Shifting Grounds of Race: Black and Japanese Americans in the Making of Multiethnic Los Angeles.* Princeton: Princeton University Press, 2008.

Kurashige, Scott. "My Initial Thoughts on the Richard Aoki Controversy." *TwitLonger.* August 20, 2012. http://www.twitlonger.com/show/iuop7v.

Kurashige, Scott. *The Fifty-Year Rebellion: How the U.S. Political Crisis Began in Detroit.* Oakland: University of California Press, 2017.

Lacan, Jacques. *The Seminar of Jacques Lacan: Book XI: The Four Fundamental Concepts of Psychoanalysis.* Edited by Jacques-Alain Miller. Translated by Alan Sheridan. New York: W. W. Norton & Company, 1998.

Lacan, Jacques. *Écrits: A Selection.* Translated by Bruce Fink. New York: W. W. Norton & Company, 2002.

Lam, Tony, dir. *Vincent Who?* Documentary. Asian Pacific Americans for Progress, 2009. Walnut, CA.

Lee, Ang, Eric Bana, and Jennifer Connelly, performers. *The Incredible Ang Lee.* Video short. Los Angeles, CA: Universal Studios, 2003.

Lee, Christopher. *The Semblance of Identity: Aesthetic Mediation in Asian American Literature.* Stanford: Stanford University Press, 2012.

Lee, Cynthia. "Beating Death Stirs Rally." *Detroit News* article. May 10, 1983a. Bentley Historical Archives, University of Michigan, Ann Arbor.

Lee, Cynthia. "Flak Stuns Judge in Chin Case: Kaufman Sentences in Slaying Assailed." *Detroit News* article, May 11, 1983b. Bentley Historical Archives, University of Michigan, Ann Arbor.

Lee, Esther Kim. *A History of Asian American Theatre.* Cambridge: Cambridge University Press, 2006.

Lee, Josephine. *Performing Asian America: Race and Ethnicity on the Contemporary Stage.* Philadelphia: Temple University Press, 1997.

Lee, Rachel, and Sau-Ling Cynthia Wong, eds. *AsianAmerica.Net: Ethnicity, Nationalism, and Cyberspace*. New York: Routledge, 2003.

Lee, Robert G. *Orientals: Asian Americans in Popular Culture*. Philadelphia: Temple University Press, 1999.

Lee, Yi-Young. "The Cleaving." *Poetry Foundation*. https://www.poetryfoundation.org/poems/50871/the-cleaving. Accessed 2 February 2020.

Lin, Tan. *Insomnia and the Aunt*. Chicago: Kenning Editions, 2011.

Lin, Tan. *tanlin* (blog). *Tumblr*. tanlin.tumblr.com. Accessed 18 May 2016.

Lin, Tao. *Taipei*. New York: Vintage, 2013.

Liu, Wen. "Complicity and Resistance: Asian American Body Politics in Black Lives Matter." *Journal of Asian American Studies* 21, no. 3 (Oct. 2018): 421–451.

Lowe, Lisa. *Immigrant Acts: On Asian American Cultural Politics*. Durham: Duke University Press, 1996.

Lowe, Lisa, and David Lloyd, eds. *The Politics of Culture in the Shadow of Capital*. Durham: Duke University Press, 1997.

Lye, Colleen. *America's Asia: Racial Form and American Literature, 1893–1945*. Princeton: Princeton University Press, 2005.

Lye, Colleen. "The Afro-Asian Analogy." Special issue, *PMLA* 123, no. 5 (October 2008a): 1732–1736.

Lye, Colleen. "Racial Form." *Representations* 104, no. 1 (Fall 2008b): 92–101.

Lye, Colleen. "The Literary Case of Wen Ho Lee." *Journal of Asian American Studies* 14, no. 2 (June 2011): 249–282.

Madrigal-Dean, Veronica, and George Czertko. "Case No. No. K-5903, Docket No. 82-273374." Psychiatric Evaluation, n.d. Box 4. American Citizens for Justice Archives. Bentley Historical Library, University of Michigan, Ann Arbor.

Maeda, Daryl. *Chains of Babylon: The Rise of Asian America*. Minneapolis: University of Minnesota Press, 2009.

Manovich, Lev. "Visual Technologies as Cognitive Prostheses: A Short History of the Externalization of the Mind." Chapter 10 in *The Prosthetic Impulse: From a Posthuman Present to a Biocultural Future*, edited by Marquard Smith and Joanna Morra. Cambridge, MA: MIT Press, 2006. pp. 203-220.

Martin, Carol. "Bodies of Evidence." *TDR: The Drama Review* 50, no. 3 (Fall 2006): 8–15.

Martin, Clancy. "The Agony of Ecstasy: 'Taipei,' a Novel by Tao Lin." *New York Times*. June 28, 2013, http://nyti.ms/19lM4aN.

Marx, Karl. "Estranged Labour." In *Economic and Philosophical Manuscripts of 1844*. Trans. Martin Milligan. Moscow: Progress Publishers, 1959. pp. 28-35. https://www.marxists.org/archive/marx/works/1844/manuscripts/labour.htm.

Massumi, Brian. "Translator's Foreword: Pleasures of Philosophy." Foreword in *A Thousand Plateaus: Capitalism and Schizophrenia* by Giles Deleuze and Felix Guattari. Minneapolis: University of Minnesota Press, 1987. pp. ix–xv.

Melamed, Jodi. "The Spirit of Neoliberalism: From Racial Liberalism to Neoliberal Multiculturalism." *Social Text* 24, no. 4 (Winter 2006): 1–24.

Mercer, Kobena. "Just Looking for Trouble: Robert Mapplethorpe and Fantasies of Race." In *Sex Exposed: Sexuality and the Pornography Debate*, edited by Lynne Segal and Mary McIntosh, 92–110. New Brunswick: Rutgers University Press, 1993.

Merleau-Ponty, Maurice. *Phenomenology of Perception*. Translated by Donald Landes. Routledge, 2012.

Mills, Charles. *The Racial Contract*. Ithaca: Cornell University Press, 1997.

Mitchell, David, and Sharon Snyder. "Narrative Prosthesis and the Materiality of Metaphor." In *The Disabilities Studies Reader*. Edited by Lennard Davis, 205–216. New York: Routledge, 2013.

Miyao, Daisuke. *Sessue Hayakawa: Silent Cinema and Transnational Stardom*. Durham: Duke University Press, 2007.

Moore, Michael. "The Man Who Killed Vincent Chin." *Detroit Free Press* article, August 30, 1987, Box 4, American Citizens for Justice Archives, Bentley Historical Library, University of Michigan, Ann Arbor.

Morley, David, and Kevin Robins. *Spaces of Identity: Global Media, Electronic Landscapes, and Cultural Boundaries*. London: Routledge, 1995.

Morrison, Toni. "On the Backs of Blacks." *Time*. 2 Dec 1993. http://content.time.com/time/subscriber/article/0,33009,979736,00.html

Moten, Fred. "Blackness and Nothingness (Mysticism in the Flesh)." *The South Atlantic Quarterly* 112, no. 4 (Fall 2013): 737–780.

Muñoz, José. *Disidentifications: Queers of Color and the Performance of Politics*. Minneapolis: University of Minnesota Press, 1999.

Muñoz, José. "Feeling Brown: Ethnicity and Affect in Ricardo Bracho's *The Sweetest Hangover (and Other STDs)*." *Theater Journal* 52, no. 1 (March 2000). pp. 67–79.

Murray, Janet. *Hamlet on the Holodeck: The Future of Narrative in Cyberspace*. Cambridge, MA: The MIT Press, 1999.

Musser, Amber Jamilla. *Sensational Flesh: Race, Power, and Masochism*. New York: New York University Press, 2014.

Nakamura, Lisa. *Cybertypes: Race, Ethnicity, and Identity on the Internet*. New York: Routledge, 2002.

Nakamura, Lisa. *Digitizing Race: Visual Cultures of the Internet*. Minneapolis: University of Minnesota Press, 2008.

Nakamura, Lisa. "Don't Hate the Player, Hate the Game: The Racialization of Labor in World of Warcraft." *Critical Studies in Media Communication* 26, no. 2 (June 2009): 128–144.

Narasaki, Karen, et al. *State of the Asian American Consumer: Growing Market, Growing Impact*. The Nielson Company. 2012. https://iibscstl.org/wp-content/PDF/State-of-the-Asian-American-Consumer-Report.pdf.

Narcisse, Evan. "The Worst Thing about Deus Ex: Human Revolution." *Time*, August 31, 2011. http://techland.time.com/2011/08/31/the-worst-thing-about-deus-ex-human-revolution/.

Ngai, Sianne. *Ugly Feelings*. Cambridge, MA: Harvard University Press, 2005.

Nguyen Tan Hoang. *A View from the Bottom: Asian American Masculinity and Sexual Representation*. Durham: Duke University Press, 2014.

Nguyễn, Việt Thanh. *Race and Resistance: Literature and Politics in Asian America*. Oxford: Oxford University Press, 2002.

Nietzsche, Friedrich. *On the Genealogy of Morality*. Edited by Keith Ansell-Pearson. Translated by Carol Diethe. Cambridge: Cambridge University Press, 1994.

Ninh, erin Khuê. *Ingratitude: The Debt-Bound Daughter in Asian American Literature*. New York: New York University Press, 2011.

Omi, Michael, and Howard Winant. *Racial Formation in the United States: From the 1960s to the 1990s*. New York: Routledge, 1994.

Pak, Greg. *World War Hulk: The Incredible Hercules*. Illustrated by Gary Frank, Leonard Kirk, and Carlo Pagulayan. New York: Marvel Worldwide, Inc., 2008.

Pak, Greg. "Re-Directing Comics: Greg Pak." In *Secret Identities: The Asian American Superhero Anthology*. Edited by Jeff Yang, Parry Shen, and Keith Chow, 55. New York: The New Press, 2009.

Pak, Greg. *The Incredible Hulk: Planet Hulk*. Illustrated by Carlo Pagulayan and Aaron Lopestri. New York: Marvel Worldwide, Inc., 2013.

Pak, Greg. *World War Hulk*. Illustrated by John Romita, Jr. New York: Marvel Worldwide, Inc., 2014.

Pak, Greg. *The Totally Awesome Hulk*. Volumes 1–4. Illustrated by Frank Cho and Sonia Oback. New York: Marvel Worldwide, Inc., 2016.
Pak, Greg. *Return to Planet Hulk*. Illustrated by Greg Land and Jay Leisten. New York: Marvel Worldwide, Inc., 2018a.
Pak, Greg. *World War Hulk II*. Illustrated by Carlo Barberi, Marco Lorenzana, Walden Wong, and Juan Vlasco. New York: Marvel Worldwide, Inc., 2018b.
Palumbo-Liu, David. *Asian/American: Historical Crossings of a Racial Frontier*. Stanford: Stanford University Press, 1999.
Parks, Suzan-Lori. *Venus*. New York: Theatre Communications Group, 1997.
Parreñas Shimizu, Celine. *The Hypersexuality of Race: Performing Asian/American Women on Screen and Scene*. Durham: Duke University Press, 2007.
Patterson, Christopher B. *Open World Empire: Race, Erotics, and the Global Rise of Video Games*. New York: NYU Press, 2020.
Phelan, Peggy. *Unmarked: The Politics of Performance*. New York: Routledge, 1993.
Prashad, Vijay. *The Karma of Brown Folk*. Minneapolis: University of Minneapolis Press, 2000.
Puar, Jasbir. *Terrorist Assemblages: Homonationalism in Queer Times*. Durham: Duke University Press, 2007.
Pulido, Laura. *Black, Brown, Yellow, and Left: Radical Activism in Los Angeles*. Berkeley: University of California Press, 2006.
Ravetto-Biagioli, Kriss. *Digital Uncanny*. New York: Oxford University Press, 2019.
Rideout, Victoria, Alexis Lauricella, and Ellen Wartella. *Children, Media, and Race: Media Use among White, Black, Hispanic, and Asian American Children*. Center on Media and Human Development, School of Communication, Northwestern University. June 2011. https://cmhd.northwestern.edu/wp-content/uploads/2011/06/SOCconfReportSingleFinal-1.pdf.
Rivera, Takeo. "Do Asians Dream of Electric Shrieks?: Techno-Orientalism and Erotohistoriographic Masochism in Eidos Montreal's *Deus Ex: Human Revolution*." *Amerasia Journal* 40, no. 2 (2014): 67–86.
Rivera, Takeo. "Ordering a New World: Orientalist Biopower in *World of Warcraft: Mists of Pandaria*." In *The Routledge Companion to Asian American Media*. Edited by Lori Kido Lopez and Vincent N. Pham, 195–208. New York: Routledge, 2017.
Robinson, Cedric. *Black Marxism: The Making of the Black Radical Tradition*. Chapel Hill: University of North Carolina Press, 1983.
Roediger, David. *Towards the Abolition of Whiteness: Essays on Race, Politics, and Working Class history*. New York: Verso, 1994.
Roggenbuck, Steve, E. E. Scott, and Rachel Younghans. *The YOLO Pages*. Tucson: boost house, 2014.
Roh, David S., Betsy Huang, and Greta A. Niu. "Technologizing Orientalism." Introduction in *Techno-Orientalism: Imagining Asia in Speculative Fiction, History, and Media*. Edited by David S. Roh, Betsy Huang, and Greta A. Niu. New Brunswick: Rutgers University Press, 2015. pp. 1–19.
Rosenbaum, Edward. "Report for the Panel of Mediators on the Financial Losses Caused by the Death of Vincent Jem Chin." Legal Report. September 23, 1986. Box 4. American Citizens for Justice Archives. Bentley Historical Library, University of Michigan, Ann Arbor.
Rosenfeld, Seth. "Man Who Armed Black Panthers Was FBI informant, Records Show." *California Watch*. August 20, 2012. http://californiawatch.org/public-safety/man-who-armed-black-panthers-was-fbi-informant-records-show-17634.
Rosenfeld, Seth. *Subversives: The FBI's War on Student Radicals, and Reagan's Rise to Power*. New York: Picador, 2013.
Ryan, Erin Gloria. "Alt-Lit Icon Tao Lin Accused of Statutory Rape and Abuse." *Jezebel*. October 2, 2014. https://jezebel.com/alt-lit-icon-tao-lin-accused-of-horrific-rape-and-abuse-1641641060.

Saïd, Edward. *Orientalism*. New York: Vintage Books, 1978.
Saïd, Edward. *Culture and Imperialism*. New York: Vintage Books, 1994.
Salamon, Gayle. *Assuming a Body*. New York: Columbia University Press, 2010.
Sanders, Katherine Elaine. "BOMB Magazine—Tan Lin by Katherine Elaine Sanders." *BOMB Magazine*. March 29, 2010, http://bombmagazine.org/article/3467/.
Sanodval, Chela. *Methodology of the Oppressed*. Minneapolis: University of Minnesota Press, 2000.
Santa Ana, Jeffrey. *Racial Feelings: Asian America in a Capitalist Culture of Emotion*. Philadelphia: Temple University Press, 2015.
Scott, A. O. "The Hulk (2003) Film Review; Tall and Green, but No 'Ho, Ho, Ho.'" *The New York Times*. June 20, 2003, http://www.nytimes.com/movie/review?res=9404E0DF1E38F93 3A15755C0A9659C8B63.
Scott, Darieck. *Extravagant Abjection: Blackness Power, and Sexuality in the African American Literary Imagination*. New York: New York University Press, 2010.
Sedgwick, Eve Kosofsky, Michèle Aina Barale, and Jonathan Goldberg. *Touching Feeling: Affect, Pedagogy, Performativity*. Duke University Press Books, 2003.
Sexton, Jared. "People-of-Color-Blindness: Notes on the Afterlife of Slavery." *Social Text* 28, no. 2 (Summer 2010): 31–56.
Shakur, Tupac. "Dear Mama." Track 9 on *Me against the World*. Interscope, 1995, compact disc.
Shimakawa, Karen. *National Abjection: The Asian American Body Onstage*. Durham: Duke University Press, 2002.
Silverman, Kaja. *The Subject of Semiotics*. New York: Oxford University Press, 1984.
Silverman, Kaja. *Male Subjectivity at the Margins*. New York: Routledge, 1992.
Sohn, Stephen Hong. "Introduction: Alien/Asian: Imagining the Racialized Future." Special issue, *MELUS* 33, no. 4 (Winter 2008): 5–22.
Song, Min Hyoung. *The Children of 1965: On Writing, and Not Writing, as an Asian American*. Durham: Duke University Press, 2013.
Spooner, Tom. "Asian-Americans Are Prolific Internet Users." *Pew Research Center*. December 12, 2001. http://www.pewinternet.org/2001/12/12/asian-americans-are-prolific-inter net-users.
Spillers, Hortense. "Mama's Baby, Papa's Maybe: An American Grammar Book." Special issue, *Diacritics* 17, no. 2 (Summer 1987): 64–81.
People of the State of Michigan v. Ebens & Nitz. Supplemental Memorandum of Law of Amicus Curiae, Chinese Welfare Council of Detroit, Chapter of the National Chinese Welfare Council and Certificate of Mailing, compiled by Larky Hiller and P. C. Hoekenga (Mich 1983). Materials Relating to the Vincent Chin Case, 1981–1990 (bulk 1983–1985). Asian American Studies Collection. Ethnic Studies Library, University of California, Berkeley.
Stephens, Michelle Ann. *Skin Acts: Race, Psychoanalysis, and the Black Male Performer*. Durham: Duke University Press, 2014.
Stiegler, Bernard. *Technics and Time, 1: The Fault of Epimetheus*. Translated by Richard Beardworth and George Collins. Stanford: Stanford University Press, 1994.
Stone, Allucquère Rosanne. *The War of Desire and Technology at the Close of the Mechanical Age*. Cambridge, MA: The MIT Press, 2001.
Tajima-Peña, Renee. "Fast Forward to History." *Amerasia Journal* 28, no. 3 (2002): 7–12.
Takaki, Ronald. "Who Really Killed Vincent Chin?" *San Francisco Examiner*. September 21, 1983, Materials Relating to the Vincent Chin case, 1981–1990 (bulk 1983–1985), Asian American Studies Collection. Ethnic Studies Library, University of California, Berkeley.
Takaki, Ronald. *Strangers from a Different Shore*. Boston: Little, Brown and Company, 1989.
Taylor, Diana. *The Archive and the Repertoire: Performing Cultural Memory in the Americas*. Durham: Duke University Press, 2013.

Terada, Rei. *Feeling in Theory: Emotion after the "Death of the Subject."* Cambridge, MA: Harvard University Press, 2001.
Thrift, Nigel. "Driving in the City." *Theory, Culture & Society* 21, nos. 4–5 (2004): 41–59.
Tran, Eric. "Amadeus Cho, Totally Awesome Hulk." In *The Gutter Spread Guide to Prayer*, 32. Pittsburgh: Autumn House Press, 2020.
Turkle, Sherry. *The Second Self: Computers and the Human Spirit*. Cambridge, MA: MIT Press, 2005.
Turner, Victor. *From Ritual to Theatre: The Human Seriousness of Play*. New York: PAJ Publications, 1982.
Uyematsu, Amy. "The Emergence of Yellow Power in America." In *Roots: An Asian American Reader*. Edited by Amy Tachiki, Eddie Wong, Franklin Odo, and Buck Wong, 9–13. Los Angeles: The Regents of the University of California, 1971.
Vizzini, Ned. "An Interview with Tao Lin." *Bookslut*. May 2007. http://www.bookslut.com/features/2007_05_011092.php. Accessed 9 April 2016.
Waldmeir, Pete. "2 Judges Let the Punishment Fit the Criminals." *Detroit News*. March 23, 1983. p. 10.
Wallace, Irving, and Amy Wallace. *The Two*. New York: Simon and Schuster, 1978.
Wark, McKenzie. *Gamer Theory*. Cambridge, MA: Harvard University Press, 2007.
Wei, William. *The Asian American Movement*. Philadelphia: Temple University Press, 1993.
Wilderson, Frank III. *Red, White & Black: Cinema and the Structure of U.S. Antagonisms*. Durham: Duke University Press, 2010.
Williams, Ben. "*Black Street Technology*: Detroit and the Information Age." Chapter 9 in *Technicolor: Race, Technology, and Everyday Life*. Edited by Alondra Nelson and Thuy Linh N. Tu. New York: New York University Press, 2001. pp. 154–176.
Williams, Linda. "Mirrors without Memories: Truth, History, and the New Documentary." *Film Quarterly* 46, no. 3 (Spring, 1993): 9–21.
Williams, Raymond. *Marxism and Literature*. Oxford: Oxford University Press, 1977.
Williams, Raymond. *Television: Technology and Cultural Form*. London: Routledge, 1990.
Wolfe, Cary. *What Is Posthumanism?* Minneapolis: University of Minnesota Press, 2009.
Wong, Sau-Ling Cynthia. *Reading Asian American Literature: From Necessity to Extravagance*. Princeton: Princeton University Press, 1993.
Wong, Sau-Ling Cynthia. "Denationalization Reconsidered: Asian American Cultural Criticism at a Theoretical Crossroads." *Amerasia Journal* 21, nos. 1 & 2 (1995): 1–27.
Worra, Bryan Thao. "Ypsilanti, 1982." In *Before We Remember We Dream*, 14. Dublin: Sahtu Press, 2020.
Wu, Cynthia. *Chang and Eng Reconnected: The Original Siamese Twins in American Culture*. Philadelphia: Temple University Press, 2012.
Wu, Ellen. *The Color of Success: Asian Americans and the Origins of the Model Minority*. Princeton: Princeton University Press, 2014.
Wu, Frank. *Yellow: Race in America Beyond Black and White*. New York: Basic Books, 2002.
Wu, Frank. "The Killing of Vincent Chin Trial Reenactment." Performed by author. YouTube video, 1:03:18. March 28, 2018. https://www.youtube.com/watch?v=-ZtGm4XMO4w.
Yang, Wesley. "Paper Tigers." *New York Magazine*. May 8, 2011, nymag.com/news/features/asian-americans-2011-5.
Yee, Kin. "Press Statement, American Citizens for Justice, June 17, 1983." Materials Relating to the Vincent Chin Case, 1981–1990 (bulk 1983–1985). Asian American Studies Collection. Ethnic Studies Library, University of California, Berkeley.
Zia, Helen. Speech to New York Violence against Asians Coalition, October 18, 1986. Materials Relating to the Vincent Chin case, 1981–1990 (bulk 1983–1985). Asian American Studies Collection. Ethnic Studies Library, University of California, Berkeley.

Zia, Helen. "ACJ Alert: Update on Federal Trial of Vincent Chin's Killers, Reported by ACJ President Helen Zia." 1984. Materials Relating to the Vincent Chin case, 1981–1990 (bulk 1983-1985). Asian American Studies Collection. Ethnic Studies Library, University of California, Berkeley.

Zia, Helen. *Asian American Dreams.* New York: Farbar, Straus and Giroux, 2000.

Index

For the benefit of digital users, indexed terms that span two pages (e.g., 52–53) may, on occasion, appear on only one of those pages.
Figures are indicated by *f* following the page number.

AAPA (Asian American Political Alliance), 42
abjection, 12–13, 72, 149–50n.8
accommodation, xix–xx
ACJ. *See* American Citizens for Justice
affective flatness
  overview, xxxiv–xxxv, 92–98
  in Tan Lin's *Insomnia and the Aunt*, 111–19
  in Tao Lin's *Taipei*, 98–111
Afro-Asian superego
  aspirations of Asian American cultural politics, 67
  concept of, 45–51
  overview, xxxiii, 42–45
  shame before Blackness in *I Dream of Chang & Eng*, 51–60
  yearning for solidarity in *After the War*, 60–66
Afro-pessimism, 47–48, 65–66, 155–56n.3
After the War/After the War Blues (Gotanda), xxxiii, 42, 44–45, 52, 60–66
Agamben, Giorgio, 105, 106
agency
  in *Deus Ex: Human Revolution*, 127–29
  in Nietzschean ressentiment, 72–73, 74, 75
"Agents of Atlas" (Pak), 70
Ahmed, Sara, 94, 104, 130–31, 161n.15
Alien Capital (Day), 162n.20
Althusser, Louis, 149n.6
alt-lit movement, 98–99
"Amadeus Cho, Totally Awesome Hulk" (Tran), 87, 88
ambient literature, 112
"American Adaptation Cycle, The" (Gotanda), 67
American Citizens for Justice (ACJ), xxxi–xxxii
  critique of model minoritarianism, 25–26
  and iteration of Asian American subject formation, 26–29
  purpose of organization, 18–19
  push for civil rights investigation, 20
  rhetorical strategy of, 19–25
  rhetoric of reflected in *Chinoiserie*, 36–37
Amin, Kadji, xxiv
analytic, masochism as, xxv, 37–41
animacies, xxvii, 116

anti-Asian propaganda by Detroit auto industry, 12–13, 13*f*
antiblackness, 45–46, 58–59, 65–66. *See also* Afro-Asian superego
anti-model minority critique, xvii–xix. *See also* Afro-Asian superego
Antinomies of Realism, The (Jameson), 95
anti-racism, 47–48, 49. *See also* Afro-Asian superego
Aoki, Richard, xxxiii, 42–44
Appadurai, Arjun, 144
Aristotelian tragedy, 157n.3
asceticism, 158n.8
Asian American Dreams (Zia), 21
Asian American Literature (Kim), xvii–xviii
Asian Americanness, 153n.3, *See also* affective flatness; Afro-Asian superego; model minority masochism; techno-orientalism
  American Citizens for Justice and, 26–29
  ethnic pride and, 26
  masculinity, techno-orientalism, and machinations of gender, xxvi–xxx
  masochism theory, xxii–xxvi
  and murder of Vincent Chin, 4–6
  overview, xiii–xvi
  of Pak's *Hulk* run, 91
  racial shadows, 84–85, 86–87, 107
  responses to becoming-machine, 17–29
  theories of Asian American subjectivity, xvi–xxii
  and *Who Killed Vincent Chin?* documentary, 11–12
Asian American Political Alliance (AAPA), 42
Asian American theater, 51–52. *See also specific playwrights; specific works*
Asian Pride Porn (Pak), 70
Asiatic ornamental feminization, xxvii
Asiatic racial form, xxvii–xxx, 9–10, 12, 71. *See also* affective flatness; becoming-machine; techno-orientalism
assemblage, 153n.6
augmentations, transhumanist, in *DX:HR*, 124–128–129, 126*f*, 130
Auslander, Philip, 113, 162n.22
auto industry in Detroit, 7–9, 12–13, 13*f*

Index

automation, threat of, 8, 9
automobile, racialization of, 12–17, 13*f*, 14*f*
avatarial capital, 126–27

Baartman, Sarah, 53–54
bad subject, 149n.3
Bakhtin, Mikhail, 154n.10
Barlow, John Perry, 122
Barthes, Roland, xix–xx
Baudrillard, Jean, 1
Beauvoir, Simone de, xxvi
becoming-machine, xxix–xxx, xxxiv. *See also* techno-orientalism
    in *Deus Ex: Human Revolution*, 127–29
    and metonymic racialization, 7–10
    and official ACJ narrative, 17–29
    and social drama of Vincent Chin, 6
    Who Killed Vincent Chin? documentary, 10–17
Beer, Matt, 10
Benjamin, Walter, 31
Benji (character in *After the War*), 63–64
Bersani, Leo, 151n.15
Best, Stephen, 155n.3
Beyond the Pleasure Principle (Freud), 150n.11
Bhabha, Homi, xviii–xix
Black exceptionalism, 47–48
Blackness as racial superego for Asian Americans
    Afro-Asian superego concept, 45–51
    aspirations of Asian American cultural politics, 67
    overview, xxxiii, 42–45
    shame before Blackness in *I Dream of Chang & Eng*, 51–60
    yearning for solidarity in *After the War*, 60–66
Black Panthers, 42–43
Black Skin, White Masks (Fanon), 92–93
Blade Runner film, 129–30
body, versus flesh, 122–23
body schema, 102–3
Boggs, Grace Lee, 44
Bostrom, Nick, 124–25
bottoming/bottomhood, xxiv, 85–87, 85*f*
Brown, Wendy, 74, 79
Bulosan, Carlos, 146
Bunker, Chang, 52–60
Bunker, Eng, 52–60
Bush, Christopher, 152n.18
Butler, Judith, xxvi, 23–24, 41, 149n.6, 151n.16
Butler-Evans, Elliott, 47

Canby, Vincent, 11
Čapek, Karel, xxviii
capitalism
    moral logics of, 75–76
    racial, xxii
Castelli, Elizabeth, 154n.13

Castronova, Edward, 126–27
Catá, Alfonso Hernandez, 159n.6
Catanese, Brandi Wilkins, 100–1
Chambers-Letson, Joshua Takano, 36
Chan, Dean, 120
Chan, Lisa, 18, 39
Chan, Sucheng, 20
Chang, Robert S., 20–21, 24–25
Chen, Mel, xxvii, 116, 135
Chen, Tina, 44
Cheng, Anne, xxi, 36, 53, 122–23, 131, 157n.5
Chickencoop Chinaman (Chin), 49–50, 157n.1
Chin, Denny, 37, 38
Chin, Frank, xviii–xx, 48, 49–50, 93, 157n.1
Chin, Lily, 2–3, 18, 20, 27–28, 32–34, 37, 154n.12
Chin, Vincent, 93–94, 154n.13
    ACJ rhetorical strategy related to, 18–29
    becoming-machine and metonymic racialization, 7–10
    Chinoiserie play, xxxii–xxxiii, 30–37
    civil rights investigation of perpetrators, 20
    and contemporary Asian American identity, xiv–xv, 4–6
    memorial plaque for, 30
    murder of, xxxi–xxxii, 3–4
    overview, 1–3
    sentencing of perpetrators, 4
    staged performances related to murder, xxxii–xxxiii, 30–31
    UC Hastings re-enactment, xxxii–xxxiii, 37–41
    Who Killed Vincent Chin? documentary, 10–17, 13*f*, 14*f*
Chinese Exclusion Act, xxi–xxii
Chinoiserie (Chong), xxxii–xxxiii, 30–37
Cho, Amadeus (character in *Hulk* comics), 72, 87–91, 89*f*
Cho, Frank, 88, 89*f*
Choi, Jimmy, 3–4, 39
Chong, Ping, xxxii–xxxiii, 30–37, 160n.10
Chow, Rey, 73, 75–76, 138–39
Choy, Christine, 10–17
Chuang, Marisa, 25–26
Chude-Sokei, Louis, xxviii
Chuh, Kandice, xv
Chun, Wendy, xxviii
class position, model minority as, xxii
"Cleaving, The" (Lee), xiii
coldness, masochistic, xxiii, 110–11. *See also* affective flatness
Coldness and Cruelty (Deleuze), xxiii–xxiv
colorblindness, 100–1
Colwell, Racine, 3–4, 38
Comay, Rebecca, 3, 27–28
complicity, Asian American, xxxiii, 45–46, 58–60, 82. *See also* Afro-Asian superego
conduct, Foucault's theorizing on, 158n.8

Index

counter-conduct, 158n.8
Crispin, Jessa, 100
Cruz, Ariane, xxvi, 121
cultural nationalism, xix–xx, 48, 77
cultural politics, 150n.10, *See also* Asian Americanness; model minority masochism; ressentiment
  aspirations of, 67
  model minority masochism as, xxvi
  of Vincent Chin affair, 5–6
cyberpunk genre, 129–30. See also *Deus Ex: Human Revolution* game
cyberrenaissance aesthetics, 124, 129–30
Czertko, George, 16–17

David, Peter, 68–69
Day, Iyko, 155–56n.3, 162n.20
Delany, Samuel, 137
Deleuze, Gilles, xxiii–xxiv, 9, 26–27, 31–32, 40, 67, 94, 105–6, 110–11
"Denationalization Reconsidered" (Wong), 46–48
Deng, Chun Hsien Michael, xiii–xv, 144
despotism, racial, 80–81
desubjectification, masochism as mode of, xxv
Detroit, 1, 7–10, 12–17, 13*f*, 14*f*, 132–33, 153n.4, 153n.5
Deus Ex: Human Revolution (*DX:HR*) game
  masochism and annihilation of self and/as other, 134–39
  overview, xxxv–xxxvi, 120–22
  racial phenomenology and transhumanist neoliberalism, 122–29
  techno-orientalism and erotohistoriography, 129–34
diaspora-focused turn in Asian American studies, 46–48
diegetic/non-diegetic distinction, 163n.6
digital uncanny, 103–4
disavowal, in ACJ rhetorical strategy related to Chin, 26–28
disidentification, xix
documentary theater, 155n.4
DuBois, W. E. B., 92
DX:HR. See *Deus Ex: Human Revolution* game

Eaman, Frank, xxxi–xxxii
East/West Quartet (Chong), 31
Ebens, Ronald, xxxi–xxxii, 3–4, 11, 15–17, 20, 24–25, 40
Edelman, Lee, 21–22
Eidos Montreal, 124. *See also Deus Ex: Human Revolution* game
Ellis, Bret Easton, 99, 160n.9
"Emergence of Yellow Power in America, The" (Uyematsu), 45–46
Enframing, 161n.17

Eng, David, xxi, 5, 49, 77
envy, versus ressentiment, 73–74
epidermal racial schema, 92–93, 124
erotohistoriography
  Chinoiserie, 31, 35
  Deus Ex: Human Revolution, xxxv–xxxvi, 121, 129–34, 137–39
Espiritu, Yến Lê, 5
"Ethnicity of Things in America's Lacquered Age, The" (Bush), 152n.18
ethnic pride, Asian American identity and, 26. *See also* panethnicity, Asian American
eugenics, 125
exclusion, and Asian American subjectivity, xxi–xxii, 72
Expeditionary Series (Tseng), 162n.20

face/faciality, in relation to affect, 105–6, 116
fairness, in ACJ rhetorical strategy related to Chin, 19–20
Fang, Jenn, 146
Fanon, Frantz, 47, 66, 92–93, 124
Fawaz, Ramzi, 77, 79–80
FBI informant, allegation concerning Richard Aoki as, 42–43
"Feeling Brown, Feeling Down" (Muñoz), 159n.5
Feeling of Kinship, The (Eng), 49
femininity
  Asian inscrutability within domain of, 96–97
  Asiatic, xxvii
  of Hulk, 77
  techno-orientalism and, xxix–xxx
feminism, women of color, 46, 155–56n.3
Ferguson, Roderick, 155–56n.3
Fernández-Vara, Clara, 130, 164n.16
Fickle, Tara, xvi–xvii
Fighting Grandpa (Pak), 70
Fillmore district, San Francisco, 61
first-person subjective view in video games, 127, 128*f*
first wave of Asian American playwrights, 156n.6
Fisher, Mark, 96
flatness, affective. See affective flatness
flesh, *DX:HR* as game about, 122–29
Ford, Henry, 7–8
foreignness
  of Asian Americans, 46–47
  in Tao Lin's *Taipei*, 106–7
Foster, Thomas, 130–31
Foucault, Michel, 74–75, 126–27, 149n.6, 149n.7, 151n.14, 151n.16, 158n.8
Freeman, Elizabeth, xxxv–xxxvi, 31, 35, 121, 132, 137
Freud, Sigmund, 15, 28, 49, 50, 150n.11
Fujino, Diane, 42
Fukuzawa, David, 22

Galloway, Alexander, 95, 102–3, 106, 118, 127, 163n.6
Galster, George, 7–8
Galton, Francis, 106
games, techno-orientalist. *See Deus Ex: Human Revolution* game
Gaming (Galloway), 163n.6
Garreau, Joel, 124–25
gender, machinations of, xxvi–xxx. *See also* femininity; masculinity
Genealogy of Morals (Nietzsche), 72
Gibson, William, 129–30
Gies, Arthur, 120
Gilmore, Ruth Wilson, 161n.16
"Glass Ceiling" test, Pi Delta Psi fraternity, xiii–xv
Goffman, Erving, 162n.21
González, Jennifer, 152n.20
Gotanda, Philip Kan, xxxii–, 42
 Afro-Asian solidarity in works of, 44–45
 diversity of work by, 51–52
 shame before Blackness in *I Dream of Chang & Eng*, 50–60
 solidarity politics of, 52, 67
 UC Hastings Chin trial re-enactment, 37
 yearning for solidarity in *After the War*, 60–66
Green, David, 106
Green Goliath. See *Incredible Hulk*
grievable, rendering Vincent Chin's life as, 23–24, 25, 36–37
Guattari, Féliz, 9, 94, 105–6, 153n.6, 161n.16
Gurley, Akai, 157n.10

Hagedorn, Jessica, 111
Harlans, Latasha, 155n.2
Harris, Cheryl, 61, 64–65
Harris, Richard, 163n.10
Hartman, Saidiya, 155n.3
Hayakawa, Sessue, 96–97
Hayes, Aleta, 30–31, 32–33
Hayles, N. Katherine, 122
hazing rituals, Pi Delta Psi fraternity, xiii–xv
HEATH (Lin), 162n.19
hegemony, racial, xv, 80–81
Heidegger, Martin, 161n.17
Hellbender (character in *Totally Awesome Hulk*), 88–90, 89*f*
"Heterogeneity, Hybridity, Multiplicity" (Lowe), xx
Higginbotham, Evelyn Brooks, 19
"History and Class Consciousness as an Unfinished Project" (Jameson), 75–76
History of Sexuality (Foucault), 74–75, 151n.16
Hitchings, Leona (character in *After the War*), 61, 62–63
Hong, Grace, 155–56n.3
Hsu, Madeline, xix
Huang, Vivian L., 96–97

Hughey, Matthew, 56
Hulk (Marvel Comics superhero)
 Amadeus Cho's Hulk, 87–91, 89*f*
 hidden Asianness of, 68–91, 69*f*
 and limits of ressentiment, 71–76
 ontology of Hulkness, 76–82
 overview, xxxiii–xxxiv
 shifts from logic of ressentiment to masochism, 82–87, 83*f*, 85*f*
Hulk film (Lee), 68–70, 69*f*
Huyssen, Andreas, 152n.19
Hwang, David Henry, 51–52, 84–85, 131, 152n.17, 164n.18
hypermasculinity, 77–78

ideal critical subject, xvii–xix, 61–62, 79–80, 146–47
identity politics of ressentiment, 73–75
I Dream of Chang and Eng (Gotanda), xxxiii, 42, 44–45, 51–60, 66
Iijima, Chris, 26
Imagine Otherwise (Chuh), xx
Imagining the Nation (Li), 153n.7
Incredible Ang Lee, The documentary, 68, 69*f*
Incredible Hulk (Marvel Comics)
 Amadeus Cho's Hulk, 87–91, 89*f*
 hidden Asianness of, 68–91, 69*f*
 and limits of ressentiment, 71–76
 ontology of Hulkness, 76–82
 overview, xxxiii–xxxiv
 shifts from logic of ressentiment to masochism, 82–87, 83*f*, 85*f*
individualist conceptualizations of racism, 11, 81–82
inscrutability, Asian, 96–97
Insomnia and the Aunt (Lin), 97–98, 111–19
Interface Effect, The (Galloway), 95

Jacques-Belletete, Jonathan, 124–25, 129–30, 132–33
"Jamaican Wash, The" (Gotanda & Jones), 67
Jameson, Fredric, xxxiv, 73, 75–76, 94–96
Japanophobia, xxxi–xxxii, 7–9
Jensen, Adam (character in *Deus Ex: Human Revolution*), 121, 125–27, 129–30, 131
Jeon, Joseph Jonghyun, 3
Johns, Adrian, xxviii
Johnson, J. E., 60
Jones, Steven Anthony, 67
"Just Looking for Trouble" (Mercer), 164n.15

Kang, Jay Caspian, xiii–xiv, xv
Kant, Emmanuel, 163n.9
Katz, Jack, 1
Kaufman, Charles, 4, 41
Keller, Helen, 163n.10

Kennedy, E. R., 99
Khoury, Edward, 4, 16
Kim, Claire Jean, 75
Kim, Daniel Y., 48, 49–50, 152n.17, 156n.4
Kim, Elaine, xvii–xviii
King, Rodney, 155n.2
Kochiyama, Yuri, 44
Koivu, Gary, 39
Koshy, Susan, xvii–xviii
Kristeva, Julia, 153n.7
Kristof, Nicholas, 149n.1
Kucich, John, 27–28, 150–51n.12, 154n.13
Kurashige, Scott, 7–8, 9, 43, 153n.5
Kwoh, Stewart, 2–3

Lacan, Jacques, 59, 150n.11
lack, and Asian American subjectivity, xxi
Lady Hellbender (character in *Totally Awesome Hulk*), 88–90, 89f
law, UC Hastings re-enactment and failure of, 39–41
Lawson, David, 38, 39
Learned Jack (character in *I Dream of Chang and Eng*), 54–60, 55f
Lee, Ang, 68–70, 69f
Lee, Chang-Rae, 160n.10
Lee, Christopher, xvii–xviii
Lee, Cynthia, 22–23
Lee, Esther Kim, 51–52
Lee, Josephine, 131, 132, 152n.17, 164n.16
Lee, Li-Young, xiii
Lee, Rachel C., xxviii, 132
Lee, Robert G., 150n.9
Lee, Spike, 56
Lee, Wen Ho, 69–70, 154n.11, 157n.2
Letitia (character in *Deus Ex: Human Revolution*), 133–34
Li, David Leiwei, 153n.7
Liang, Peter, 157n.10
liberalism, xv, 5
liberationist negativity, xxiv
Lillian (character in *After the War*), 63
Lin, Tan Anthony, 97–98, 111–19
Lin, Tao, 97–111, 117–19
"Literary Case of Wen Ho Lee, The" (Lye), 154n.11
Liu, Wen, xv
Lloyd, David, 150n.10
Lopresti, Aaron, 80–81
Los Angeles riots, 155n.2
Lowe, Lisa, xx, 150n.10
Lukács, György, 75–76
Lye, Colleen, xvi–xvii, xxvii, 9, 12, 46, 50, 71, 154n.11, 157n.2

machinic, associations of Asians with, xxviii. *See also* becoming-machine; techno-orientalism

Madrigal-Dean, Veronica A., 16–17
Maeda, Daryl, 149n.4
magical negro, 56–57
"Mama's Baby, Papa's Maybe" (Spillers), 122–23, 156n.5
Mantlo, Bill, 68–69
Mapplethorpe, Robert, 164n.15
Martin, Carol, 155n.4
Martin, Clancy, 99
martyrdom, 154n.13
Marvel Comics. *See Incredible Hulk*
Marx, Karl, 15
Mary-Louise (character in *After the War*), 63–64, 66
masculine masochism, 110. *See also* masochism
masculinity. *See also* model minority masochism
  in ACJ rhetorical strategy related to Chin, 21–22, 24–25
  Afro-Asian superego, 48–50
  and masochism theory, xxiii
  method and theory behind book, xxx–xxxi
  overview, xiii–xvi
  in Pak's *Hulk* run, 71, 76–84, 88–91
  and resistance to model minoritarianism, xviii–xix
  techno-orientalism and machinations of gender, xxvi–xxx
masochism. *See also* model minority masochism; techno-orientalism
  and ACJ rhetorical strategy related to Chin, 24
  affective flatness and, 92–98
  Afro-Asian superego and, 49–50, 66
  Chinoiserie play, 31–37
  and Detroit labor force, 15
  in *Deus Ex: Human Revolution*, 134–39
  disavowal and, 26–28
  of Ebens, 16–17
  erotohistoriography, 132
  and fetish substitute of melancholia, 3
  Freudian, 150n.11
  in Pak's *Hulk* run, xxxiii–xxxiv, 71, 82–87, 83f, 85f, 88–91
  in relational psychoanalysis, 150–51n.12
  versus ressentiment, 154n.8
  in Tao Lin's *Taipei*, 109–11, 118–19
  techno-orientalism and, xxix, 93–94
  theories of, xxii–xxvi
  UC Hastings re-enactment and, 31, 37–41
  and Vincent Chin affair, 5–6
masochistic coldness, xxiii, 110–11
Massumi, Brian, 159–60n.7
master narratives, xx
M Butterfly (Hwang), 131, 152n.17, 164n.18
Melamed, Jodi, 159n.4

melancholia
  in ACJ rhetorical strategy related to Chin, 24
  in *Chinoiserie* play, 36–37
  overview, xxi–xxii
  and photograph of Vincent Chin, 2–3
  versus ressentiment, 157n.5
  and social drama of Vincent Chin, 6
Melancholy of Race, The (Cheng), xxi
Mercer, Kobena, 164n.15
Merleau-Ponty, Maurice, 102–3, 104
metonymic racialization, 7–10
Miek (character in *Hulk* comics), 71–72, 78–80
Mills, Charles, 125, 163n.9
mimicry, versus model minoritarianism, xviii–xix
mirror stage, 59–60
model anti–model minority, xviii–xix
"Model Minority" (Rivera), 140–43
model minoritarianism, 142, 144
  Afro-Asian superego and, 43–45, 65–66, 67
  and Asian American subjectivity, xvi–xx, xxi–xxii
  and *Chinoiserie* play, 37
  historiographic framing, xxxi
  in official ACJ narrative, 25–26, 27–29
  and politics of respectability, 19
  and techno-orientalism, xxix
model minority masochism, 139. *See also* techno-orientalism
  general discussion, 146–47
  historiographic framing, xxxi
  masculinity, techno-orientalism, and machinations of gender, xxvi–xxx
  masochism theory, xxii–xxvi
  method and theory behind book, xxx–xxxvi
  overview, xiii–xvi
  theories of Asian American subjectivity, xvi–xxii
  theses of, xxv–xxvi
  in *Totally Awesome Hulk*, 91
  and Yang's campaign for presidency, 145–46
Monkawa, Chet (character in *After the War*), 61–62, 63–66
moral economy of ressentiment, 14–15, 16–17. *See also* ressentiment
moral masochism. *See* masochism
Morley, David, xxviii
Morrison, Toni, 58–59
Mortis, Joe, 2–3
Moten, Fred, 155–56n.3
Motor City. *See* Detroit
Moy, Afong, 53
Muñoz, José, xix, 96, 159n.5
Musser, Amber Jamilla, xxiii, 123

Nakamura, Lisa, 122, 127, 129–30
Narcisse, Evan, 133
National Abjection (Shimakawa), 149–50n.8, 153n.7

neoliberalism, xv, 44
neoliberal transhumanism, 124–29, 130
Neuromancer (Gibson), 129–30
new sexless man, 27
Ngai, Sianne, xxviii, 73–74
Nguyen Tan Hoang, xxiv, 86
Nguyễn, Việt Thanh, xviii–xix, 79–80, 149n.2
Nietzsche, Friedrich, 72
Ninh, erin Khuê, 152n.17
Nitz, Michael, xxxi–xxxii, 3–4, 15–16, 20, 24–25
No No Boys, xvii–xviii, 60–61
normativity, racial, 159n.5
nostalgic racial liberalism, xv

Oback, Sonia, 88, 89*f*
objecthood. *See also* becoming-machine; techno-orientalism
  and masochism, xxvi–xxvii
  and social drama of Vincent Chin, 6, 10
Okada, John, 60–61
Omi, Michael, 80–81
ontology of Hulkness, 76–82
optimistic masochism, xxiv
orientalism, xxvii–xxx, 104, 161n.15. *See also* techno-orientalism
Ornamentalism (Cheng), xxvii

Pagulayan, Carlo, 80–81
Pak, Greg
  Amadeus Cho's Hulk, 87–91, 89*f*
  background and work of, 70
  Incredible Hulk run overview, xxxiii–xxxiv, 70–72
  ressentiment in ontology of Hulkness, 76–82
  shifts from logic of ressentiment to masochism, 82–87, 83*f*, 85*f*
Palumbo-Liu, David, xvii–xviii, 122
panethnicity, Asian American, xiv–xvi, xxxi, 4–6, 79–80. *See also* Afro-Asian superego; Asian Americanness; model minority masochism
"Paper Tigers" (Yang), 92–94
parahuman femininity of Asian women, xxvii
Parks, Suzan-Lori, 53
patriotism, in ACJ rhetorical strategy, 22–23
Patterson, Christopher B., 121
Pêcheux, Michel, 149n.3
penetrability, in queer of color critique, xxiv
"People of Color Blindness" (Sexton), 47–48
performance event, Vincent Chin affair as
  becoming-machine and metonymic racialization, 7–10
  overview, 5–6
  Who Killed Vincent Chin? documentary, 10–17
performance studies, xxx
Phelan, Peggy, 10

phenomenological embodiment
  in *Deus Ex: Human Revolution*, 122–29
  overview, xxxiv–xxxv, 92–93, 97–98
  in Tan Lin's *Insomnia and the Aunt*, 111–19
  in Tao Lin's *Taipei*, 97–111
Pi Delta Psi fraternity hazing rituals, xiii–xv
Planet Hulk (Pak), xxxiii–xxxiv
  ressentiment logic in, 70, 71–72, 76–82
  shifts from ressentiment to masochism, 82–87, 85f
playwrights, Asian American, 51–52. *See also specific playwrights*
political consciousness, 75–76
Political Unconscious, The (Jameson), 73
politics of bottomhood, 86
Politics of Culture in the Shadow of Capital, The (Lowe and Lloyd), 150n.10
politics of respectability, 19
Postmodernism (Jameson), 94–95
postmodernity, 95–96
postraciality, xv, 100–1
power, and Nietzschean ressentiment, 74–75
Prashad, Vijay, xxxiii, 42
Presentation of Self in Everyday Life, The (Goffman), 162n.21
Price, Lee, 9
property, racialization and, 64–65
Protestant Ethnic and the Spirit of Capitalism, The (Chow), 73
Psychic Life of Power (Butler), 151n.16
psychoanalytic writings on Asian American subjectivity, xxi
Puar, Jasbir, 153n.6

queer theory, xxiv
"Question Concerning Technology, The" (Heidegger), 161n.17

R&L (Rivera), 142–44, 145–46
Rabelais and His World (Bakhtin), 154n.10
racial capitalism, xxii
Racial Castration (Eng), xxi
Racial Contract, The (Mills), 163n.9
racial despotism, 80–81
Racial Feelings (Santa Ana), 159–60n.7
racial form, Asiatic, xxvii–xxx, 9–10, 12, 71. *See also* affective flatness; becoming-machine; techno-orientalism
racial hegemony, xv, 80–81
racialization. *See also* affective flatness; model minority masochism; techno-orientalism
  of automobiles, techno-orientalism and, 12–17, 13f, 14f
  clash of narratives of, 61–66
  comparative, between Asianness and Blackness, 47
  metonymic, 7–10
  property and, 65
  subject formation and, xx–xxi
racial liberalism, xv
racial melancholia. *See* melancholia
racial normativity, 159n.5
racial phenomenology. *See* phenomenological embodiment
racial power, 75
racial ressentiment. *See* ressentiment
racial schema, epidermal, 92–93
racial shadows, 84–85, 86–87, 107
racial thing, 3
racial Uncle Toms, xviii–xx, 48
racism, 161n.16, *See also* Afro-Asian superego
  and defensive nature of panethnic identity, 79–80
  modeled by Asian Americans, xiii–xv
  UC Hastings re-enactment and, 39–41
radicality, Asian Americanist, xxxi, 44, 46, 144, 147
Ravetto-Biagioli, Kriss, 103–4
recuperative capacity of masochism, 84–87
Redford, Robert, 114–15
relational psychoanalysis, 150–51n.12
reparations, 36
resistance
  to model minorityism, xvii–xix
  and Nietzschean ressentiment, 75–76
  under racial despotism, 80–81
respectability
  in ACJ rhetorical strategy related to Chin, 21–22
  politics of, 19
ressentiment, 147
  versus masochism, 83–84, 154n.8
  versus melancholia, 157n.5
  in Nietzschean tradition, 72–76
  in Pak's *Hulk* run, xxxiii–xxxiv, 70–71, 72, 76–82, 89–90, 91
  and social drama of Vincent Chin, 6
  in *After the War*, 63, 66
  in *Who Killed Vincent Chin?* documentary, 14–15, 16–17
Rivera, Takeo, 120–21, 140–44, 145–46
Robins, Kevin, xxviii
Robinson, Cedric, xxii
Robot Stories (Pak), 70
Roggenbuck, Steve, 98–99
Romita, John, Jr., 80–81, 82–83
Rosenbaum, Edward, 18
Rosenfeld, Seth, 42–43
Rudolph, Angela, 3–4, 32–33, 37

sadism, xxiii, 15, 118, 132, 151n.13, 151n.14
Salamon, Gayle, 123–24
Samurai among Panthers (Fujino), 42
Sandoval, Chela, 159n.4

San Francisco, 61
Santa Ana, Jeffrey, 159–60n.7
Saperstein, Bruce, 4
Sartre, Jean-Paul, xxvi
scenarios, xviii, 54
Scott, A. O., 68–69
Scott, Darieck, 86, 137
screens, in Tao Lin's *Taipei*, 102–5
Second Skin (Cheng), 122–23
second wave of Asian American playwrights, 51–52
Secret Identities (Pak), 70
Seldin, Naomi, 118–19
self-annihilation
   in *Chinoiserie* play, 35–36
   in *Deus Ex: Human Revolution*, 134–39
self-objectification, 150n.10
Sensational Flesh (Musser), xxiv–xxv
Seven Controlled Vocabularies and Obituary 2004. The Joy of Cooking (Lin), 112
Sexton, Jared, 47–48, 58–59
sexuality, in ACJ rhetorical strategy related to Chin, 21–22, 24–25, 26–28
Shakur, Tupac, 1–2
shame precipitated by Afro-Asian superego, 50–60
Shimakawa, Karen, 72, 149–50n.8, 153n.7
Shimizu, Celine Parreñas, xxix–xxx, 151n.16
Silverman, Kaja, 10, 83–84, 158n.8
simulacrum, face as, 105, 106
Siroskey, Robert, 39
slavery, Chang and Eng Bunker's complicity in, 57–60
slavery reparations, 155n.3
social drama, Vincent Chin affair as
   becoming-machine and metonymic racialization, 7–10
   overview, 5–6
   Who Killed Vincent Chin? documentary, 10–17
Sohn, Stephen Hong, xxxiv, 96
solidarity, Afro-Asian. *See* Afro-Asian superego
Spikes (in *Planet Hulk*), 84–87
Spillers, Hortense, 122–24, 156n.5
standpoint theory, 75–76
Stephens, Michelle Ann, 123
stereotype, living under weight of dominant, 92–93
Stiegler, Bernard, xxxiv
Stone, Allucquère Rosanne, 122, 162n.4
Strange Affinities (Hong and Ferguson), 155–56n.3
strategic racial positioning by Asian Americans, xix
subjectivity, Asian American. *See also* Afro-Asian superego; Asian Americanness; becoming-machine; model minority masochism
   American Citizens for Justice and, 26–29
   masculinity, techno-orientalism, and machinations of gender, xxvi–xxx

   masochism theory, xxii–xxvi
   method and theory behind book, xxx–xxxvi
   overview, xv
   and social drama of Vincent Chin, 10
   theories of, xvi–xxii
supercrip, 163n.10
superego. *See* Afro-Asian superego
superhero comics. *See Incredible Hulk*
superhero teams, 79–80
suspense, masochistic, in *Chinoiserie* play, 31–35

Taipei (Lin), 97–111, 117–19
Tajima-Peña, Renee, 10–17
Takaki, Ronald, 5, 9
Taylor, Diana, xviii, 54
techno music, 153n.4
techno-orientalism, xxv
   affective flatness and, xxxiv, 92–98
   becoming-machine and metonymic racialization, 7–10
   in *Deus Ex: Human Revolution*, 128–34, 137–39
   masculinity and machinations of gender, xxvi–xxx
   and official ACJ narrative, 25, 27–28
   and social drama of Vincent Chin, xxxi–xxxii, 6
   in Tan Lin's *Insomnia and the Aunt*, 111–19
   in Tao Lin's *Taipei*, 98–111
   and *Who Killed Vincent Chin?* documentary, 12–17, 13*f*, 14*f*
television, in Tan Lin's *Insomnia and the Aunt*, 113, 114–15, 116–17
Terada, Rei, 159–60n.7
theater, Asian American, 51–52. *See also specific playwrights; specific works*
thingliness, ornamental, xxvii
Third World Liberation Front (TWLF), 42, 79–80
Thousand Plateaus, A (Deleuze and Guattari), 105–6
Threadgill, Burney, 42–43
"Three Essays on the Theory of Sexuality" (Freud), 150n.11
Thrift, Nigel, 127–28
Till, Mamie, 154n.12
Totally Awesome Hulk, The (Pak), 87–91, 89*f*
Tran, Eric, 87, 88
transhumanism, in *Deus Ex: Human Revolution*, 124–128–129, 126*f*, 130
transnational turn in Asian American studies, 46–48
trial re-enactment at UC Hastings, xxxii–xxxiii, 37–41
Tseng Kwong Chi, 162n.20
Turkle, Sherry, 126–27, 130, 163n.13
TWLF (Third World Liberation Front), 42, 79–80
Two, The (Wallace and Wallace), 60

UC Hastings, Chin trial re-enactment at, xxxii–xxxiii, 37–41
Uncle Tom minorities, xviii–xx, 48
United Auto Workers (UAW), 8–9
utopian potentials of masochism, xxiv
Uyematsu, Amy, 45–46

"Vamp and the Machine, The" (Huyssen), 152n.19
Venus (Parks), 53
video games, techno-orientalist. *See Deus Ex: Human Revolution* game
View from the Bottom, A (Nguyen), xxiv
Vincent Chin Trial Reenactment, UC Hastings, xxxii–xxxiii, 37–41
Vincent Who? documentary, 2–3

Wallace, Amy, 60
Wallace, Irving, 60
waning of affect, xxxiv, 94–96. *See also* affective flatness
Warbound group (in *Hulk* comics), 79–80
Wash, The (Gotanda), 67
"We Asian Americans Are Not the Virus, but We Can Be Part of the Cure" (Yang), 145
Weber, Max, 75–76
whiteness
  claims to in *After the War*, 66
  in *Deus Ex: Human Revolution*, 124–25, 126–27
  face as, 105–6
  property interest in, 61, 64–65
  racial normativity, 159n.5
white racist violence modeled by Asian Americans, xiii–xv
white ressentiment, 16–17
Who Killed Vincent Chin? documentary, 10–17, 32–33

Wilderson, Frank, III, 47–48
Williams, Ben, 153n.4
Williams, Linda, 11
Williams, Raymond, 113
Wilson, August, 60–61
Winant, Howard, 80–81
Wolfe, Cary, 125
women of color feminism, 46, 155–56n.3
Wong, Sau-Ling, xxviii, 46–48, 65, 84–85, 107, 132, 165n.20
World War Hulk (Pak), xxxiii–xxxiv
  ressentiment logic in, 71–72, 76–82
  shifts from ressentiment to masochism, 82–87, 83*f*
World War Hulk II (Pak), 90
Worra, Bryan Thao, 7
Worthing, Earl (character in *After the War*), 61–62, 63–66
Wu, Ellen, xix, 149n.5
Wu, Frank, xxxii–xxxiii, 4–5, 37, 39–40
Wynter, Sylvia, 125

Yang, Andrew, 144–46
Yang, Wesley, 92–94, 106
Yankee Dawg You Die (Gotanda), 51–52
Yee, Henry, 18
Yee, Kin, 18, 22–23
"yellow power" movement, 45–46
Yohen (Gotanda), 52
YOLO Pages, The (Roggenbuck et al.), 98–99
"Ypsilanti, 1982" (Worra), 7

Zhao Yun Ru (character in *Deus Ex: Human Revolution*), 134–39, 134*f*, 136*f*, 138*f*
Zia, Helen, 2, 3–4, 18, 21–22, 154n.11